Greenhill Books

HITLER'S
GREY
WOLVES

HITLER'S GREY WOLVES

U-BOATS IN THE INDIAN OCEAN

Lawrence Paterson

GREENHILL BOOKS ✦ LONDON
STACKPOLE BOOKS ✦ PENNSYLVANIA

Greenhill Books

Hitler's Grey Wolves: U-Boats in the Indian Ocean
first published 2004 by
Greenhill Books, Lionel Leventhal Limited, Park House,
1 Russell Gardens, London NW11 9NN
www.greenhillbooks.com
and
Stackpole Books, 5067 Ritter Road, Mechanicsburg, PA 17055, USA

British Library Cataloguing in Publication Data
Paterson, Lawrence
Hitler's grey wolves : U-boats in the Indian Ocean
1. World War, 1939-1945 – Naval operations – Submarine
2. World War, 1939–1945 – Naval operations, German
3. World War, 1939–1945 – Campaigns – Indian Ocean
I. Title
940.5'429

ISBN 1-85367-615-2

Library of Congress Cataloging-in-Publication Data available

Edited, designed and typeset by Roger Chesneau

Printed and bound in Great Britain by
MPG Books Ltd, Bodmin, Cornwall

*This book is dedicated to
the München U-Bootkameradschaft*

Contents

Illustrations

The first glimpse of the mysterious Far East for a German U-boat crew

Georgetown pictured from the conning tower of a U-boat

A U-boat approaches her berth at Swettenham Pier

A German welcoming party at Swettenham Pier

U 183, *U 188* and *U 532* at Penang

Crewmen aboard *U 861* relax with coffee and cake

Korvettenkapitän Wolfgang Erhardt and *Fregattenkapitän* Wilhelm Dommes

Members of a U-boat crew at their billet

A sports event between German crewmen and their Japanese hosts

A sample of the opulence in which the German crews were housed in Malaysia

A view over Penang, with Pulau Jerejak in the distance

Local girls, often hired by the *Kriegsmarine* staff

The funicular railway between Penang Hill and Georgetown

Interaction betwen the Oriental and Occidental cultures

German and Japanese servicemen overcoming the racial divide

Goodwill from the Imperial Japanese Army

Crewmen from *U 861* try their hand at touring by pony

Dönitz listening to an address by a Japanese naval officer

Kapitänleutnant Konrad Hoppe and two of his Japanese naval staff

U-boats at rendezvous during their return from the East

The platform provided for the launch of the *Bachstelze* rotor-kite

Another view of the *Bachstelze* platform, seen from the '*Wintergarten*'

The *Bachstelze* stowed within one of the upright canisters

Manning the *Naxos* radar alarm atop *U 861*'s conning tower

War correspondent Kiefer's watercolour painting in *U 861*'s guest book

An example of 'Ultra' decryption of the German Enigma code network

The wide sweep of the Type IXD2's deck

A reload torpedo is withdrawn from its port-side storage container

A torpedo is tipped and lowered to the U-boat's interior torpedo room

A crew member about to carry out a check on suspected damage

Obersteuermann Berthold Wendelmuth aboard *U 861*

Heinz-Wilhelm Eck's *U 852* wrecked and beached on the Somalian
  coast
Petty officers aboard *U 861* relax for the camera in 1944
Jürgen Oesten and Günther Kuhnke after *U 861*'s arrival at
  Trondheim

*Unless indicated otherwise, all photographs are from the author's
collection*

Preface

On 29 August 1943 a small warship entered the Malaysian harbour of Georgetown on the island of Pilau Pinang, known to Westerners as Penang. The Malay peninsula, to which the island was adjacent, was no stranger to naval activity since having fallen to Japanese invaders in December 1941. Almost immediately after its victorious and brief campaign of conquest, the Imperial Japanese Navy had begun to station submarines in Penang following their deployment in action within the Bay of Bengal. However, the low silhouette that approached Swettenham Pier on that humid August day was not that of a large Japanese cruiser-submarine but rather *U 178*, a German Type IXD2 U-boat. The arrival of this vessel heralded nearly two years of operational U-boat presence in the Far East as *Grossadmiral* Karl Dönitz sought to open fresh hunting grounds for his force.

In his memoirs, published in Germany in 1958, Dönitz related the tempestuous events of his own life, largely in the context of his naval service as a member, and later commander, of Germany's U-Boat Service. However, within over 500 pages and thousands of words of text there are only 42 lines summarising one of the most unusual applications of German U-boat force during the Second World War. In total, nearly 50 U-boats were assigned to penetrate the Indian Ocean, as far north as the Arabian Sea, in search of targets before proceeding to Malaysia, where rudimentary bases awaited them, serving alongside troops of the Imperial Japanese forces. To clarify its area, the 28,400,000 square miles that comprise the Indian Ocean make it the third largest body of water in the world. It stretches from the northern boundary of southern Asia and the Indian subcontinent to Antarctica, bordered on the west by the Arabian Peninsula and Africa running to the 20° east longitude off the Cape of Good Hope, and on the east by the Malay Peninsula, the Sunda Islands and Australia. The ocean has been of great value to European trade since the time that the first Portuguese explorer, Vasco de Gama, rounded the Cape of Good Hope in 1487 and made landfall in India; and the opening of the Suez Canal in 1869 rendered control of the Indian Ocean supply arteries of enormous importance to Britain and her interests within the almost landlocked Mediterranean. Although the *Kriegsmarine*'s war in the Indian Ocean began with auxiliary cruisers and surface raiders, laying the foundations upon which U-boat operations could be built, that subject must necessarily form mere background information for this study: it would require separate treatment to tell the complete story of the surface raiders in this distant arena of combat.

In October 1942 the *crump* of torpedoes exploding off the eastern coast of South Africa indicated the arrival of German U-boats for the first time within the Indian Ocean. Detached from supporting the *Eisbär* group's attack against South Africa, the first Type IXD2 U-cruisers then entered the action, their incredible range enabling the *Kriegsmarine* to begin U-boat operations within fresh hunting grounds of enormous potential. Over the months that followed, more U-boats sailed for the burgeoning battlegrounds around the Cape of Good Hope and Madagascar. Finally granted permission by the Japanese occupation forces to use Malaysia as an operational station, they began stretching their limits northwards to the Arabian Sea before continuing eastwards to Penang and their new base. There German and Japanese forces mixed on a hitherto unseen scale, serving not only to spread U-boat activity throughout the Indian Ocean and into the Pacific but also to bring into stark relief the fundamental differences between the German and Japanese war aims. The two nationalities were before long joined by a third—the crews of Italian supply submarines. Relations between the fighting men of the three main Axis powers were often brutal and almost constantly turbulent.

This, then, is the story of a forgotten campaign, waged by U-boats as far to the east as New Zealand and fought to the very shores of India and the entrance to the Persian Gulf. Fighting Allied naval and air power, tropical storms, malaria and that implacable foe the ocean, Germany's 'Grey Wolves' persevered in the face of appalling casualties to take their fight into the Far East. This is the story of these *Monsun* U-boats.

ACKNOWLEDGEMENTS

The writing of a book like this would be impossible for me without the support and help of a great number of people. First of all I would like to thank my wife Sarah, as well as my family (Audrey, Shane, Ray, Megan and James Paterson, and Julia Hargreaves) for their constant encouragement.

I would also like to mention Maggie Bidmead, the former Keeper of Archives at the RNSM, who always helped willingly with information, inspiration and afternoon chats in her office—and then embarked on a career as an excellent freelance proof-reader: my thanks for your work in eliminating those nagging 'typos' from the manuscript. Thanks go also to Tonya Allen for her impeccable proofreading.

The preparation of this manuscript was made possible by my barricading myself into Elizabeth Burbridge's study ('the Bunker'), for which I am deeply indebted. You can have it back now! Lionel Leventhal and the entire staff of Greenhill Books have made the production of this book, and my previous work, a pleasure.

For information, help or plain inspiration I am very grateful to the following people: Lt Goh Keng Loon, Royal Malaysian Air Force; Carlo Guzzi; Ralf Bublitz; Jürgen Weber and the München U-Boot-Kameradschaft; Deborah Eaton, Head Librarian and Keeper of the Emden Naval Collection, St Edmund Hall, Oxford; Jurgen Schlemm, Editor of the excellent *Das Archiv*; Ulrich and Cristel Zimmermann; Peter 'More Krustenbraten' Carlow; David 'Gepeto' Beasley; Saint Peter and his never-ending supply of paper; Ian Kilminster; Eddie Clark; Phil Taylor; Phil Campbell; Mick Burston; Pete Gill; Mikkey Dee; the mighty Beamer; Big Col of MH-fame; and the courteous and helpful staff at Kew's Public Records Office. Horst and Annmarie Bredow of Altenbruch's U-Boot Archiv also provided much time for me to peruse the fascinating collection of documents within their walls.

My most sincere thanks go to the many veterans of the Second World War who have shared their knowledge and memories with me. I would like to begin by mentioning the special credit that I owe to Jürgen Oesten

(*U 61*, *U 106* and *U 861*) and Hans-Joachim Krug (*U 219*) for the time that they spent talking of their experiences within the Far Eastern U-boats and correcting mistakes that had crept into the text. Moreover, *Herr* Oesten has permitted the reproduction of many of his unique photographs from *U 861*'s journey to and from the Far East: taken by an onboard photographer, they offer an unsurpassed glimpse into life aboard the Type IXD2 as well as in occupied Penang and Singapore. Of course, there are many other veterans who have helped with their time and willingness to talk about their experiences before during and after the war. Of those who had helped me, I would particularly like to mention Georg Seitz (*U 604* and *U 873*), Hans Rudolf Rösing (*U 48*), Georg Högel (*U 30* and *U 110*), Gerhard Buske (*U 226*) and Ludwig Stoll (*U 148*). The hospitality that these men and their families have extended to my wife and me made researching this subject an enormous pleasure on a professional and personal level. I offer my apologies to those not listed by name, but they have my enduring gratitude.

Lawrence Paterson
2004

Glossary

A	(German) *Achtzig Meter*. KTB shorthand meaning 'eighty metres'. Thus a boat at a depth of 110 metres could be referred to as 'A+30'.
ASDIC	Term applied to the sonar equipment used for locating submerged submarines. A powerful and effective weapon, it emitted a distinct 'ping' when locating the target. 'ASDIC' is an acronym for 'Anti-Submarine Detection Committee', the organisation that began research into this device in 1917.
AGRU Front	(German) *Ausbildungsgruppe Front*. The technical branch that handled the final tests and training of boats and crews before they left for the front.
BdU	(German) *Befehlshaber der Unterseeboote*. Commander U-Boats.
Betasom	(Italian) Italian submarine command for operations in the Atlantic. Established in Bordeaux during 1940, it became operational in September that year and had an establishment of 32 submarines before Italy's surrender in September 1943. The name was a simple derivative of two words—'B' for 'Bordeaux' and 'SOM' as an abbreviation for *Sommergibile* ('submarine' in Italian). Within the Italian military, the letter B was indicated as 'Beta', and thus the combination of the two created the name '*Betasom*'.

Bold	(German) Short for *Kobold* (goblin), an acoustic decoy known also as the 'submarine bubble target'. It comprised a small cylindrical mesh container filled with calcium hydride. When ejected from a submerged U-boat the compound reacted with seawater and gave off hydrogen bubbles and hence a false echo to ASDIC operators. It was simple but effective.
DF	Direction-finding. Locating U-boats by pinpointing their radio transmissions.
Eel	(German *aal*) Slang expression for torpedo.
Enigma	(German) Coding machine used by German Armed Forces throughout World War II.
FdU	(German) *Führer der Unterseeboote*. Flag Officer for Submarines, responsible for a particular geographical region.
FRUMEL	Fleet Radio Unit Melbourne. Allied intelligence monitoring service in Australia.
grt	Gross registered tons (one ton = 100 cubic feet of cargo capacity). A standard way of judging merchant shipping size.
HF/DF	High-frequency direction-finder. Used to locate U-boats by detecting radio emissions.
(*Ing.*)	(German) *Ingenieur*. Engineering grade, e.g. *Kaptitänleutnant (Ing)*.
Kriegsmarine	(German) Navy of the Third Reich.
KTB	(German) *Kriegstagebuch*. War Diary. Kept by the commander during a U-boat's patrol. His handwritten version was later typed for the official records. Included torpedo firing diagrams.
LI	(German) *Leitendre Ingenieur*, Chief Engineer.
Luftwaffe	(German) Air Force.
OKM	(German) *Oberkommando der Kriegsmarine*. Supreme Navy Command.
OKW	(German) *Oberkommando der Wehrmacht*; Supreme Armed Forces Command.
Ritterkreuz	(German) Knight's Cross of the Iron Cross.

U-Bootwaffe	(German) U-Boat Service.
Wachoffizier	(German) Watch Officer. There were three separate U-boat watch crews, each consisting of an officer, a petty officer and two ratings. The ship's First Watch Officer (IWO) would be the Executive Officer (second-in-command), the Second Watch Officer (IIWO) the ship's designated Second Officer and the Third Watch Officer (IIIWO) often the *Obersteuermann* (Navigation Officer).
Wehrmacht	(German) Armed Forces.
'Wintergarten'	(German) Nickname given to the open railed extension astern of the conning tower, built to accommodate increased flak weaponry. Known to the Allies as a 'bandstand'.

Table of Ranks

German	Japanese	British/American
Grossadmiral	–	Admiral of the Fleet/ Fleet Admiral
Admiral	Taisho	Admiral
Vizeadmiral (V.A.)	Chujo	Vice-Admiral
Konteradmiral (K.A.)	Shosho	Rear Admiral
Kapitän zur See (K.z.S.)	Taisa	Captain
Fregattenkapitän (F.K.)	Chusa	Commander
Korvettenkapitän (K.K.)	Chusa	Commander
Kapitänleutnant (Kptlt.)	Shosa	Lieutenant-Commander
Oberleutnant zur See (Oblt.z.S.)	Tai-i	Lieutenant
Oberleutnant der Reserve (Oblt.d.R.)	–	Lieutenant of the Reserve
Leutnant zur See (L.z.S.)	Chu-i	Sub-Lieutenant/ Lieutenant (j.g.)
Fähnrich	Sho-i	Midshipman/Ensign
Stabsobersteuermann	–	Senior Quartermaster/ Warrant Quartermaster

Obermaschinist	–	Senior Machinist/ Warrant Machinist
Bootsmann	–	Boatswain
Oberbootsmannsmaat	–	Boatswain's Mate Second Class
Bootsmannsmaat	–	Coxswain
Mechanikermaat	–	Torpedo Petty Officer
-maat (the man's trade inserted at dash)	–	Petty Officer
Maschinenobergefreiter	–	Leading Seaman Machinist
Funkobergefreiter	–	Leading Seaman Telegraphist
Matrosenobergefreiter	–	Leading Seaman
Maschinengefreiter	–	Able Seaman Machinist
Matrosengefreiter	–	Able Seaman

One

The Genesis of German Far Eastern Involvement

THE WAR in Europe was three years old before the sound of exploding German torpedoes from the spearhead group of U-boats fighting their way around South Africa reverberated within the Indian Ocean. However, in order to understand the reasoning behind the stationing of German submarines so far from the vital Atlantic convoy routes it is essential to understand the strategic importance of the British supply lines that traversed the Indian Ocean. It is also important to realise that submarines and other naval forces of both Germany and Italy had already been operating within the Indian Ocean long before the arrival of the former's Grey Wolves.

The idea of stationing U-boats within the Far East could rightly claim to have grown from roots first established during German-Japanese naval co-operation at the end of the nineteenth century, when Japan was waging her war against Russia. Later, during the First World War, Berlin and Tokyo found themselves on opposite sides of the conflict, although their only potentially major naval confrontation was averted as Japanese troops occupied the German protectorate of Kiaochao in 1914 at the behest of the British. Kiaochao boasted the German colonial outpost of Tsingtao, an important military and trading hub which had also housed the German East Asia Squadron before its withdrawal at the first sign of possible combat with Japan's overwhelming naval might. Indeed by 1914 Germany possessed a scattering of recently claimed colonies, including several within the Pacific Ocean in what are now known as Papua-New Guinea, Micronesia, Samoa, the Marianas and

Nauru. The period of war between 1914 and 1918 deprived Germany of all her acquisitions.

Years later relations between Berlin and Tokyo improved, particularly after Hitler's accession to power and the rise of the aggressive military *junta* in Japan, but even before the advent of the National Socialist state in Germany U-boat commanders and engineers who had seen action between 1914 and 1918 travelled to Japan to advise and assist in designing submarines for her Imperial Navy (*Teikoku Kaigun*).

During the mid-1930s the two countries moved inexorably closer to one another, until on 25 November 1936 they signed the Anti-Comintern Pact in Berlin. Dedicated to resisting the influence of spreading international communism, the Pact concentrated in particular on the containment of the Soviet Union and Stalin's potentially expansionist leanings as Emperor Hirohito's government and Adolf Hitler prepared to indulge theirs. The alliance was soon joined by Italy, and the resulting so-called Triple Axis was established by November 1937. However, there was little unity of purpose in the various protocols signed by the three nations. Within mainland Europe, Italy adopted the role of a passive member, Mussolini's colonial aspirations lying in North and East Africa, while Hitler hoped that the treaty would dissuade Stalin's regime from interfering with Germany's planned extensions to the south—into Czechoslovakia and Austria. While keeping Stalin in check, Germany could strengthen her enlarged borders before directly confronting the Soviet Union at a time of Hitler's choosing. In Tokyo, the Japanese government also hoped to avoid Soviet interference, this time in their war of conquest on mainland China.

Disharmony between the two major Axis powers followed soon afterwards when, shortly before its attack on Poland in September 1939, Hitler's government concluded a non-aggression pact with its ideological enemy, Russia. Japan protested vigorously and stated baldly—and correctly—that it violated the Anti-Comintern pact, but Hitler, soon flushed with the success of his *Wehrmacht* and victory against the Poles, blatantly ignored the Japanese protest. However, Erich Raeder, the head of Germany's small *Kriegsmarine*, cherished hopes of German-Japanese naval co-operation despite the brusque reaction of his commander-in-chief to the Japanese complaints. Raeder realised that Germany's navy was in no position seriously to threaten British dominance on the world's oceans, notably the Atlantic, and reasoned that, by utilising the strength of the large and powerful Imperial Japanese Navy operating along the same lines as his own, the supremacy of Britain's Royal Navy could be diluted by its need to maintain sufficient strength in several geographically spread regions. Raeder also wished to lease some of Japan's large cruiser-submarines to augment the tiny U-boat force under the command of *Fregattenkapitän* Karl Dönitz, as well as bases within the Far East from which to strike at the trade arteries that traversed the Indian Ocean and kept alive British interests in the Middle East and North Africa. Indeed, although Hitler failed to grasp this most fundamental of issues, German domination of the Mediterranean could lead directly to control of North Africa and the Middle Eastern oilfields, spreading as far as the southern borders of the Caucasus. From there India—and, ultimately, the entire Indian subcontinent—lay vulnerable to attack and exploitation. The course of war against Britain could thus have been altered dramatically by German naval success in the Mediterranean Sea and land victory in Egypt. On 8 December 1939 the German naval command formally requested that Japanese bases be made available for *Kriegsmarine* units, an appeal that prompted protracted negotiations in Tokyo between Japanese authorities and *Kapitän zur See* Joachim Lietzmann, the German Naval Attaché. During these inconclusive initial discussions the Japanese proposed that German naval units could perhaps be allowed to lease sites in the Caroline, Aleutian, Marshall or Amchitka Islands. Nevertheless, ultimately no real headway was made in reaching a successful conclusion to the talks.

In the meantime, by mid-1940 Germany had spectacularly defeated her enemies on mainland Europe and successfully invaded Norway by means of combined amphibious and parachute landings. Importantly for Allied security within the Red Sea and Middle East, Italy had also finally declared war on Britain and France on 10 June, Australia, Canada, India, New Zealand and South Africa correspondingly declaring war on Italy hours later. Britain's Mediterranean possessions now appeared to face a direct threat from Mussolini's modern Roman legions, a situation exacerbated within a fortnight when the *Wehrmacht*, in a lightning military campaign, comprehensively defeated France. Strategically, Italy, with her large naval and air force units, was well placed to threaten the otherwise unhampered supply of material bound for Britain from the oil-producing regions of the Middle East. The countries fringing the coasts of the Persian Gulf lay within the British sphere of influence and were either Allied or pro-Allied neutral countries, although Persia remained a dubious friend at best. To the south-east, Arabia maintained close ties with Britain, also securing the eastern shores of the Red Sea and its important entrance to the Suez Canal. At the southern end of Arabia, Aden was a British colony. On the western shore of the Red Sea, Egypt and the Anglo-Egyptian Sudan were squarely within Allied control; further south, French and British Somaliland lay on the southern shores of the Gulf of Aden. However, between the Sudan and Anglo-French Somaliland were the linked Italian colonies of Eritrea, Ethiopia and Italian Somaliland, bordered to the south by British Kenya. This small but strategically vital empire—Italian East Africa—gave Italian air and naval forces the potential to cut crucial Allied supply routes to Suez that trailed through the cramped passage of the Red Sea, particularly the southern entrance channel at Bab el Mandeb. Within the small port of Massawa in Eritrea, seven destroyers, eight submarines and two torpedo-boats of the *Regia Marina* lay ready for action against Allied merchant shipping, both within the Red Sea and Indian Ocean. Furthermore, it was not merely the naval threat that concerned Britain: Italian army units stationed within the region were also theoretically powerful enough to conquer both British and French Somaliland, thereby posing a serious threat to the Sudan and Kenya. The Italians' one major problem was of supply to their distant colonies, the only effective route left open to them an aerial link from Libya.

While Italy prepared for her Middle Eastern and North African adventures, amongst the spoils of war from conquered Europe that Hitler could not readily claim were French and Dutch colonial possessions. Many such territories lay within the Pacific, a region considered by the Japanese as their personal area of authority. In order to allay fears in Tokyo over German trespass within their domain, the Japanese proposed a new pact detailing territorial claims and pledging conditional mutual assistance, particularly in the event of an attack on Japan by nations not already involved in the European or Chinese conflicts. Signed in Berlin on 27 September 1940, the Tripartite Pact declared that

> The Governments of Germany, Italy and Japan . . . have decided to stand by and co-operate with one another in regard to their efforts in Greater East Asia

and the regions of Europe, respectively, wherein it is the prime purpose to establish and maintain a new order of things calculated to promote mutual prosperity and welfare of the peoples concerned.

Alongside the main treaty clauses were two Secret Supplementary Protocols exchanged between the three countries. The Axis powers had already determined to establish joint military and naval commissions as well as a joint economic commission within the clauses of their main treaty, the secret addendum stating more bluntly that the three countries would

> . . . undertake to exchange from time to time without delay all useful inventions and devices of war and to supply one another with war equipment, such as airplanes, tanks, guns, explosives, etc., which each party may reasonably spare, together with technical skill and men, should they be required.

However, once again none of the parties bound by the Treaty appeared to view it as much more than a convenience for their own separate ambitions. Japan in particular, paranoid about German interest in the Pacific, was gratified when Hitler declared no territorial claim on the colonies of his recently subjugated foes (particularly the Dutch East Indies oilfields, which were crucial for Japanese imports of crude oil), although the German leader demanded guarantees from Tokyo that Germany could gain access to reasonable amounts of raw materials that might be found on the small islands.

While Berlin and Tokyo negotiated, Rome began to suffer the first of many unpredicted and devastating military upsets that would seem to characterise Mussolini's war. Italian possessions within the Middle East were staggering under the hammer blows of precisely targeted and extremely effective Allied attack, although not totally without retaliation. Four of the eight Italian submarines stationed in Eritrea had been accounted for within ten days of action. On 14 June 1940 *Macallé* ran aground, becoming a total loss. Two days later *Galieleo Galilei* made the sole sinking of a merchant ship by the group during June when she torpedoed and sank the 8,215-ton Norwegian MT *James Stove*. Captain Olaus Eliassen had been taking his tanker from Singapore to Aden, carrying 10,800 tons of aviation fuel bound for British forces, when *Galieleo Galilei* intercepted the ship and signalled her to stop. The crew were given an opportunity to abandon ship in lifeboats before two torpedoes sent her under. On 19 June it was *Galilei*'s turn as the armed trawler

Moonstone captured her following a surfaced gun duel in the Gulf of Aden during which the Italian commander and several men were killed.[1] On 23 June, off the coast of French Somaliland, the submarine *Evangelista Toricelli* was scuttled after taking severe damage from the destroyers HMS *Kandahar*, *Khartoum* and *Kingston*, supported by the sloops *Shoreham* and *Indus*. During the fierce action, which comprised much surface gunnery, *Shoreham* was hit and damaged, while an Italian shell also hit *Khartoum*, splinters ricocheting against stored torpedoes which exploded and caused the destroyer to sink in shallow water off Perim Island. The submarine *Galvani* sank the 661-ton Indian patrol boat *Pathan* with a torpedo before being sunk herself by the sloop HMS *Falmouth* the following day. The last success of an Italian submarine within the Indian Ocean was the sinking of Greek tanker SS *Atlas* on 6 September 1940, by a torpedo from *Guglielmotti*.

On land, Italian forces had greater success at first, moving from Ethiopia to attack British Somaliland and border posts in Kenya and the Sudan. The British evacuated the Somali capital, Berbera, on 14 August, Italian troops entering the town five days later. However, their success was to be relatively short-lived. In January 1941 the British and Dominion campaign to drive the Italians from East Africa began in earnest. Eritrea was invaded from the Sudan by largely Indian forces, while East African and South African troops attacked Italian Somaliland from Kenya to the south. The Indian advance into Eritrea was held up for most of February and March by the battle for Keren, which controlled the road through the mountainous interior that led to the Eritrean capital Asmara and the vital port of Massawa. However, to the south, Mogadishu, the capital of Italian Somaliland, was swiftly captured on 25 February, British forces pushing north-west into Ethiopia immediately afterwards. By 1 April the capture of Eritrea on the Red Sea coast of Italian East Africa was accomplished when Asmara was occupied, the strategically vital port of Massawa falling to Allied troops seven days later. On 6 April Addis Ababa, the capital of Ethiopia, was taken, confining Italian resistance to the rugged northern highlands of Ethiopia.

Before the fall of Massawa the eight surviving Italian destroyers and torpedo-boats had been lost in action or scuttled in last-ditch attacks on Port Sudan and convoy traffic near the Eritrean coast. The Italian armed merchant cruiser *Ramb 1* was located within the Indian Ocean near the

Maldive Islands and sunk by the New Zealand cruiser HMNZS *Leander* as she attempted to break free of the East African débâcle and make for open seas and a potential raiding voyage. However, the four remaining Italian submarines had indeed managed to make good their escape. After fourteen unsuccessful patrols between September 1940 and February 1941, *Archimede, Ferraris, Guglielmotti* and *Perla* managed to escape from the Indian Ocean, rounding the Cape of Good Hope and eventually reaching Bordeaux, France, where they would join the *Betasom* command established within that port. With Italian naval forces either defeated or fleeing, the Allies once again considered the Red Sea and Indian Ocean to be secure.

The end of Axis power within the region was hastened after a pro-German *coup* in Iraq on 1 April 1941 had threatened Allied oil supplies, prompting British and Indian units to enter the country through the Persian Gulf, advance on Baghdad and occupy the city on 1 June. Later that month Allied troops invaded Vichy French Lebanon and Syria, concerned about growing German influence within the region. An armistice signed in the middle of July brought the fighting to an end, but paranoia over spreading pro-German sentiment in the Middle East had already begun to swell. During August the possibility of a pro-Axis *coup d'état* led Anglo-Soviet forces to invade and occupy Persia. A cease-fire was announced within four days, but violations of its terms led to Teheran being occupied by the British in the middle of September. By the month's end, with the exception of small parts of Ethiopia, the whole of the Middle East and East Africa, with its vital oilfields and pipelines, was now firmly under Allied control. Success was complete when the last Italian forces surrendered at Gondar in the northern mountains of Ethiopia near Lake Tana on 27 November 1941. The Italian East African empire had ceased to exist.

Tensions within the Indian Ocean were not completely assuaged by these events. In response to the British seizure off South Africa on 3 November 1941 of five merchant ships that comprised a Vichy convoy bound from Madagascar to Europe, two Vichy submarines were ordered by Pétain's government to operate against Allied shipping. The submarine *Le Héros* subsequently sank Captain This Jørgensen's 5,757-ton Norwegian steamer SS *Thode Fagelund* east of East London on 17 November. Travelling from Chittagong and Madras to Britain via Cape

Town with a cargo of scrap iron, jute and tea, the steamer was hit by a single torpedo in the stern near No 5 hold and the subsequent damage caused her to sink immediately, although all 35 crewmen successfully abandoned ship and were later rescued. Initially their report to the South African authorities on the circumstances of the attack caused great suspicion in Cape Town, where the Allied representatives at first refused to believe that enemy submarines or aircraft were active in that area. The possibility of Axis mines within the region was also denied, and the suspicion of sabotage was unfairly placed on the ship's First Mate before Jørgensen categorically stated that it had been a torpedo that had hit his ship. His statement culminated with the assertion that after the initial explosion he had definitely spotted a conning tower and periscope to port of his sinking ship. Eventually Cape Town reported to the Admiralty that a Vichy French submarine had indeed torpedoed *Thode Fagelund*, their conclusion aided by knowledge of the Vichy convoy capture as well as intercepted radio communications between the French authorities and the convoy's escorting destroyer *d'Iberville*, which had been allowed to return to Madagascar. The submarines *Le Glorieux* and *Le Héros* were thought to have departed Dakar for Madagascar as part of the escort for a different convoy but had not returned with the recalled merchant ships and were therefore potentially active within the Indian Ocean.

German raiders had also long been in action within the region, the first wave of two fast diesel-powered pocket battleships leaving Germany during the very first days of the war and a second wave of disguised warships—armed merchant cruisers—departing in 1940.[2] By January 1941 six of the original seven AMC raiders were still at sea, joined in February by the pocket battleship *Admiral Scheer*, which operated successfully off Madagascar before returning to Germany after five months in the Atlantic and Indian Oceans with 16 sinkings totalling 99,000 tons to her credit. On 8 May the heavy cruiser HMS *Cornwall* found and sank the German AMC *Pinguin* north of the Seychelles—the first surface raider to be hunted down successfully and sunk. She had accounted for 28 merchant ships totalling 136,000 tons.

While the Allied war against Germany and Italy continued unabated, tensions with Japan also increased dramatically. During July 1941 Vichy France acceded to Japanese demands for bases in southern Indo-China, allowing Japanese troops to enter the country. Britain, the Dutch government in exile and the United States immediately protested and froze Japanese assets. Nevertheless, Japanese troops continued to march into their new occupation areas as the Dutch East Indies cancelled existing oil delivery arrangements with Tokyo and America imposed her own oil embargo. At a stroke, therefore, Japan had lost her primary sources of oil, and, as stocks rapidly began to dwindle, she stepped up her preparations for war. In October 1941 the last nail was driven into the coffin of peace when the Japanese War Minister, *Taisho* (General) Hideki Tôjô, became Prime Minister after the resignation of Prince Konoye.

During the month of November talks regarding the Japanese presence in South-East Asia dragged on, the United States demanding the departure of Japanese troops from China as well as from French Indo-China, while the Imperial Japanese Navy's Pearl Harbor Strike Force sailed into the North Pacific. Britain's limited naval deterrent to Japanese expansion, the capital ships *Prince of Wales* and *Repulse*, met at Colombo, Ceylon, on 28 November, en route to Singapore, where they hoped to convey the potential threat of entanglement with British forces to Tôjô's military *junta*. However, without the fleet carrier *Indomitable*, due to join the pair but damaged after grounding near Jamaica, they had no viable aircraft support—a fact soon to bear fruit for Japan.

Despite the lauded co-operation of the Axis' three military powers, Hitler had refused to give warning to Japan of his attack on Russia during June 1941 and, likewise, Japan provided no firm indication of her strike against Pearl Harbor once Tokyo had obtained Germany's written pledge to support Japan and enter into any future war that might break out between Japan and the United States.[3] On 7 December 1941 the almost inevitable escalation of the political stand-off burst over Pearl Harbor, Hawaii, as aircraft carrying the emblem of the Rising Sun launched their raid against the American naval base on the island of Oahu in what President Roosevelt famously described a 'day of infamy'.[4] On 11 December 1941, four days after the Japanese strike, Germany and Italy dutifully declared war against the United States, Hitler jubilantly remarking, 'We can't lose the war at all. We now have an ally which has never been conquered in 3,000 years!'[5]

The three Axis countries signed yet another treaty that same day to cover the realities of joint warfare, precluding any signatory from establishing a separate peace with the Allied nations ranged against them. This last accord was followed by the further secret Tripartite Military Agreement signed on 18 January 1942. Enhancing the protocols already established, this also provided a foundation for increased naval co-operation between the three nations in terms of strategy and operations, 'in order to ensure operational co-operation among one another and to destroy the fighting capacity of the enemy as quickly as possible.'[6] At the same time a firm delineation of the world's oceans was created between the Western and Eastern Axis powers. The longitude of 70° east, bisecting the Indian Ocean and mainland west of the Maldives and Bombay, was chosen. Crucially, however, Article Three allowed the zones of responsibility to be crossed, stating that 'In the Indian Ocean each side may carry out operations across the above-agreed boundary according to the situation.'[7]

As well as the combat possibilities entailed by the Tripartite Pacts, both the Japanese and German governments expressed great interest in the possibilities for the exchange of materials and technology. For the Japanese there seemed to be great potential in examining German design ideas and adapting them for their own use. While Japanese technicians often lacked the initial inventive flair that would lead to such German developments as jet and rocket fighters and highly specialised production tools, they had complete mastery of the ability to copy and enhance an already proven product.

With the outbreak of war in the Far East on 7 December 1941, Japanese submarines were immediately active within the Indian Ocean and in the waters around South-East Asia. Indeed on 10 December it was *I-156* that spotted and unsuccessfully attacked HMS *Repulse* and *Prince of Wales*, the submarine's subsequent sighting report bringing aircraft from Saigon to torpedo and sink the British behemoths that lacked air cover of their own. In total, 31 submarines of the Imperial Japanese Navy were deployed within the Indian Ocean, sinking 41 ships and damaging five by April 1942. In turn Japanese carrier groups had by this time launched devastating raids against Darwin to the south and Ceylon to the west, a mixed destroyer and cruiser group also prowling the Bay of Bengal and savaging British merchant and naval strength.

Japanese naval strategy focused firmly on harassing shipping around Hawaii, New Zealand and Australia and making the occasional raiding

forays to South Africa, the Panama Canal and the west coast of the
United States, concentrating on cutting vulnerable supply and communications lines that stretched from the United States over thousands of
miles of ocean. The Japanese Southern Command area would also deploy its naval forces into the Indian Ocean and off Australia's west coast
in order to interdict the sea lanes leading into the Atlantic and Indian
Oceans.

During the swift subjugation of Malaysia by Imperial Japanese forces,
Penang was first bombed by 27 Japanese aircraft during the morning of
11 December 1941, starting a wholesale emigration by town residents
into the countryside. As the brief raid developed, many people crowded
on to the streets to watch, believing the aircraft to be from the British
carrier HMS *Eagle*, which was said by locals to be sailing to Singapore.
One bomb exploded beside the minaret of the Kapitan Kling Mosque;
others fell on Ah Qwee Street, Kampung Kolam and Chulia Street.
Twelve people were killed within that small area of town, while elsewhere there was apparently considerable damage and loss of life, although records are difficult to access. Georgetown's fire station was
amongst those buildings hit by high-explosive bombs, and flames quickly
raged unchecked through the narrow streets. Two more days of bombing followed and people fled the city, which was soon quiet and covered
with a pall of smoke, the streets of Georgetown virtually deserted apart
from small groups of looters.[8] Despite having been given the grandiose
title of 'Fortress Penang', Georgetown was defended by four anti-
aircraft guns and around 500 largely untrained troops. On 16 December
1941 the British evacuated the island to crowd within the doomed fortress of Singapore, the withdrawal limited to personnel of British birth,
fuelling despair and anger among the Asiatic population who felt abandoned at a time when they wanted leadership from the Imperial forces.[9]
Penang was soon occupied after unopposed fast-moving soldiers of the
Kobayashi Battalion of the Japanese 5th Infantry Division landed on
the island during 17 December. The battered, narrow, Chinese-style
streets of Georgetown and the British-built fortifications of Fort
Cornwallis, completed on the order of Francis Light decades earlier,
were soon crowned with the flag of Imperial Japan's Rising Sun.

Almost immediately the Detached Workshop of the 101st Office of
Naval Construction arrived in Penang, establishing a naval presence on

the island for the first time in order to provide routine repairs and maintenance for Japanese submarines. The new base was opened for use on 20 January. In short order the Workshop was enlarged to form a more permanent base, absorbed into the headquarters of *Shosho* Ishizaki Noboru's 8th Submarine Squadron (Sixth Fleet) on 17 April 1942. This group, expanded on 12 September 1943 with the arrival of the 30th Submarine Unit (including three I-class boats) as command changed from Ishizaki to *Chujo* Ichioka Hisashi, eventually comprised a total of ten submarines, four of them I-class with seaplanes embarked within capacious deck hangars. The 8th Submarine Squadron was divided during 1942 into three divisions: the 1st, comprising *I-10* (the flagship), *I-16*, *I-18* and *I-20*; the 3rd, comprising *I-21*, *I-22* and *I-24*; and the 14th, consisting of *I-27*, *I-29* and *I-30*. The 1st Division (*Kô*) that spearheaded the Penang contingent to their new base had originally been stationed at Kwajalein Atoll in the Marshall Islands but had been redeployed as part of a planned major offensive against Allied merchant shipping and sea communication lines in the Indian Ocean. As Mochitsura Hashimoto, wartime commander of *I-58*, related,

> Our losses [in the Indian Ocean] were small and the harvest large, while in the Pacific it was just the other way around . . . Compared with the bases in the southern seas, Penang was better equipped in every way and was very popular with submarine crews, and the Indian Ocean campaign was regarded almost as a paradise compared with the 'Hell War' in the Pacific.[10]

From there Japanese forces, following the urgings of the *Kriegsmarine*, launched their attempts at disrupting Allied merchant and military supply lines and communications arteries within the Arabian Sea. In turn, success in these endeavours could have had a decisive effect on the *Wehrmacht*'s land operations aimed at capturing Egypt and the Caucasus before defeat at El Alamein, Stalingrad and the Solomons had deflected the Axis powers from their paths to victory. However, a major strategic difference between the Japanese and German submarine forces lay in the fact that while the latter concentrated on attacking merchant shipping, naval targets were the primary focus for the Japanese, merchant shipping generally being regarded as a secondary objective.

Accompanied by the auxiliary cruisers *Aikoku Maru* and *Hôkuku Maru*, which were acting as supply ships, the Japanese 1st Submarine Division (8th Flotilla) had attacked Royal Navy forces in Madagascar's

Diego Suarez harbour, recently surrendered to British invaders by its Vichy French garrison. Fearing that Japanese might establish bases on Madagascar, Winston Churchill telegraphed Roosevelt: 'A Japanese air, submarine, and/or cruiser base at Diego Suarez would paralyse our whole convoy route both to the Middle East and to the Far East. . .' To the Allies, Madagascar represented the key to the Indian Ocean, and the Allied operation 'Ironclad' therefore got under way with British land-ings on 5 May at Diego Saurez: concerned about the Japanese carrier sorties into the Indian Ocean and the vulnerability of the Cape of Good Hope/Middle East convoy routes, Britain had decided to take the strate-gically positioned port in northern Madagascar. French forces resisted fiercely for two days before the anchorage was in British hands.[11]

Japanese midget submarines launched from *I-16* and *I-20* penetrated the harbour defence at Diego Suarez on 31 May and badly damaged the battleship HMS *Ramillies*, which was forced to withdraw to Durban for repairs. The 7,000-ton tanker *British Loyalty* was also hit and sunk, but both midget submarines were lost, *I-16*'s disappearing without trace and *I-20*'s beaching on Madagascar, her crew being killed by British commandos. By the end of June 1942 the 1st Division had also sunk twenty merchant ships plying the waters of the Mozambique Channel, seriously hampering the logistical supply for Britain's Eighth Army in North Africa in what was one of the single most successful Japanese midget submarine operations.

In mid-June four of the Division's five submarines retired to Penang, their auxiliary cruiser supply ships docking in newly conquered Singapore. Singapore had been a small island settlement when Sir Stam-ford Ruffles first arrived while searching for a suitable location for a British port in January 1819. Ruffles, along with Major William Far-quahar, had chosen Singapore because of its strategic location in rela-tion to the trade routes between the Far East and Europe, and because of the fact that it possessed a deep-water harbour. Leased annually by the Crown from Malaysia, Singapore rapidly expanded as a free port; Brit-ish naval power even managed to control piracy within the region. Its strategic importance increased dramatically for Britain when the Suez Canal opened in 1869, allowing quicker transit between Europe and Asia, and the increasing desire for Malaysian rubber added to its pres-tige. It was not until the mid-1930s that Britain, alarmed at Japanese aggression against China, built Singapore's naval base. Completed in 1938, the island bastion was considered virtually impregnable by the British, but 'Fortress Singapore' possessed a major Achilles' heel in that its 'back door' faced the Malay peninsula—a vulnerability soon demonstrated following the outbreak of war with Japan in late 1941. Japanese forces of the Twenty-Fifth Army soon landed on the Malay peninsula and raced southward, herding thousands of refugees and disorganised Allied troops before them, until by 31 January 1942 over a million refugees and British troops were penned within Singapore Island. The island's major defence, the formidable guns of the Jahore battery are often recorded as 'facing the wrong way' prepared to defend against amphibious assault, but this is untrue: in fact they were indeed turned towards the mainland and the impending Japanese assault, but they had been supplied with the wrong ammunition, unsuitable for use against land combat troops.

The British garrison commander, General Sir Arthur Percival, was left in an untenable position. He was forced to defend a northern shore over 30 miles long across a strait less than a mile wide with virtually no air support and little in the way of naval defence as the British had attempted to destroy their own naval base. Facing him was *Taisho* Tomoyuku Yamashita, who skilfully feinted, stretching the already thin defenders, and then invaded on 8 February. Despite their best efforts, the defending Australian troops rapidly crumbled, and within a week Yamashita had surrounded the city proper and was in possession of the reservoirs which supplied the city with water. Fearing a civil disaster, Percival surrendered on 15 February, his command defeated by a Japanese force that they outnumbered by three to one and who had virtually run out of ammunition. The victorious Japanese renamed the city Shonanto, or 'Light of the South', and 130,000 British and Australian prisoners-of-war were marched across the island to a hastily constructed facility at Changi, where years of torment and labour would follow. Indian and Malay soldiers were urged to transfer allegiance to the Rising Sun, those that refused facing imprisonment, torture or death. However, it was the Chinese who bore the worst initial brunt of the Japanese ferocity: within three days of the defeat at Singapore all Chinese males were screened by the *Kempeitai* for potential anti-Japanese elements and thousands were executed in makeshift jails or herded on to Changi Beach and shot. The fall of Singapore had been an Allied disaster of a magnitude previously unseen—arguably even worse than defeat in France and the forced evacuation of troops from Dunkirk and other French ports.

Elsewhere the Dutch East Indies fell rapidly to advancing Japanese soldiers of the Sixteenth Army. On 1 March 1942 Japanese amphibious forces landed on Java, Batavia witnessing the Rising Sun banner within five days and the final Dutch surrender being achieved on 9 March. On land the Japanese had secured their southern boundary; at sea the battle continued.

The fifth Japanese submarine to have taken part in the first successful attack into the Indian Ocean, *I-30*, headed west instead of towards Singapore, rounding the Cape of Good Hope. She was the first Japanese boat to reach occupied France as a part of the *Yanagi* supply missions, tying up in Lorient on 5 August 1942 and bringing news of the easy successes against merchant shipping within the Indian Ocean. *Chusa* Shinobu Endo had loaded his huge submarine with a cargo of 1,500kg of mica and 660kg of shellac for transfer to German hands and would return to Japan carrying German goods—including a torpedo data computer, *Bold*, *Seetakt* radar, *Metox*, Enigma machines and G7a and G7e torpedoes. *I-30* began her return voyage, codenamed '*Kirschblüte*' ('Cherry Blossom'), on 22 August and reached Singapore on 13 October, stopping for only 6½ hours before sailing for Japan. Outbound from Singapore harbour she strayed into a Japanese defensive minefield and was sunk with the loss of fourteen of her 110 crewmen. Nevertheless this had been the first example of a submarine of the Tokyo–Berlin Axis entering a partner's harbour, and from the German point of view it represented a successful importation of Eastern raw materials.

Japanese naval deployment within the Indian Ocean, though west of the 70° demarcation longitude, suited Germany's plans that were unfolding in North Africa. With the Mediterranean closed to British merchant shipping, the Eighth Army, facing Erwin Rommel's *Afrika Korps*, was dependent on supplies shipped through the Indian Ocean into the Red Sea and Egypt. By May 1942 Rommel stood at the gates of Egypt itself and the war in North Africa hung in the balance, with British forces pushed back, their situation critical and reliant on the supplies pouring into the Mediterranean through the Suez 'back door'. It was at this moment that a Japanese advance against Ceylon, dominating the Indian

Ocean supply arteries, could have swung the balance irreversibly, leading to British defeat and a possible linking of German and Japanese
forces in India. As early as 1940 Japanese military planners had toyed
with the idea of striking west against Ceylon before attacking the United
States, but they had decided against it in favour of the raid on Pearl
Harbour and landings elsewhere. The establishment of the Greater East-
Asia Co-Prosperity Sphere, providing the legitimacy for Japan's war of
conquest, did not originally include India. However, once again plans
were drawn up in Tokyo during June 1942—mainly on the urging of the
Army High Command, which had originally opposed the idea when
first debated the previous year—for an invasion of Ceylon and an advance by the Army through India. All eyes rested on Rommel, for the
Japanese government decided that German victory in North Africa would
spur their plan into action.

However, the Imperial Japanese Navy suffered the humiliating loss
of four carriers and their aircraft at Midway during June 1942 and remained cautious of the ambitious undertaking, not realising that American codebreaking had revealed details of the bold Japanese invasion
plan and allowed the Midway force to be so successfully intercepted.
Although the IJN was in agreement with the Army that British forces,
under pressure from Rommel, were weakened and ripe for defeat if attacked from the Indian quarter, naval air power was crucially low after
Midway. Thus preparations were made for preliminary raids by capital
ships supported by meagre aerial reconnaissance assets based in
Singapore, Sabang and Rangoon augmented by shipboard catapult seaplanes.

However, the interlocking fortunes of Japan and Germany defeated
the Ceylon operation. The latter half of 1942 saw German fortunes fad-
ing in Africa and the disaster of Stalingrad looming over the *Wehrmacht*'s
immediate future. Hitler's preoccupation with Russia and ignorance of
the strategic importance of success in North Africa (and, as a corollary,
Axis control of the Mediterranean) meant that the moment when victory could have been seized had passed. Vague attempts were made at
interdicting Allied supply ships by U-boats in the Mediterranean—
against Dönitz's better judgement—once the former had passed through
the Suez Canal, but these failed. As Japan vacillated over whether to
begin the operation in the face of German retreat and increasing British

strength, American forces landed on Guadalcanal during August 1942, necessitating a diversion of Japanese strength from the Indian Ocean to the contested Solomon Islands. During September the rest of the island of Madagascar was also finally invaded by Allied troops, the capital, Tananarive, being wrested from Vichy hands on 23 September (although the last Vichy forces did not surrender until early November). The moment when Japan could have subjugated the Indian Ocean without challenge was lost never to be regained. As *Chujo* Ugaki Matome, Chief of Staff of the Combined Fleet, wrote,

> How brilliant was the first-stage operation up to April [1942]. And what miserable setbacks since Midway in June! The invasions of Hawaii, Fiji, Samoa and New Caledonia, [the] liberation of India and [the] destruction of the British Far Eastern Fleet have all scattered like dreams.[12]

However, the sudden Japanese naval probes toward Ceylon that would have preceded invasion had produced benefits for future German raiding expeditions. Suffering grievous losses, the British Eastern Fleet had retreated to East Africa, sufficiently beyond Japanese carrier aircraft range, guarding the southern entrances to the Red Sea and therefore the Mediterranean. As the Japanese, too, had withdrawn the bulk of their strength from the Indian Ocean, there suddenly existed a vacuum of power within the region. If U-boats could arrive in strength, the Indian Ocean could become an almost unopposed German hunting ground.

NOTES

1. Ironically, it had been HMT *Moonstone* that had rescued the survivors of the MT *James Stove*.
2. The pocket-battleships (heavy cruisers) *Admiral Graf Spee*, *Deutschland* and *Admiral Scheer* were the first three raiders sent to sea, the last also not until 1940. *Spee* and *Scheer* were the only two to round the Cape of Good Hope and enter the Indian Ocean; the former was later cornered and scuttled off Montevideo, Uruguay, after her return to the South Atlantic.
3. It cannot have come as a complete surprise, however: the German Ambassador in Tokyo, General Eugen Ott, judged during November that war between Japan and the USA and Britain was likely in the foreseeable future.
4. Japanese strategic planning was aided enormously by British military documents captured by the German raider *Atlantis* from the British merchant ship *Automedon* on 11 November 1940. The papers included a full appreciation of British military strength in the Far East and allowed Japanese planners to anticipate their enemy's defensive capabilities and probable reaction to a strike on Pearl Harbor. For this action *Atlantis*'s captain, Bernhard Rogge, was awarded

the Sword of the Samurai by the Japanese—one of only three given during the war.

5. Ian Kershaw, *Hitler. 1936– 1945: Nemesis*, p. 442.
6. *Reluctant Allies*, Appendix D, p. 259.
7. *Ibid.*
8. Later, looted goods offered for sale in stalls and markets were known as 'Axe Brand' items because they had been obtained by breaking down the doors of shops and houses with axes.
9. Not all the British left Penang: Dr Evans, of the General Hospital, remained behind to care for his patients and was later allowed by the Japanese to continue his work.
10. Mochitsura Hashimoto, *Sunk*, p. 38.
11. *Le Héros* was sunk by air attack on the last day of fighting in the port.
12. Krug, Hirama, Sander-Nagashima and Niestlé, *Reluctant Allies*, p. 55. Quoted from Ugaki diary, p. 319.

Two

Polar Bears at Cape Town

B Y 1942 the exchange of technology for raw materials amongst the three Axis partners was reaping enormous benefits for Germany. Despite the Nazis' ambitious—and doomed—Four-Year Plan for independence from imported goods, they remained highly dependent on natural resources from outside the Reich's borders. Before war had begun in 1939, Germany had managed to amass a small reserve of basic raw materials required for the *Wehrmacht* to conduct operations. The conquest of France, Norway and the Ukraine added to the stockpile of various goods, although these did not include such vital elements as tin, quinine, opium and—perhaps most crucially—rubber.

Since the end of the First World War, Germany had forged ahead in the creation of synthetic rubber, known as *Buna* and available in three steadily improved versions—*Buna, Buna-S* and *Buna-N*. However, despite these advances, synthetic compounds were unable to supplant the natural product and large quantities of raw rubber were still required in Germany. An increasingly tight Royal Navy blockade combined with anti-German political pressure on the countries concerned soon cut off supplies from South America, and so Hitler looked to the East for his new source of rubber, metals, ore and edible oils.

Before June 1941 the Trans-Siberian railway was available for the shipment of some supplies from Japan, but Hitler's attack on Russia closed this link. By 1941 24 large German merchant ships lay within several scattered Far Eastern harbours, caught by the outbreak of war and unable or unwilling to put to sea. Twelve of them were diesel-powered and highly suited to requisition by the *Kriegsmarine* and the task of blockade-running supply missions to Europe. Augmented by four motor ships chartered from the Japanese government and two prize vessels captured by raiders, the number of craft capable of being used as *V-Schiffe* by the *Kriegsmarine*'s Supply Service stood at seventeen by April 1941.[1]

The Italian Naval Command added four of its own cargo ships stationed in the East to the German blockade-running effort, and within the months between April 1941 and February 1942 fifteen ships, including three Italian, departed during the first season of blockade-running. Timed to pass the areas of greatest danger from Allied attack during winter months, all the voyages were routed across the Pacific and around Cape Horn. Despite the loss of three vessels at sea and the recall to Japan of a fourth, eleven freighters carrying 74,960 tons of goods (including 32,000 tons of rubber) out of a total of 104,233 tons loaded in Japan reached occupied Bordeaux, which the Germans had designated the European home port for these vessels.[2] In turn, five ships carrying 32,540 tons of mainly technological cargo reached Japan from Europe, fulfilling the Japanese demand for a *quid pro quo* from the Germans.[3] As well as the material for transfer to Japan, the five ships also carried equipment and supplies for the other German ships and departments located in the East.

The success of this first season of blockade-running prompted an escalation of the entire project, German demands and projections for imported goods increasing correspondingly. With the Japanese entry into the war during December 1941 and the swift subjugation of Malaysia and Indonesia, German ships were able to shorten the length of time that would be necessary to traverse the great distances required as they were now able to pass through the Sunda Strait, refuelling in Batavia (the old Dutch colonial title for Jakarta, renamed in early 1943) and proceeding via the Cape of Good Hope to Europe.

As the war progressed into 1942 and German naval strength was focused on the struggle over North Atlantic convoy routes, the Indian Ocean still held great importance and potential for the *Kriegsmarine*. Not only the importation of scarce raw materials but the possibility of hampering troop transport routes from British Dominion territories and South Africa could reap enormous benefit for the *Wehrmacht* on land. However, the development of a German offensive capability within the Indian Ocean was largely dependent on events in the Atlantic. While the *Kriegsmarine*'s few surface raiders travelled into the South Atlantic and Eastern seas in search of targets, U-boats were tied firmly to Dönitz's centre of operations—cutting the trade arteries between Britain and the United States. Moreover, the backbone of the U-Boat Service was the medium-sized Type VIIC, which was incapable of travelling further than the Caribbean on the western Atlantic fringe and Freetown on the eastern seaboard—and even then only with dedicated refuelling available.

During 1941 the 2nd U-Boat Flotilla, based at Lorient, began operating significant numbers of the Type IXC U-boat, a cruiser design that was capable of ranging 13,450 miles and patrolling distant targets. In October, after much pressure from his superiors, Karl Dönitz finally saw the value of striking towards the Indian Ocean with these and he directed four of the flotilla's U-boats towards Cape Town. Spearheaded by *Kapitänleutnant* Nicolai 'Nico' Clausen's *U 129*, which departed on 21 October, the *Kapstadt* group illustrated a determination by Dönitz to find fresh hunting grounds for his burgeoning U-boat fleet. A temporary dearth of targets in the North Atlantic and the greater availability of the Type IXCs—not to mention considerable pressure from within the higher echelons of the *Kriegsmarine* command—persuaded Dönitz to plan for offensive operations in distant and as yet untested arenas of combat. West Africa, particularly the vital Allied central Atlantic stopover port of Freetown, had long been under fire and the opportunity for a fresh onslaught against an unprepared enemy attracted his attention. *Abwehr* operatives within South Africa had reported upwards of 200 ships passing through Cape Town in recent months and as many as 50 moored within the harbour and its approaches at any given time.

Clausen's *U 129* was joined by Joachim 'Jochen' Mohr's *U 124*, with her distinctive Edelweiss emblem, Karl-Friedrich Merten's *U 68* and Hans Eckermann's oddity, *U A*—all scheduled to be refuelled and armed from the tanker *Python*. The boats were strictly forbidden to attack shipping once past the Equator until they were within their allocated zone of operations, but the *Kapstadt* plan ultimately misfired as a direct result of British penetration of the *Kriegsmarine*'s Enigma code net. The Admiralty had learned from decrypted Enigma messages that the raider *Atlantis* and supply ship *Python* were both active within the South Atlantic and promptly ordered the cruisers *Devonshire*, *Dorsetshire* and *Dunedin* to track them down independently and destroy them. While a miraculous long-distance torpedo shot from *U 124* destroyed *Dunedin*, *Devonshire* found and sank *Atlantis*, survivors of the raider being taken aboard by *U 126* and transferred to *Python*. Disaster then struck once more for the Germans when on 1 December HMS *Dorsetshire* appeared on the horizon as *Python* was in the act of refuelling *U 68* and *U A*. Within minutes the tanker was under attack and scuttled in the face of accurate artillery fire as the U-boats dived to safety, too far to attempt a retaliatory attack. After *Dorsetshire* had departed the scene, hundreds of survivors from the two ships were scattered amongst lifeboats and the pair of submarines. Dönitz thereupon ordered *U 124* and *U 129* to assist in the rescue, and all plans for the *Kapstadt* assault on Cape Town were abandoned.

It was not until August 1942 that another attempt at attacking South Africa was mounted. Dönitz elected once again to send four experienced U-boats, in a group designated *Eisbär* (Polar Bear)—the name a vague attempt at disguising the group's destination. The four chosen were Werner Hartenstein's *U 156*, Merten's *U 68*, Fritz Poske's *U 504* and Carl Emmermann's *U 172*, supported by the *Milchkuh* tanker *U 459* commanded by *Korvettenkapitän* Georg von Wilamowitz-Moellendorf (a First World War veteran more commonly known within the U-Boat Service as 'Wild Moritz'). Although designated a group within BdU operational records, the four attack boats were detailed to operate independently of one another beyond the initial co-ordination of timing their opening assault. Following behind the first wave would come four larger U-cruisers destined to reinforce the attack and round the Cape, crossing for the first time the 20° east meridian that bisects Cape Agulhas and separates the Indian Ocean from the wild expanse of the Atlantic.

With complete surprise a precondition of the success of the operation, a paranoid SKL issued 'Operations Order 52' via BdU that not only outlined the planned method of attack but also, once again, forbade any engagements en route after the boats had passed the Equator except in the case of 'attacks on battleships and aircraft carriers . . . provided firing data is certain.' Although recognising that results were indeed dependent on surprise, Dönitz ensured that his four commanders were well aware of their freedom to attack enemy shipping before the

Equator was reached; however, torpedoes could not be spared for insignificant targets. This 'free-fire' area was later enlarged by SKL to reach 5° south, an extension that would prove of great consequence to Hartenstein.

The first pair of *Eisbär* boats, *U 156* and *U 172*, sailed on 19 August, *U 459* departing Bordeaux that same day en route to quadrant GG, where she would hold her refuelling station. *U 156* and *U 172* were tasked with making a thorough reconnaissance of the Cape Town roadstead before beginning their own attacks, which would act as a signal for the remaining boats to open fire. *U 68* was given the operational area southwest, south and south-east of areas mined by the German raider *Doggerbank* earlier that year, while *U 504* was ordered to cover the seas to the north, north-east and north-west of Cape Town.

On 12 September, as the *Eisbär* U-boats were well on their way to Cape Town, disaster appeared once again to strike the mission. Already having been diverted to attack convoy SL.119 east of the Azores, *U 156* was approaching the new cease-fire latitude of 5° south when Hartenstein torpedoed and sank the SS *Laconia* with her cargo of passengers and Italian prisoners-of-war. Faced with the disaster, Hartenstein began rescuing survivors and was forced to retire from the *Eisbär* operation.

Although *U 156* was no longer on the strength of the attacking force, Hitler furiously demanded that the Cape Town U-boats resume their journey, leaving the problem of rescuing *Laconia*'s survivors to Hartenstein and other nearby boats working the waters off Freetown. Later the German submarines transferred the survivors to the Vichy ships *Gloire*, *Annamite* and *Dumont d'Urville* sailing from North Africa and the remaining *Eisbär* boats and their tanker, *U 459*, continued according to their original orders. Merten's *U 68* took over the role of Hartenstein's boat for the planned assault as Helmut Witte's *U 159* was diverted from her own patrol to join the group.

After a final refuelling from *U 459* south of St Helena, the U-boats took up their positions. *U 68* and *U 172* rendezvoused north-west of their objective, Merten going aboard *U 172* to confer with *Kapitänleutnant* Carl Emmermann over coffee regarding their best methods of approach. However, instead of there being dozens of enemy ships lying vulnerably at anchor in the roadstead to the South African port, Emmermann later reported it empty, while Merten radioed the presence of a heavy searchlight barrage off Table Bay and thick traffic in small patrol craft between Robben Island and Fort Wynard. There were no targets— an inauspicious beginning to an assault on South Africa.

Dönitz responded by radio that same night, giving the *Eisbär* group freedom of action as of 8 October. At BdU headquarters Dönitz guessed that the presence of Japanese submarines off Madagascar during the previous months may have alerted the Allies to Cape Town's potential vulnerability. A lack of practical co-operation between Germany and Japan had directly forestalled U-boat operations: the German authorities had wrongly assumed that Japanese naval forces would continue to keep pressure on the African coast throughout 1942 after an earlier intimation of this possibility had come from the Japanese Naval Attaché in Berlin.

In October 1942, although the *Eisbär* operation had begun in a less than promising fashion, things rapidly improved for the German commanders. When the U-boats began their individual attacks on 8 October—Carl Emmermann opening fire prematurely the day before and sinking two ships, later blaming 'garbled reception' of Dönitz's radioed instructions—they managed to sink thirteen more merchant ships within three days. *Kapitänleutnant* Witte's *U 159* had also prematurely opened her attack (though only by five minutes in German time), torpedoing the SS *Boringa*. Merten's *U 68* despatched six merchantmen in less than 27 hours as the U-boat assault commenced in full. Further south Poske's *U 504* failed to find any targets until 17 October, when she hit and sank the 5,970-ton SS *Empire Chaucer*, travelling from Calcutta to Liverpool via Cape Town and carrying 2,000 tons of pig iron and 6,500 tons of general cargo, including tea and bags of mail. *Empire Chaucer* was fresh from the shipyards, having been completed in Sunderland earlier in 1942 as part of the Ministry of War Transport's Emergency Shipbuilding Programme that resulted in the new-build 'Empire' range of merchant ships, and was registered to W. J. Tatem Ltd. At 0615hrs local time Master Roy Jennings's unescorted vessel was hit by torpedoes from *U 504* about 450 miles south-east of Cape Town. Three crew members died during the attack and subsequent sinking, but Jennings and 46 survivors, including a single passenger, were later rescued by British merchant ships—fifteen of them after having spent 23 days drifting in an open lifeboat. Although the significance of the sinking may have been lost on

Poske and his men, this was the first Allied merchant ship sunk by direct German U-boat action east of the meridian where the Atlantic officially ends and the Indian Ocean begins. Poske then ranged further east and sank four more merchant ships before beginning his return to France.

Bolstering the attack on South Africa were the new Type IXD2 U-cruisers from the 10th U-Flotilla, the first to arrive, *U 179*, opening fire simultaneously with the *Eisbär* boats. However, after one sinking—the 6,558-ton SS *City of Athens*—*U 179*'s combat career ended when she was sunk by depth charges that same day.

The presence aboard *U 179* of 29-year-old Paul Temme as navigation officer has caused much post-war speculation as to a possible alternative mission scheduled for that boat. Temme had been navigator aboard the German sailing ship *Kyloe*, used by the *Abwehr*'s Ausland IV department to deliver agents to foreign shores. This small 34-ton, 22.1m sailing ship, equipped with an auxiliary 30hp diesel engine, was commanded by *Leutnant zur See* (*Sonderführer*) Christian Nissen and carrying five crew, including Temme, when, during 1941, she departed St-Malo on a voyage south to deposit the South African-born German agent Robby Leibbrandt north of Cape Town on a mission to assassinate General Smuts (Operation '*Weissdorn*').[4] The Boer Leibbrandt had been born in the Transvaal in 1914 to Irish/German parents, later becoming a champion heavyweight boxer and appearing as a member of the South African team at the 1936 Berlin Olympic Games. Impressed by his time in Berlin, he remained in thrall to the Nazis after his return to South Africa and travelled back to Germany in 1938 to study at the Reich Gymnastic Academy. Upon the outbreak of war he stayed and joined the German military, where he qualified first as a glider pilot and later as a paratrooper. His mission to South Africa was ultimately a failure, although he spent months building a small but dedicated Nazi group modelled on the SS within the fiercely anti-British *Ossewabrandwag* organisation.[5]

Paul Temme had navigated the small yacht to Mitchell's Bay, where Leibbrandt was landed with his radio operator. By October 1942 the *Ossewabrandwag* organisation was mounting small sabotage raids against 'English' targets in South Africa. Interestingly, *U 179* was sunk very close to the area where Leibbrandt had disembarked, leading to speculation that the U-boat may have been carrying *matériel* for transfer ashore under Temme's expert guidance or perhaps was being prepared to embark somebody from shore. Unfortunately this remains, at present, only interesting speculation.

By mid-October the notorious weather off the Cape of Good Hope began to deteriorate into hurricane-force winds and the rash of sinkings died away as the *Eisbär* boats were forced from Cape Town in search of milder weather. By 1 November they had destroyed 22 ships in total, many laden with valuable war material and including three huge troop transports. Three fresh Type IXD2 boats—*U 178*, *U 177* and *U 181*—had arrived to continue applying pressure as the exhausted *Eisbär* group began its return to France. Merten and Emmermann departed the region first, each sinking one further ship as they headed north.[6] However, just as the German U-boats were celebrating their success off South Africa, the *Afrika Korps*, which stood to benefit most from their victory, was finally forced into retreat, the disastrous material loss at El Alamein putting it into a withdrawal that would never be halted.

The Type IXD2s that had arrived to bolster the onslaught were the largest of the Type IX series of ocean-going cruiser-submarines. Initially Dönitz had advocated the construction of the bulky planned Type XI U-boat—albeit without its planned burdensome deck-mounted gun turrets—but the drain on German resources that would be brought about by building a completely new type of U-boat was deemed unjustifiable. Instead, the tried and tested Type IXC design provided the basis of both an enlarged cruiser version and one capable of higher speeds. The Type IXD1 would be given six combined 1,500hp Daimler-Benz *Schnellboot* engines, the total 9,000hp, 20-cylinder powerplant providing a higher than normal surface speed to satisfy the latter requirement, while the Type IXD2 would use the same diesels as the IXC but with an additional diesel-electric drive. The living and stowage spaces and outer hull on the IXDs were enlarged and the bows and stern extended, providing a boat nearly 11m longer and displacing, on the surface, 400 tons more than the IXCs because of an additional accommodation compartment forward of the conning tower, balanced with extra engines within an added section towards the stern. The real bonus of the Type IXD2, however, was its fuel capacity—442 tons compared to the 214 of the Type IXC—giving, potentially, a surfaced cruising range for the new boat of 23,700 miles at 12kts with a standard diesel load or more with a little careful husbandry. In fact the IXD2s were capable of 32,000 miles at 9kts if five of the eight diving cells were used as fuel bunkers at the beginning of a voyage and the boat floated on three cells only.[7]

Because the larger boats were double-hulled, the fuel tanks were wrapped around the pressure hull and offered a massive capacity for diesel fuel. However, these capabilities came at a price: the Type IXD2 was even slower to dive and harder to control than the 'Sea Cow', the standard Type IXB and C. This ponderous diving time was belatedly addressed later in the war when the upper forward deck was reshaped into an 'hour-glass' configuration. The large flat plane that comprised the standard wide deck was a major cause of delay in submerging as it interacted with the plane of the sea surface, holding the boat pinned for priceless seconds as sheer weight gradually dragged it through and below the waves.

The three large boats took over where *Eisbär* had left off, cruising in atrocious conditions off Cape Town and battling through the 'Roaring Forties' but continuing slowly to add to the grim harvest of enemy shipping. Although all were fresh from Germany and on their maiden patrols, they were all captained by experienced commanders and largely veteran crews. One was *U 178*, commissioned on 14 February 1942 in the Bremen shipyard of A. G. Weser. After months of trials and exercises within the Baltic the boat was ready for her first patrol, bearing one of the more unusual emblems painted on a U-boat's conning tower. The pictures that graced each flank showed a swan, wings outstretched and beak open. The inspiration for such a painting had been an incident in the Baltic when, in the course of a submerged drill, a swan had proceeded to attack the U-boat's periscope that had rudely arrived from below and disturbed its quiet day.

Aboard *U 178* there was little harmony among the officers and crew. *Korvettenkapitän* Hans Ibbeken had served in the German Navy since 1918, captaining the *Kriegsmarine*'s *U 27* before the war, occupying the briefly established post of FdU West in September 1939 and later taking command of *U 178* as she neared completion within the shipyards. Ibbeken was backed by *Oberleutnant zur See* Wilhelm Spahr as IWO and Chief Engineer *Kapitänleutnant (Ing.)* Hans Gottwald, but neither man maintained any respect for his commander.[8] Ibbeken, nicknamed 'Ibbo', was considered by his crew to be overly cautious and unwilling to attack. Several merchant ships were sighted by lookouts before Ibbeken opted to change course and ignore the potential targets. He also insisted on smoking unguarded cigarettes at night on the bridge when the glowing tip of burning tobacco could easily betray his boat to a careful observer. Minor disagreements became heated argument among the ship's officers, creating an air of tension that soon rubbed off on the crew. Furthermore, a provisioning error showed that *U 178* did not have enough food stored aboard for the planned journey. Tempers rose in tandem with the boat's internal temperature as *U 178* cruised into the equatorial heat en route to South Africa.

With the elements battering the three boats, greater freedom of action was finally given by BdU and the submarines proceeded into calmer waters, sailing north-east towards Lourenço Marques, the capital of Portuguese East Africa (now Mozambique) that sprawled lazily along the north bank of the Espiritos Santos river. This, with its deep-water harbour near to the Rand, South Africa's industrial and mining heartland, was an important supply point for Allied shipping, but there was little local protection for merchant shipping and they suffered accordingly. On 28 November *Kapitänleutnant* Robert Gysae's *U 177* made perhaps the most tragic sinking of the fresh offensive when he torpedoed the SS *Nova Scotia* south-west of Lourenço Marques during the morning of 28 November. En route from Aden to Durban, the British steamer was carrying 769 Italian civilian internees and prisoners-of-war, the majority from sunken and captured ships that had been based in Eritrea, as well as their British and South African guards.

Gysae, described even by the Admiralty in its top-secret 'Anti-Submarine Warfare Report' for June 1944 as an 'outstanding seaman', had left Kiel on 10 September. The boat suffered her first casualty only sixteen days from harbour when *Bootsmannsmaat* Erwin Henning was washed overboard during a morning watch rotation atop the conning tower in heavy weather. *U 177* made her first kill with the successful torpedoing of the Greek steamer SS *Aegeus* in late October. She then rounded the Cape and embarked on an unsuccessful chase of a laden tanker, loosing off five torpedoes for no result and being forced to break northwards toward Durban for fear of airborne retaliation summoned by the tanker's crew. On 19 November Gysae made his second successful sinking after torpedoing the 7,006-ton tanker SS *Scottish Chief,* whose crew disappeared with their ship despite attempts by Gysae to locate and assist survivors. The tanker's fiery destruction was reported by the American Liberty ship SS *Pierce Butler* as 'off our stern'—a signal intercepted and used by *U 177* to find and sink the American. Then disaster struck, with Gysae's misidentification of the zig-zagging *Nova Scotia* as an armed merchant cruiser.

The steamer was hit by three torpedoes in a submerged attack. *Nova Scotia*'s gun crew fired at the visible periscope until they were virtually waist-deep in water and forced to abandon their ship, which was sinking rapidly by the head. It was only after closing the lifeboats to assist survivors that the identity of the victim was ascertained. Gysae immediately radioed BdU, urging them to contact the Portuguese authorities at Lourenço Marques and assist in rescue efforts. Two Italians taken on board related tales of panic aboard the ship as fire instantly spread through crowded holds and cabins; well over 200 people were killed during the sinking. Mindful of the recent *Laconia* débâcle, Gysae distributed what water and medical supplies he could and reluctantly departed. The survivors struggled amid choking oil and floating corpses as sharks began to converge on the tragic scene. Forty-eight hours later the Portuguese destroyer *Alfonso de Albuquerque*, commanded by *Capitão* Josè August Guerreiro de Brito, arrived and began plucking exhausted people from the warm equatorial waters, his search for survivors lasting well into the following day. In total the Portuguese destroyer picked up 117 Italians and 64 South African and English soldiers—only 181 of the estimated 1,200 people aboard the SS *Nova Scotia*. Six hundred and fifty-two Italians disappeared for ever into the Indian Ocean, and for weeks afterwards bodies continued to be washed ashore on the beaches of Zinkwasi, north of Durban—the area now known locally as 'Eyetie's Bay'.

Gysae's next successful attack netted the largest ship sunk of his career when he intercepted and torpedoed the 10,786-ton liner *Llandaff Castle* of the Union Castle Line. After carrying the first child evacuees from England to South Africa during 1940, the *Llandaff Castle* had been rushed into service as a troopship between South and East Africa in support of the British campaigns in Abyssinia and North Africa and had subsequently taken part in Operation 'Ironclad', the invasion of Vichy-held Madagascar. At 1730hrs local time she was torpedoed three times by Gysae 100 miles off Zululand. When *U 177* surfaced to confirm the

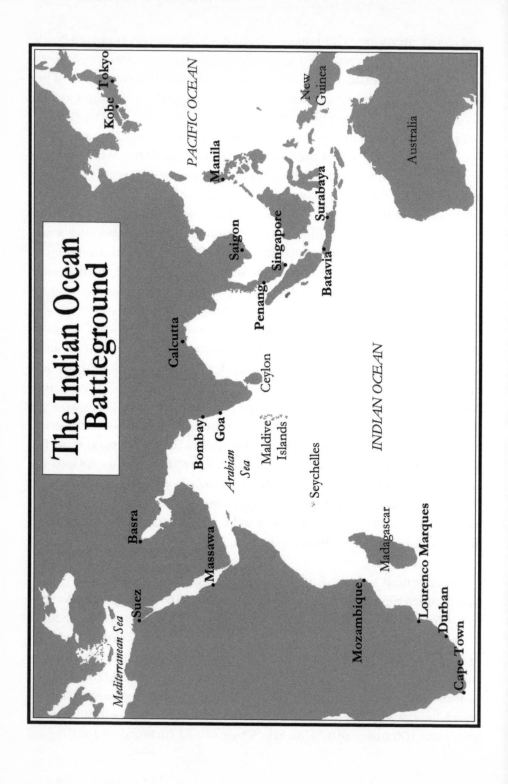

The Indian Ocean Battleground

name and manifest of the ship, voices in the water replied 'Hardship' and 'Queen Mary'. Gysae's questions as to whether there were any wounded that needed assistance were answered in a similar vein when he was told that they were only 'wet'. Amused by his enemy's spirit, Gysae departed and only two British lives were lost as a result of the sinking.

Gysae would despatch three more ships using the last of his torpedoes during this, his first operational sortie into the Indian Ocean. *U 178* and *U 181* accounted for a total of eighteen sunk and another damaged. Lüth, who sank twelve of the victims, had suffered under the exhausting attentions of the destroyer HMS *Inconstant* and the corvettes HMS *Jasmine* and *Nigella* on 15 November after having been spotted running surfaced. Dozens of depth charges battered *U 181* and forced Lüth to a depth of 570ft, his boat suffering leaks but no catastrophic flooding, until the attackers finally gave up their hunt during the evening.

Although there has been a tendency to overstate the usefulness of information supplied by German agents as opposed to the effective German decoding of British naval signals, the U-boats' first successful forays into the Indian Ocean were aided to some degree by *Abwehr* intelligence reports. This seemed to be reflected in many of the survivors' eyewitness accounts diligently collected by Allied naval intelligence to help provide a picture of U-boat operations, although among them *U 181* was incorrectly identified as an Italian 'Pisani' class submarine by the crew survivors from the SS *Excello*. For example, after the American freighter SS *Jeremiah Wadsworth* had been intercepted and sunk by a torpedo from Hans Ibbeken's *U 178*, the U-boat surfaced and approached the three lifeboats that floated on the lazy swell:

> Four officers were on the conning tower. The oldest, probably the commander, was bearded; the other three very young blondes. . . The commander asked in broken English, with an Austrian or Bavarian accent, where bound, where from, tonnage and type of cargo. He did not ask for the ship's name, and the survivors think that he already knew.[9]

Similarly, after Lüth sank the freighter SS *East Indian* on 3 November headed from Cape Town to New York and carrying 3,500 tons of manganese ore, 500 tons of tea and 560 tons of general cargo, *U 181* also approached the survivors, providing them with water and asking for information regarding their victim:

Five minutes after the ship sank, [*U 181*] surfaced about 50 yards from the lifeboat and questioned the 3rd Mate who was the ranking survivor . . . 'What is the name of your ship? . . . What flag? Etc. . . Why did you zigzag? If you had not been zigzagging I would have gotten you about 9 o'clock this morning and saved you 100 miles of rowing!'

The commander had a notebook in his hand and was apparently checking off the information supplied, indicating that he already knew most of the information.[10]

Lüth had indeed known of the *East Indian*'s departure from Calcutta, informed by intelligence transmitted by a covert radio on land. Perhaps the most dramatic example of this *Abwehr* net in action was within the neutral port of Marmugao, a natural harbour at the mouth of the Zuari estuary within the humid Portuguese colony of Goa. There three German merchant ships were lazily swinging at anchor in the harbour. Two diesel-powered merchantmen, the MVs *Brauenfels* and *Ehrenfels*, and the steamer SS *Drachenfels*, all owned by the German Hansa company, were accompanied by a fourth Axis ship, the Italian MV *Anfora*, within the fetid backwater as war raged across the world's oceans. Conforming to international neutrality regulations, all four ships had had their means of wireless communication removed upon taking refuge in the port, but on board *Kapitän* Röfen's *Ehrenfels*, hidden within a nondescript compartment marked 'Danger of Death! High Voltage!' to deter crewmen curious as to its content, was a small but powerful transmitter and the myriad lead-bound code books that would facilitate communication with combat U-boats. A German agent ashore in Goa regularly visited Röfen's ship, passing valuable information concerning Allied merchant ship sailings to *Ehrenfels'* First Officer, who in turn encoded the details and transmitted them at a prearranged time into the ether. Lüth received the broadcasts and was able to formulate his plans accordingly. By post-war reckoning, at least three of the ships that he intercepted and sank had been betrayed by the agent's coded messages— one of them the SS *East Indian* mentioned above.

The information originated from Indians working within docks and shipping companies who, while not necessarily pro-Nazi, were definitely anti-British. Dedicated to the cause of Indian independence, they adhered to a more direct form of subversion advocated by the Indian nationalist Subhas Chandra Bose rather than to the passive resistance of Mohandas Gandhi. Bose, the son of a knighted Indian scientist, was President of the Indian National Congress Party and formerly the mayor of Calcutta. Cambridge-educated, he had been imprisoned during 1940 by the Imperial powers in India for his anti-war activities but paroled in 1941, whereupon he fled first to Kabul and then onwards through Russia and Italy to Berlin. There he lived on Sophienstrasse in the former residence of the United States Ambassador and holding an Italian passport in the name of Orlando Mazzotta. Bose was received by Hitler who somewhat grudgingly supported his idea of creating an Indian Legion that could fight alongside German troops and eventually help free India from British rule.[11] However, despite his outward interest in the scheme, in private Hitler never fully supported Bose's and the Japanese' proposals for promoting Indian independence, primarily because of his own racial prejudice. His ideas are reflected in private conversations with his chief lieutenants: he feared the establishment of a 'Yellow Man' supremacy within Asia, replacing the white rule of colonial Britain. Indeed soon after Japan attacked British possessions in the Far East he said, 'Strange that with the help of Japan we will destroy the positions of the white race in East Asia and that England fights in Europe with the Bolshevik swine.'[12]

Many in India had received the vociferous radio broadcasts that Bose made from Berlin with relish. For four hours each day starting on 7 January 1942, 'Free India Radio' (*Azad Hind Radio*) broadcast to the Indian subcontinent from its transmitter in Berlin, advocating a nationalist uprising. Bose and others delivered stirring appeals to enlist the aid of fighting men and also those who chose a more shadowy method of resistance.

The information from such spies that reached *Ehrenfels'* transmitter concerned merchant sailings from Bombay, ships' departure times, routes and cargoes, allowing precise interception by *U 181*. The British authorities were already aghast at the sudden and severe attrition rate within the Indian Ocean brought about by Dönitz's attack, but with their concern came also a realisation that ships carrying cargoes of the highest priority were frequently attacked in lieu of other targets, pointing to espionage as the probable reason. Acting upon their suspicions, they soon managed to pinpoint the source of the frequent furtive radio broadcasts emanating from the Goanese port of Marmagao—not on land but from within the harbour itself. With three German ships at anchor within the port, the conclusion was obvious. However, Portuguese neutrality was a matter of extreme importance to the British. If the Portuguese were provoked, and retaliated by opting to join or actively assist the Axis powers, severe complications could be expected along the Portuguese coast. Thus far-reaching and disastrous consequences could affect supplies to Gibraltar and the control of the entrance to the Mediterranean. Official protest regarding the transmitter was deemed unlikely to succeed, and accordingly the Special Operations Executive was delegated the task of dealing with it. Soon the location of the transmitter was narrowed to one ship — *Ehrenfels*.

The most modern of the three German ships, *Ehrenfels* had been built in 1935 and also posed the alternative threat of her conversion to an armed merchant raider should she choose to break out of the port and proceed to Japan for armaments. A brief attempt at bribing Röfen into leaving harbour and either sinking his ship or surrendering her to the British failed, and direct action was put forward as the only real alternative. The first move was to kidnap the main German agent in Goa, codenamed 'Trompeta', but even in his absence the messages were still transmitted . Aboard the German ships the assembled captains were aware of their precarious position following the British approach to Röfen. *Ad hoc* defences were prepared, as was the final option of self-destruction should the enemy succeed in a direct assault.

The Allied SOE thrived on unconventional warfare and, unable to use regular British commandos or troops, entrusted a last-ditch mission to destroy *Ehrenfels* to a small group of territorial soldiers—the Calcutta Light Horse, augmented by a few men of the Calcutta Scottish. Made up of middle-aged civilians, the Light Horse and Scottish were primarily engaged in polo matches, cricket tournaments and games of rugby rather than actual military service and hence were the most unlikely candidates for a commando raid—and perfect for SOE's purpose. Accordingly, in the early hours of 9 March 1943 a handful of greying British accountants, bankers, solicitors and tea planters attacked the *Ehrenfels* after approaching the harbour aboard a nearly derelict mud-dredging barge named *Phoebe* (officially, Hopper Barge No 5). The 30-year-old *Phoebe* had sailed from Calcutta, loading the men of the raiding party at Cochin, whither they had travelled discreetly by train. Aided by an SOE-organised carnival ashore, which distracted the majority of officers and crewmen from the ships, the boarding party entered Marmagao Harbour and successfully disembarked on *Ehrenfels*, causing her and her three Axis companions to scuttle themselves and thereby denying Lüth and his comrades any further radio intelligence. The cause of the sinkings was later reported in national and international newspapers as resulting from internal unrest within the crews—a cover story 'leaked' to them by the SOE:

> [The crews] took this desperate step in order to scotch a plan which they feared other members of the crew might carry out to elude the guards and make a dash for Singapore or some other Japanese-occupied port. The two groups are reported to have engaged in violent fighting and some of the Germans set fire to a few of the ships, which were burnt out. The men escaped ashore, where they were rounded up and detained.[13]

As the three Type IXD2 cruisers disengaged and began their return to France the original *Eisbär* boats were already docking in Lorient and St-Nazaire, streaming success pennants from their raised periscopes that represented the sinking of 28 ships grossing 182,174 tons—and thus one of the most successful single U-boat offensives of the war.[14] Flushed with this success, Dönitz immediately decided to reinforce his opening effort with another foray to South Africa using Type IXCs. The only available IXD2 cruiser-U-boats were still engaged in the Indian Ocean and would eventually amass victories of 25 ships destroyed (134,780 tons). Dönitz therefore judged that, by refuelling within the South Atlantic, the new group—named *Seehund* and, like *Eisbär*, a group in name only—would be able to repeat the success of the first, arriving on location as the winter storms subsided. A single Type IXD2, *U 182*, became available to augment the group and was in fact the first to depart port for the fresh attack, leaving Horten, Norway, on 9 December 1942. Staggered over the following three weeks, *U 506*, *U 509*, *U 516* and *U 160* all departed for Cape Town, supported by refuelling during January and February from *U 459* in quadrant FU, 600 miles south of St Helena.

However, the situation around the Cape had changed dramatically. Instead of single-sailing merchant ships there were now tightly knit and heavily defended convoys, often hugging the coastline to benefit from land-based radar as well as the available escort naval vessels and aircraft. The German 'Triton' Enigma net had also been compromised and pickings for the *Seehund* group were slim, although each boat achieved some success. Again the group moved north-east to Lourenço Marques, but the U-boats were unable to repeat earlier successes in the region.

The most dramatic breakthrough was made by *U 160* when it attacked DN.21, the first convoy to be hit by a U-boat south of Durban. In the course of two attacks *Kapitänleutnant* Georg Lassen sank four ships and damaged two others. The convoy comprised eleven large merchant ships under escort by a single corvette and three ASW trawlers. Lassen's first attack was launched a little before midnight local time, sank the SS *Harvey W. Scott* and *Nipura* and damaged the Dutch MT *Tibia*. Barely one and half hours later Lassen launched his second attack, sinking the SS *Empire Masheer*, while a third separate attack sank the SS *Marietta E.* and damaged the SS *Sheaf Crown*. The *Marietta E.* added several small vessels to Lassen's score as she had been carrying 4,865 tons of government and commercial stores as well as eight landing craft as deck cargo, all of which went straight to the seabed alongside four crewmen and a naval gunner.[15] Despite Lassen's brief bonanza *Seehund*'s results were relatively meagre for the distances traversed. Seventeen ships were confirmed sunk, totalling 100,577 tons, and a further three suffered damage. Moreover, both *U 506* and *U 509* each sank only a single ship during nearly five months at sea.

After being briefly transferred back towards the Cape by BdU, the *Seehund* operation ended during April and all five U-boats headed home. It had been a frustrating patrol for most of the group, and one made worse by the loss of *Korvettenkapitän* Nicolai 'Nico' Clausen's *U 182* during the return voyage. Knight's Cross holder Clausen, a veteran naval officer and U-boat commander who had achieved probably his greatest success while captain of *U 129* in the Caribbean, sank his last ship on 1 May with the torpedoing of the Greek steamer *Adelfotis*—the fifth victim of his patrol. Clausen could feel at least some contentment with his victories during the boat's first combat mission, and he was also carrying two captured captains, one from *Adelfotis* the other the master of the British SS *Aloe,* for internment in Germany.

During the sinking of the *Aloe*, en route from Australia to Durban with 5,000 tons of wheat, 1,500 tons of lumber, 320 tons of lead and mail for South Africa, Clausen had been 'identified' by British survivors of the ship, prompting another of the many legends about covert U-boat landings causing chaos within Allied merchant ports:

[*U 182*] surfaced after the vessel had sunk and went alongside the lifeboats. One of the officers, who spoke good English, did all the talking. He asked if a distress signal had been sent and then commented the sub had heard it. He then inquired and received truthful answers about the name, cargo, point of departure and destination. They then took the Master prisoner and the officer apologised for torpedoing the ship without warning and expressed his regrets at not being able to give them any supplies, but they said they would soon be rescued. The sub's crew were all smiles and talking and taking pictures . . . On the conning tower, painted clearly and plainly, were the words 'Westward Ho!' and 'Deutschland' below. The commander had a very heavy black beard. Some survivors claimed to have met him in a bar in Lourenço Marques some time last year [1942] before sailing to Australia.[16]

However, the contentment aboard *U 182* was short-lived as she encountered convoy UGS.8, comprising fourteen LSTs en route from the United States to Gibraltar and under escort by two destroyers, northwest of Madeira on 16 May. *U 182* was picked up while running surfaced by radar aboard the escort destroyer USS *MacKenzie*. Clausen crash-dived as soon as the enemy threat was spotted, but *MacKenzie* maintained ASDIC contact and attacked twice, augmented by half-hearted assistance from the USS *Laub*, the senior destroyer of the escort pair. *MacKenzie* violated operational doctrine by not opening fire with her main armaments while approaching the radar fix, while *Laub* made neither radar nor ASDIC contact. Both destroyers left the area after about 90 minutes, unsure as to their success. At 0500hrs, about 45 minutes after the final depth-charge attack, two underwater explosions, nine minutes between them, were reported aboard the Americans, who scoured the sea surface for an explanation of the noise. Despite the lack of debris to prove the U-boat's destruction, those explosions marked the end of Clausen and his 60 crewmen.[17]

Meanwhile, combined with the desire to exchange goods and technology between Japan and Germany was the need for key personnel to travel between the two allied combatants. The Japanese steadfastly refused German proposals for what would have been the difficult establishment of an air link, and as the surface blockade-runners faced crisis during 1943 at the hands of enemy hunting groups the only remaining option appeared to be by submarine. On 9 February the new Type IXD1 *U 180* prepared for her first combat mission into the Indian Ocean. The experimental high-speed diesels had thus far appeared satisfactory during trials within the Baltic, and as *Korvettenkapitän* Werner Musenberg prepared his boat for sea within Kiel's sheltered military harbour the diesel crew were confident about their high-speed machinery. The evening before departure the majority of the boat's crew were ashore, *Obermaschinist* Hermann Wien holding watch duties aboard the stocked U-boat: 'So at 2100 the post guard who was watching the boat announced that a private car had arrived on the dock. An officer of the flotilla came up carrying some suitcases, identified himself, and told us to keep quiet and stow away his baggage.'[18]

The following day *U 180* slipped from Kiel's military harbour to the cheers of well-wishers and family members, easing out of the confined port and into Kieler Förde. Sailing slowly northward, Musenberg suddenly ordered the boat's engines cut as *U 180* lay off Laboe, before the imposing red brick naval memorial. A small boat approached and two passengers disembarked to come aboard the submarine, the mysterious suitcases' owners arriving to accompany *U 180* on her voyage. The most important arrival was none other than the Indian nationalist Subhas Chandra Bose, referred to by the German ratings aboard *U 180* as the 'Indian Adolf', although Musenberg announced to his crew initially that the pair were engineers heading to Norway to build U-boat bunkers. It was only after departing Norway following refuelling, the pair making no effort to disembark, that the crew were informed of their real identities and destination. Accompanied by his adjutant, the Arab nationalist leader Dr Habid Hassan, Bose had camouflaged his departure from Berlin, his voice having been recorded for later broadcast on 'Radio Free India' after *U 180* had sailed.

Unable to match the Type IXD2's endurance at sea, Musenberg was ordered to prepare for an Indian Ocean rendezvous with a Japanese submarine and to pass the two passengers over to Japanese forces for the remainder of their journey. However, despite the propaganda value of transporting the nationalists to their homelands, the transfer of Bose and Hassan was not Musenberg's primary objective. Alongside the two men and their bulky cases *U 180* carried mail for the German embassy in Tokyo, samples of various German weapons and machine parts, a sample of quinine for future Japanese shipments and blueprints for jet engines and V 1 and V 2 rockets, as well as 432 '*Bold*' capsules in three crates for Japanese technical evaluation. In turn, Musenburg was to receive eleven tons of cargo, including three torpedoes for German scrutiny and two tons of gold bars within 146 crates bound for the Japanese Embassy in Berlin. Also due to be put on board were blueprints of the

'Akagi' fighter (for use in the construction of the carrier *Graf Zeppelin*) and the Type A midget submarine, an experimental gas pressure gun, half a ton of mail and documents and various Japanese inventions. Musenberg would also replace his departing passengers with two Japanese officers bound for Germany—*Chusa* (Commander) Emi Tetsushiro (the former captain of *I-8*), a member of the Japanese Navy's Technical Department, and *Shosa* Hideo Tomonaga, a submarine design specialist involved in the *Kriegsmarine*'s midget submarine project, both of whom had been tasked with observing U-boat building techniques in Germany. To round out *U 180*'s mission, Musenberg was allowed freedom to operate aggressively against enemy shipping if such opportunity presented itself, though was urged only to attack those targets sailing independently.

U 180 proceeded largely without incident through the Atlantic. She rounding the Cape of Good Hope in April and entered the Indian Ocean after refuelling from *U 462* in quadrant BD 8111, taking 60m³ of diesel for the temperamental and thirsty engines. The diesel plants had begun to show numerous technical problems and the Chief Engineer and his crew struggled to keep them on line. Not only did they 'smoke like an old coal burning tramp' when changing from low to high revolutions but they also generated a temperature of 60°C within the submarine's pressure hull—an almost unbearable heat, particularly apparent as *U 180* was within tropical latitudes. Coupled with the heat was the constant battle to keep the engines cool, their own water-cooling system repeatedly malfunctioning. Bose took several days to find his sea legs, suffering almost constant seasickness until he adapted to the pitch and yaw. Once acclimatised to his new surroundings he became a constant visitor to the conning tower.

Bose created an odd impression on the crew. He was often quiet and reserved, though proved well-versed and knowledgeable if drawn into halting discussion with his less than perfect German. During the voyage he diligently worked within the cramped U-boat's wardroom on a manuscript entitled 'My Struggle for Indian Freedom'. Oxford-educated Hassan, on the other hand, spoke rather better German, with a distinct Berlin dialect. As *Obermaschininst* Hermann Wien remembered, 'I talked with him often, because he had the bunk over me. You could say he was a joke teller and he had many about the Third Reich. He knew a lot of them and didn't hold back.'[19] Bose and Hassan also added their own touches to the menu aboard *U 180*, apparently impressing the initially dubious crew with a touch of Eastern cuisine.

On 18 April Musenberg sighted the MV *Corbis* and sank her in a submerged torpedo attack. The 8,132-ton British tanker, travelling from Abadan to Cape Town, stood little chance, loaded as it was with 11,310 tons of diesel oil and 50 tons of highly volatile aviation spirit. She was hit at 0126hrs local time and Master Stanley Wilfred Appleton, 47 of his crewmen and two naval gunners were lost in either the ensuing inferno or within the expanse of the Indian Ocean after the launch of two din-ghies was observed by the German lookouts and the occupants pro-vided with some water and food.[20] A second attack on a solo ship two days later was foiled by a combination of loss of depth-keeping control and *U 180*'s perpetually smoking engines:

> 1048hrs: KQ 7764, Steamer 100 degrees, because we are giving off clouds of smoke, immediate alarm.
> Before attack, break surface three times. Steamer turns to ram so go to depth. Surfaced to follow smoke sighted through periscope. Broken off, since diesels failed and the steamer always manages to hold us astern. (Smoke cloud!)[21]

U 180 instead headed for the rendezvous point in quadrant KR 5276, some 400 nautical miles south-south-west of Madagascar. The weather quickly deteriorated and Musenberg had to batter through storm condi-tions towards his meeting with the Japanese.

On 20 April 1943 the Japanese submarine *I-29* had slipped from Pen-ang harbour carrying her store of supplies and two additional Japanese officers for transfer to *U 180*. Rumours spread quickly through the large Indian community in Penang, the boat's cooks having bought quantities of supplies for the creation of Indian meals for their prestigious guest. *Chusa* Juichi Izu's *I-29* also carried flotilla commander *Taisa* Teraoka aboard, an unusual step for a routine combat patrol and the source of further speculation. *I-29* made good time towards the rendezvous within the Mozambique Channel, arriving at the meeting point on 25 April, a day earlier than expected. She cruised within the prescribed area until, as darkness fell the following day, *U 180* emerged from over the gloomy horizon. After a difficult transfer in the rough sea of a German officer and signalman from *U 180* to *I-29*, the two submarines cruised slowly on a north-easterly course, waiting for the conditions to moderate.

Optimistically Bose wrote his farewell message within *U 180*'s KTB on the first day of the two submarines' meeting:

> For a civilian, life in general within a U-boat is not very comfortable. However, I cannot claim this myself. The commander, the officers and the entire crew not only spoiled me throughout the voyage, but turned it into a happy experience. From the first time I came aboard, I wondered, how would I endure this long time within such cramped circumstances.
>
> Now the time of our parting comes, and it is no exaggeration to confess that I have the feeling that I am leaving a comfortable home with a heavy heart. Also nature was merciful to us and we could absorb and admire some unforgettable beauties of the sea and sky during the trip.
>
> We give our wholehearted thanks to the officers and men, in particular the Commandant, for always showing us friendship and being helpful during the whole trip. We wish the boat *U 180* a happy and proud homecoming into her base, decorated with victory pennants and garlands. The sun and the stars may bear witness to the strikes that this boat will deliver to our common enemy. When we have succeeded in striking England in the distant Far Eastern Front, then we will always think back with joy to this trip on *U 180*, that leads us to victory and to freedom.
>
> [Signed] Subdhas Tchandra [*sic*] Bose and Abid Hassan, Adjutant.[22]

Izu suggested to Musenberg that they proceed to Sabang together until the sea calmed, but Musenberg declined on account of his having insufficient fuel to complete the journey safely. Unable to converse by radio because of the need to maintain silence and avoid Allied direction-finding equipment, communications men flashed their Morse messages by signal lamp and semaphore flag as the boats proceeded slowly in company. The two submarines continued until 27 April, Musenberg becoming increasingly worried about his fuel situation. He communicated his concern to Izu and the decision was made to attempt the transfer as conditions had abated somewhat. The waves were still high, but neither the Japanese nor the Germans were inclined to continue their dangerous surfaced passage any longer.

A strong rope was connected between the two submarines and the transfer began. Bose and Hassan rode a rubber raft to *I-29*, clinging to the rope and inching their way across cresting waves, aware of the omnipresent threat of lurking sharks as German crewmen stood ready with machine guns to deter any potential predators. Finally, drenched to the skin, Bose and Hassan at last climbed aboard *I-29*—to an enthusiastic welcome—and Tetsushiro and Tomonaga in turn made their way back to *U 180*. The transfer of the vital and heavy equipment took considerably longer aboard three large inflatable rafts, while both submarines sailed with torpedo hatches open in what Izu later called 'a dive-bomber's dream come true'.

Finally, after hours of back-breaking labour, the first exchange of personnel at sea between the *Kriegsmarine* and Imperial Japanese Navy was completed. *U 180* was able to depart and she laid course for the West once more, the heavy gold broken free of its large crates and distributed along the boat's bilges to attempt to regain some measure of trim control. *I-29* in turn began her own monotonous return trip, landing the two passengers at Sabang, an isolated offshore island north of Sumatra, on 6 May 1943 in order to avoid possible detection by British spies in Penang. Once ashore, Bose was met by Colonel Yamamoto Bin, head of the Hikari Kikan spy unit and the Japanese-Indian liaison group. Yamamoto had met Bose before, while Assistant Military Attaché in Berlin. Bose and Yamamoto flew from Sabang to Tokyo, arriving on 16 May, and Bose was later received by Premier Hideki Tôjô and by the Japanese Emperor Hirohito himself. Bose's subsequent return to India provided a stimulus for the Independence movement, the agitation that ensued leading to intense British concern within India's borders. Although the 'Indian Legion' sanctioned by Hitler never fully developed beyond several scattered units, the possibility of further Indian insurgence could rightly claim to have acted as a deterrent to any immediate Allied offensive action within the region.

For Musenberg the return journey to France was tiresome in the extreme. His boat was now loaded with eleven tons of Japanese cargo and the unwelcome presence of cockroaches, beetles and fleas that had come with it. Musenberg briefly took *U 180* closer to the South African coast in search of shipping targets, but all he found were aircraft. His boat was spotted by an Avro Anson, on a training flight and therefore unarmed. The aircraft was driven away by an accurate barrage of flak, but it was followed soon afterwards by a Hampden bomber that proceeded to attack *U 180*. According to Musenberg's War Diary, the boat's flak crews again earned their keep by hitting and bringing down their new assailant, but by that stage Musenberg had had enough. His temperamental engines continued to malfunction periodically, and even when they were running well they billowed clouds of smoke into the air, advertising the U-boat's position to anyone within sight. Accordingly Musenberg turned about and headed into the Atlantic for the home run to France. A second solo sailing merchant ship, the 5,166-ton Greek SS *Boris*, was encountered and sunk on 3 June before *U 180* refuelled from *U 530* west of the Canary Islands. Originally *U 180* had been ordered to take diesel from the *Milchkuh U 463*, but the large Type XIV had been sunk during May by a Halifax bomber south-west of the Scilly Isles. The loss of *U 463* had a particular resonance aboard *U 180*— *Obermaschinist* Hermann Wien's brother Eberhard, his opposite number aboard the tanker, was killed along with the remaining 55 crewmen. Musenberg entered Bordeaux's inland harbour on 3 July under destroyer escort, relieved to have reached his home port safely with his passengers and cargo intact and determined that the Type IXD1 would not sail again. The landing itself was not without its fraught moments. A group of Gestapo officers and Military Police (*Feldgendarmerie*, known colloquially as 'Chained Dogs' on account of the metal gorgets worn around their necks on small chains) were on hand to supervise the unloading of the precious cargo: 'Everybody was running around and then all hell broke loose. A bar of gold had been discovered missing. After they looked and looked they found it hidden under the mud of the bilge in the engine room.'[23]

The operational home of the 12th U-Flotilla in Bordeaux had opened for service as the fifth U-boat base on the French Atlantic coast during January 1943 with the arrival of *U 178* from the Indian Ocean. Before that date other surface units of the *Kriegsmarine*'s 4th *Sicherungs-division*, as well as the Italian *Betasom* boats, had shared the harbour. Bordeaux was the only U-boat base in France to not be directly located on the coastline, lying some 80km from the sea along the Gironde river, itself vulnerable to enemy aerial minelaying. The 12th U-Flotilla had been formed on 15 October 1942 and differed from the majority of combat flotillas in that it consisted solely of long-range boats, transport and resupply submarines. In command was *Korvettenkapitän* Klaus Scholtz, Knight's Cross holder and veteran captain of the Type IXB *U 108*. By the time of Musenberg's arrival in the brown swirling waters of the Gironde, the U-boat base had been crowned with the now familiar edifice of virtually bomb-proof concrete shelters to accommodate the boats of the 12th U-Flotilla.

Situated in the third basin of Bordeaux's working port—the *Bassin Alimentaire*—and accessible through two locks, the U-boat pens stretched over 41,400m² of ground. Their building had begun in September 1941 and the first pens were ready by January 1943. Unlike other sites where the *Organization Todt* constructed such shelters, the ground chosen at Bordeaux was solid enough to be built upon without the aid of extensive foundations, thus reducing the time necessary for completion. In total there were eleven separate pens, seven of them drydocks, and as well as attached workshops a separate bunker 800 metres behind the main pens held 4,000m³ of fuel and lubricating oils, fed to the pens via subterranean pipeline.

The bustling streets of the nearby Bordeaux city centre, architecturally impressive in many quarters although slightly decayed at the edges, were an enormous attraction for both Italian and German submariners between patrols. While the *Kriegsmarine* also requisitioned *châteaux* within the nearby countryside for their men, the Italian commander *Ammiraglio* Parona politely refused offers from his *Kriegsmarine* liaison, and later FdU West, *Korvettenkapitän* Hans-Rudolf Rösing to do the same, stating that his men liked to be near to the city, not stranded in some 'god-forsaken wilderness'.

As Musenberg eased *U 180* along the expanse of the Gironde towards Bordeaux, his was not the only U-boat of that type to be condemned as wholly unsatisfactory in action. In early March the first of seven U-cruisers had departed Europe, the new *U 198* leaving Germany to begin another major penetration of the Indian Ocean. Six of the seven were Type IXD2s, the seventh *U 195*, sister-boat to *U 180*. Dönitz reckoned on his new force operating independently of one another and being able to remain in action through resupply for a prolonged period before having to return to Europe. The commanders chosen to captain the large boats were older than average and combat veterans, five of them already holders of the *Ritterkreuz* for previous service.

The first of the new wave to depart was Werner Hartmann's *U 198* on 9 March 1943, followed four days later by Eitel-Friedrich Kentrat's *U 196*. A week later, and with a maximum five-day gap between the remainder, *U 195*, *U 181*, *U 178*, *U 177* and *U 197* left their bases in Bordeaux and Kiel, the last putting out from harbour on 3 April.

As the seven U-boats sailed for the Indian Ocean, the Italian submarines *Da Vinci* and *Cagni* were already active within the region, having been despatched independently to Cape Town from Bordeaux's

Betasom command. *Capitano di Corvetta* Giofranco Gazzana Priaroggia's boat, *Da Vinci*, was among five ordered to patrol either the Brazilian or South African coasts, their patrols cumulatively proving to be the most successful Italian voyages of the war. *Da Vinci* attacked and sank six ships during her voyage, earning her commander the *Ritterkreuz* from Dönitz and the Italian Gold Medal.[24] These were to be the last Italian submarine sinkings within the Indian Ocean.

As the seven 12th U-Flotilla boats sailed, they began the series of U-boat patrols that would be the longest of the entire war, the punishing lengths testimony to the discipline and spirit of their crews and the leadership of the captains concerned.[25] The seven boats independently patrolled south-east of the Cape of Good Hope, achieving only moderate success until mid-June: a combined total of eighteen ships (89,625 tons) were sunk and one other damaged. Once again it seemed that a great distance had been traversed to achieve relatively little.

While Lüth had sunk one and Buchholz two ships during their transit through the Atlantic Ocean, the first blood drawn past 20° longitude by this group was Lüth's torpedo sinking of the 5,232-ton SS *Tinhow* in quadrant KP 4777. From then the new offensive steadily collected victims until a temporary lull occurred during the middle of June in which the boats could refuel. Lüth's *U 181* had destroyed three ships in the Indian Ocean, including the tiny, 193-ton South African steamer SS *Harrier*, hit by a torpedo and completely demolished, her cargo of explosives detonating on impact. As Lüth remarked in his War Diary, 'There is a strong smell of gasoline and nothing more to see of the ship except for small fragments no larger than a man's arm . . . The crew probably still doesn't know that their ship was blown up . . .'

Kentrat's *U 196* had managed a single victory, sinking the SS *Nailsea Meadow* on 11 April; Heinz Buchholz, in the temperamental *U 195*, managed only a single damaged target after hitting the American steamer SS *Cape Neddick* the following day. *U 178* had acquired a new commander before beginning her second voyage to the Far East. *Korvettenkapitän* Wilhelm Dommes, a former merchant seaman and watch officer aboard the battleship *Scharnhorst* before taking over the captaincy of the Mediterranean boat *U 431* in April 1940, came aboard *U 178* already wearing the Knight's Cross for his exploits within the Mediterranean. However, great success eluded him on this voyage: *U 178* also managed only one victory, the destruction of Dutch steamer SS *Salabanka*. In fact Dommes succeeded only in damaging the ship with a torpedo hit, turning away in frustration as one of the torpedoes fired at the target failed to explode. The hulk eventually sank that evening while under friendly tow in storm conditions. Robert Gysae's *U 177* sank a pair of ships from convoy CD.20 under escort by four armed trawlers during the night of 28 May, one of them the American steamer SS *Agwimonte* and the other the Norwegian tanker MT *Storaas* travelling in ballast. Three torpedoes were needed before the stubborn Norwegian would go under.

The most successful boat—just—during this first period at sea before refuelling was Werner Hartmann's *U 198*. The experienced commander had managed to destroy one ship from convoy LMD.17 (and had claimed a second hit that was never confirmed by Allied sources) during a day-light attack on 17 May and went on to sink three more ships before requiring replenishment from Germany's tanker within the Indian Ocean.

Although the achievements of the German submariners were not ex-travagant, the hardships they endured aboard the seven boats were be-yond their previous experiences. A constant battle was waged against boredom, the captains organising various sporting endeavours when cir-cumstances allowed as well as competitions, musical events and onboard newspapers. Beards grew thick and long and hygiene became another source of major concern as the U-boats sailed through heavy, humid seas, the interiors of the pressure hulls reliant on open hatches to allow rank air, dripping with moisture, to be changed for fresh. The U-boats carried no air conditioning and soon the interiors became as ovens, stink-ing of unwashed bodies and perishing food. As the boats also carried very little refrigeration, non-preserved foodstuffs rotted and crews were limited to what had been stored aboard in tins or as salted produce. Occasionally fish were caught to augment rations: shark was a favourite with men who had tasted it before, but unfortunately often a challenge to inexperienced cooks who regularly destroyed the succulent flesh dur-ing preparation until it could only be jettisoned.

The true qualities of the various U-boat commanders and their offic-ers were tested to the limit during such long and monotonous voyages, and aboard *U 196* Kentrat was found to be lacking by many of his men. While other boats organised diversions and entertainments that could occupy crewmen, Kentrat resorted to harsh discipline and rigid control. Harking back to bygone days of sailing ship navies, constant weapons drills and threats of temporary imprisonment or loss of pay were used to keep the boat's crew in line, breeding resentment and hostility towards the boat's officers and towards Kentrat in particular. Sunburn for those above decks and sweating stickiness for those below added to the general feeling of despondency aboard *U 196*.

However, it was not only the crews that were adversely affected by the temperature. The Type IXD2 was a difficult boat to handle at the best of times. It was large and clumsy on the surface and its relatively slow diving time made it vulnerable to air attack. Conversely, while proceeding at periscope depth in any seas above a Force 4 the boat would yaw and pitch wildly, often 'broaching' (breaking the surface) and potentially alerting its intended target or inviting attack from above. Crucially, German torpedoes also suffered from the humid environment aboard the boats once they passed the Tropic of Cancer. Maintenance of the electric G7e, with which the boats were mostly equipped, became virtually impossible as the batteries within the 'eels', designed for use within European climates, deteriorated rapidly. Correspondingly, their performance in action was erratic: the torpedoes frequently travelled more slowly than normal, rendering all but the most secure firing solutions void. Despite the conditions, however, the marathon trek of the Type IXD U-boats continued into June 1943, their presence a worrying thorn in the flesh of British naval dominance within the Indian Ocean.

NOTES

1. One ship, the 6,528-ton MS *Ermland*, had already departed Kobe on 28 December 1940 in ballast in order to rendezvous with the raider *Admiral Scheer* and take on 350 prisoners, who were landed in Bordeaux on 4 April 1941.
2. The MV *Elbe* was sunk by aircraft from HMS *Eagle* on 6 June 1941; the USS *Omaha* seized the MV *Odenwald* on 6 November 1941; and the MV *Spreewald* was sunk by accident by *U 333* on 31 January 1942. A total of 19,200 tons of cargo was lost from these three ships.
3. The tanker MT *Benno* was the sole loss during this first season of blockade-running from the Far East blockade-runners, sunk by RAF attack near Carino, Spain.
4. *SS-Obergruppenführer* Ernst Kaltenbrunner later awarded the Knight's Cross to one of the crew, *Leutnant zur See (S)* Heinrich Garbers, on 1 November 1944 after similar missions in command of another covert delivery ship. His award

followed the successful landing of ten tons of freight in Argentina on 5 July 1944, including forged British pound notes, SS rings and literature, copies of Hitler's *Mein Kampf* and many small items (gifts) for use by the South American *Abwehr* operatives.

5. Leibbrandt was at large until 21 December, when he was captured. Tried for treason, he was condemned to death, a sentence commuted to life imprisonment by Smuts, who had admired his father as a 'courageous Boer warrior' during the war against the British at the turn of the century. Leibbrandt was released in 1948 and died of natural causes in 1966.

6. For Merten, his last attack was a chilling reminder of Hartenstein's *Laconia* experience. Sinking what he took to be an 8,000-ton cargo freighter, he torpedoed the steamer SS *City of Cairo*, which carried 125 passengers on board, mainly women and children. Unable to rescue survivors both for practical reasons and because of Dönitz's 'Laconia Order', Merten sailed U 68 amongst the lifeboats, directing the rescue of people in the water through a megaphone. Eleven days later he was awarded the Knight's Cross by radio for the claimed sinking of over 200,000 tons (but proved to be a confirmed total of 27 ships amounting to 170,248 tons).

7. Information by courtesy of Jürgen Oesten, 14 September 2003.

8. Spahr had been the *Obersteuermann* aboard *U 47* when Günther Prien made his legendary attack on Scapa Flow and sank the battleship HMS *Royal Oak*.

9. Survivor's accounts compiled by US Naval Intelligence (Author's collection).

10. *Ibid.*

11. Interestingly, Penang hosted a major base for the Indian National Army that had rallied to Bose's banner and there were an estimated at 10,000 men on the island in September 1942. There was also a training school, situated at the site of the Penang Free School on Green Lane and named the 'Swaraj Institute', for the training of agents who were to be sent into India for espionage and propaganda work.

12. Kershaw, *Hitler*, p.953, App., n. 291.

13. *The Statesman*, March 9 1942. Unsurprisingly, the truth of this remarkable story formed the basis for a book by James Leasor and, subsequently, the film *The Sea Wolves*, starring Gregory Peck, David Niven and Roger Moore. However, it has become increasingly difficult to weed the facts of these matters from dramatic 'fictionalisation' with regard to the events that took place.

14. Even the often-discussed success of the U-boat assault on the United States in January 1942, Operation '*Paukenschlag*', netted fewer victims than the *Eisbär* boats—25 ships sunk, totalling 156,939 tons. Indisputably the most successful U-boat assault had been Operation '*Neuland*', the February 1942 assault on the Caribbean. Forty-one ships had been sunk, eighteen of them tankers, and eleven other merchant ships had been badly damaged. The five boats that had mounted the 'Neuland' attack had sunk altogether 222,651 tons of Allied shipping.

15. The eight landing craft destroyed were LCP(R) 673, 680, 684, 685, 689, 692, 693 and 727.

16. Survivors' accounts compiled by US Naval Intelligence.

17. The commanders of both destroyers were severely criticised for their half-hearted and badly handled operations, described as 'a sad pair of attacks' by US Navy assessors. The likelihood that they had destroyed U 182 only became known through post-war analysis.

18. Wiggins, *U-Boat Adventures*, p. 91.
19. *Ibid.*, pp. 95–6.
20. Only four crewmen and six gunners survived, to be rescued by an SAAF launch after drifting for thirteen days in an open boat.
21. Jochen Brennecke, *Haie im Paradies*, p. 42.
22. *Ibid.*, p. 45.
23. Wiggins, *op. cit.*, p. 100.
24. *Da Vinci* was sunk with all 64 crewmen while returning from this patrol, destroyed by depth charges from HMS *Ness* and HMS *Active* west of Cape Finisterre on 24 May 1943.
25. It was this patrol by *U 181* that prompted Wolfgang Lüth to compose his controversial 'Problems of Leadership' lecture.

Three

Blockade

O N THE PENULTIMATE day of January 1943 Karl Dönitz had been appointed *Oberbefehlshaber der Kriegsmarine*. While assessing the general state of his navy he briefed Hitler on 26 February 1943 that German surface blockade-runners carrying war materials to and from the Far East were suffering unacceptably high losses and were unable to fulfil their missions. Despite the initial success of the first season of blockade-running, the second was hampered by a combination of increased Allied naval and aerial power within the Atlantic as well as by the penetration of German naval codes. Only ten of the seventeen ships despatched between September 1942 and April 1943 from France reached Japan. Worse still for Hitler, out of sixteen that departed Japan carrying the vital raw materials to an increasingly overstretched German war economy, only four reached France intact. It was a crippling blow to the planned importation of goods via surface blockade-runners and it led to delays in mounting fresh attempts until October 1943. When all but one of these attempts in turn failed, the entire programme was cancelled on 18 January 1944.

Although the end of blockade-running by surface ships still lay in the future, Dönitz suggested in February 1943 that further such trade could perhaps be carried out by submarines—a concept that dated from the First World War and the U-cruisers *Deutschland* and *Bremen*. A week prior to Dönitz's proposal the *Kriegsmarine* command had discussed the possibility of converting a number of Type VIIC U-boats into transport submarines, although the idea was soon dismissed on the grounds that, although the potential cargo space reached a maximum of 250 tons, combat boats could not be spared for adaptation to unarmed vessels.

In fact the original stimulus for the project of constructing U-boat transports had come directly from Hitler himself when, during a naval conference on 19 November 1942, he requested that such vessels be constructed for the purpose of supporting an invasion of American-occupied Iceland and the establishment there of a *Luftwaffe* base. Although using Hitler's 'inspiration' as a useful key to unlocking production possibilities within the Third Reich where construction priorities remained fiercely competitive between the four services, OKM quietly viewed the idea of transport submarines as primarily related to the matter of Far Eastern material imports.

Despite being unwilling to utilise fighting boats purely for transport missions, Dönitz strongly recommended that nine of the large, slow-diving Italian submarines based at Bordeaux be transformed into long-range supply submarines to traverse the Atlantic and Indian Oceans. Unsuitable in German eyes for the rough and tumble of war in the Atlantic, some of the larger, ponderous Italian vessels were theoretically capable of reaching Indonesia from Europe without the need to refuel en route. Hitler at first turned down the idea, but after Dönitz had flown to Rome and secured agreement regarding his suggestion from the Italian dictator Benito Mussolini and *Ammiraglio* Arturo Ricardi, the C-in-C of the *Regia Marina*, the *Führer* relented and allowed the project to begin. However, the agreement with the Italians carried a price: in return for their submarines being taken out of combat, the Germans would have to provide Italy with ten new Type VIIC/41 U-boats as replacements.[1]

The concept of submarine blockade-runners was so vigorously pursued by the *Kriegsmarine* that, as well as toying with the principle of towed freight storage containers during 1943, shipyards in Kiel, Bremen and Hamburg were also commissioned to build a new large ocean-going transport submarine, designated Type XX and numbered from *U 1601* to *U 1800*. The new submarines would have displaced 2,708 tons surfaced and a colossal 3,425 tons submerged. They would have been capable of transporting up to 800 tons of freight, though they were not equipped with torpedo tubes. However, these new boats would not have become operational in the *Kriegsmarine* until spring 1944 at the earliest, and as the production of this design clashed with plans for the Type XXI and XXIII electro-boats their construction was suspended on 27 May 1944.

Dönitz had decided to use the Type IXD1 and IXD2 boats as well as the refitted Italian ocean-going submarines of Bordeaux's *Betasom* command. Thus on their return from patrol during January and February 1942 *Alpino Bagnolini*, *Barbarigo*, *Cappellini*, *Reginaldo Giuliani*, *Finzi*, *Tazzoli*, and *Luigi Torelli* began refitting as transport submarines. Their attack periscopes, deck guns and torpedo tubes were removed and the ammunition stowage areas were converted to fuel bunkers, enabling the boats able to carry between 100 and 240 tons of freight, depending on their class. The entire group was codenamed '*Aquila*' (Eagle) *I* to *IX*. In the meantime, in Singapore (Shonan), the Italian Navy organised a new base for its submarines. Logistical support was to be provided by *Capitano di Fregata* Mario Jannucci's *Eritrea*, which had arrived in Japan from the Red Sea during March 1941 carrying two officers and about 30 soldiers. This small gunboat, which transferred to Singapore in June 1943, would provide liaison services between the Italian sailors and their Japanese hosts as well as escorting Italian submarines during the final leg of their voyage to Singapore. The first conversions were completed so quickly that *Aquila I* (*Tazzoli*) departed Bordeaux in May, followed immediately by *Aquila II* and *III* (*Giuliani* and *Cappellini*). Two more Italian boats, *Aquila V* and *VI* (*Barbarigo* and *Torelli*), followed during June, although ultimately only three would reach Singapore during July and September.

Meanwhile Dönitz had continued to oppose any diversion of German combat submarine strength to the Indian Ocean while Atlantic operations still held promise. The vast distances to be traversed made such undertakings hazardous and potentially unprofitable in his eyes, and during the early months of 1943 there remained a good deal of work to be done in order to provide a home port for German boats and crews. Hitler, in fits of paranoia about phantom Allied invasion forces, was demanding that much of Germany's submarine strength be deployed away from the main convoy routes and instead near Gibraltar, the Azores and Norway, and the last thing that Dönitz wished to do was further to deprive the Atlantic battle of fighting strength—a point made by Winston Churchill in his own history of the war:

The U-boat attack was our worst evil. It would have been wise for the Germans to stake all upon it. I remember hearing my father say, 'In politics, when you have got hold of a good thing, stick to it'. This is also a strategic principle of importance. Just as Göring repeatedly shifted his targets in the Battle of Britain in 1940, so now the U-boat warfare was to some extent weakened for the sake of competing attractions.[2]

However, with the reversal of German fortunes in May 1943 and the sinking of 43 boats, BdU withdrew from the North Atlantic battle. His U-boats beaten from the area by Allied sea power, Dönitz opted once again to despatch U-boats to such far-flung areas as the Indian Ocean, where merchant shipping was reported still to be sailing largely unescorted. Although it would later transpire to have been the moment of final Atlantic defeat, Dönitz viewed the withdrawal as temporary, hoping that by sending boats into the Indian Ocean significant Allied naval forces would be tied down away from the Atlantic until Germany was able to resume U-boat operations there. Dönitz correctly reasoned that May was too late in the year to despatch boats to Malaysia as they would arrive in the Indian Ocean during the harsh weather and mountainous seas of the monsoon season, when opportunities to attack were likely to be slim at best.

 Thus on 5 April *U 178*, one of the six Type IXD2 boats active south of Madagascar, was ordered to continue her voyage east rather than return to Bordeaux. She was instructed to dock in Penang in order to co-ordinate facilities for the U-boats that were to follow. Any ideas that were harboured about using all six for the continuation of this voyage were soon discarded, however. They had already loosed off nearly half of their torpedo stocks and were therefore unable to launch the concerted attack against the northern regions of the Indian Ocean with which Dönitz wished to open his new offensive. The technique of sudden surprise attacks from a number of large boats had reaped rewards off the East Coast of United States, in the Caribbean and off South Africa during 1942 and the stage seemed set for yet another devastating 'drumbeat' against apparently unprepared Allied forces. Therefore the six others already in action were to refuel from a tanker (*Charlotte Schliemann*) and remain stationed around Madagascar, Dommes alone heading east and towards the unknown territory of Malaysia.

 As far back as November 1942 the German Naval Attaché in Tokyo, Admiral Paul Wenneker—who had first been the Tokyo Attaché before

1937, though was replaced for three years by Lietzmann before returning to Tokyo in March 1940—had suggested that German naval bases
be established within selected Japanese ports. There the *Kriegsmarine*
would have been better able to utilise its own logistical capabilities for
the support of the various blockade-running ships and the future deployment of combat and transport U-boats. In Tokyo Wenneker was
responsible for all *Kriegsmarine* activities in the Asian theatre from the
beginning of the war, although he was originally concerned primarily
with the *Etappendienst der Kriegsmarine* (Naval Supply Service) that
serviced and advised German raiders and blockade-breakers operating
within East Asia. As part of the requirements of the blockade-runners
Wenneker was also responsible for the Asian end of the *Marinesonder-
dienst* (Special Naval Service) that had been established pre-war by the
Abwehr and later placed under OKM command. His assertions that dedicated facilities would enhance the blockade-breaking operation were
initially greeted with enthusiasm in Berlin.

The Japanese continued to delay any such German deployment, however, by making protracted demands and requesting guarantees limiting
any European claims within the 'New Order for Asia' that Tokyo envisaged. Specifically, Japanese interests were best suited by having outbound German cargo ships traversing the Java Sea before heading
through the Allied blockade to Europe, stopping along the way at various Japanese ports and serving as local transports for the Japanese forces
in lieu of the IJN's own vessels. Having the ships loaded with goods for
Europe in Jakarta and Surabaya (previously known by the Dutch as
Soerabaja) would have precluded much of this, and it was not until the
beginning of 1943 that work proper began on the German sites. Indeed
during December 1942 the Japanese authorities finally offered the
Kriegsmarine its desired bases, stating that it would be beneficial to the
joint Axis war effort if 'the maritime forces of the Axis could be deployed in stronger measures to the Indian Ocean.'[3]

The offer was made to Germany and Italy, although both continued to
view Japanese motives with suspicion. Aware that the major Japanese
naval effort was being directed at the Solomon Islands, the European
partners viewed the Japanese offer as unreliable and likely to change
should the Japanese situation improve elsewhere. However, the opportunity was too great to ignore and the suggestion was accepted by both

Berlin and Rome. Instructions issued from OKW on 28 December for work to commence at the chosen ports.

Wenneker's relationship with *Shosho* Ichioka Hisashi, commander of the local Eighth Submarine Group of the Imperial Japanese Navy, has been described as excellent, and swift progress followed.[4] During spring 1943 ports in Java (Dutch East Indies)—Jakarta (Batavia) and Surabaya—and at Singapore were made ready for use, loading and clearing German blockade-running U-boats, while the small island of Penang alongside Malaysia's west coast would be used by combat boats between patrols.[5] The first such site to become classified operational for the *Kriegsmarine* was Singapore, which was reported to be at readiness on 17 May 1943.

The principal port for the U-boats was to be Georgetown, a safe, sheltered harbour on the north-eastern promontory of the island (Pulau Pinang), where the former Imperial Airways seaplane installation at Swettenham Pier had already been converted to military use for Japanese submarines. It had been in the sixteenth century that the first Europeans had arrived at Penang, Portuguese explorers stumbling across the already inhabited island and naming it Pulo Pinaom, probably because of the abundance of 'pinang', or betel nut palm, on the 177-square-mile island. The sailing ships of the era began to use the small, lush island regularly as a last stopover in order to replenish their supplies of fruit and fresh water before embarking on long ocean voyages. By the middle of the following century the island had also become a popular place for pirates to hide and launch viscious lightning raids on passing ships before disappearing once more among its jungle-fringed coves. During the eighteenth century, however, British power reached a dominance in Asia and in 1765 Francis Light, under instructions from his company, Jourdain, Sullivan & de Souza, left England aboard the *Speedwell* for Sumatra and the Malay peninsula in order to establish better trade links with the region. In little over two decades he had established the first British settlement in this region, on the island of Penang. During 1786, following negotiations with the Sultan of Kedah, Light officially took possession of the island and named it Prince of Wales Island. He also established Georgetown, named after the King of England, George III.

The small island was virtually ignored by the colonial powers during the years of British rule that followed despite its strategic position at the

SEE INSET

Andaman Sea

South China Sea

Georgetown

Pulau Penang   Butterworth

Pulau Jerejak

INSET

Kuala Lumpur

Singapore

Sumatra

Borneo

Celebes

Java Sea

Batavia

Indian Ocean

Surabaya

Java

Timor

The Far East

north entry to the Malacca Strait. The Malay peninsula was secured for Britain at the turn of the century and named 'Province Wellesley' after the then-Governor of India, Richard, Marquis of Wellesley, and the significance of the more tantalising harbour at Singapore began to eclipse that of Georgetown. In 1832 the Straits Settlement was formed, comprising Malacca, Singapore and Penang; the latter became the capital, a title usurped by Singapore within two years. It was not until 1910—and the increasing popularity and availability of the automobile within the Western world and the consequent demand for rubber—that Penang, by then a Crown Settlement of the British Empire, once more became a major port, for the shipping of Malaysian rubber abroad. By 1937 over half the world's rubber was produced within the British Empire, and 79 per cent of it was Malaysian.

Despite the bustling trade arteries that flowed through Georgetown, Penang, after decades of being passed over in deference to Singapore, had hosted no naval presence. It hosted merchant shipping, and a base for the flying boats of Imperial Airways was established within the small sheltered harbour. The ungainly aircraft would land in Georgetown, making fast at the elongated wooden pilings of Swettenham Pier. The Malacca Strait, the narrow channel that passed between Georgetown and the main Malay peninsula, spanned only just over a mile, the jungle-shrouded hills of the mainland and the bustling streets of the town of Butterworth plainly visible from Penang. During the First World War Penang had witnessed an attack by the German raider SMS *Emden* at dawn on 28 October 1914 when, with the sun barely risen, the German warship had sailed through the Northern Channel disguised as the British cruiser HMS *Yarmouth* before hoisting the *Kaiserliche Marine* ensign and successfully torpedoing and shelling the Russian light cruiser *Zhemtchug*. As the Russian disappeared beneath the surface, the French torpedo boat *Mousquette* attempted retaliation but soon joined *Zhemtchug* on the seabed.[6] Interestingly, two of the dead Russian crewmen were buried on Pulau Jerejak off Penang's south-east coast. It has been strongly rumoured that this 150-acre (362-hectare) island hosted the *Monsun* U-boats, although no evidence exists to support this claim. Pulau Jerejak boasted a small shipyard that had sprung into existence when British powers considered the idea of establishing a major naval base there. However, the plan was stillborn in 1805 with the ascendancy of Royal Navy power following the Battle of Trafalgar and the subsequent development of Georgetown. If the *Kriegsmarine* had considered basing its units on Pulau Jerejak it would have vastly complicated already tortuous logistical matters: fundamentally, there were no docking facilities that could have accommodated operational submarines. The Japanese occupation had largely ignored Pulau Jerejak (which hosted a leper colony), and the events of the Second World War generally passed unremarked within the jungle-infested interior.

After three years of a second world conflict Dönitz had good reasons for continuing to embrace the concepts of his war of attrition against enemy merchant shipping, reasoning that merchant ships sunk anywhere on the world's oceans would still constitute a drain on Allied resources. However, a major factor unbeknown to Dönitz that had aided the U-boat assaults against South Africa and within the Atlantic in 1942 had been the Allies' loss of access to the priceless 'Triton' Enigma code net. During most of that year the introduction of a fourth rotor on 1 February to the standard U-boat's Enigma machine and the implementation of a new code net (Triton) had 'blacked out' Allied codebreakers. The dawning of 1943 had seen this situation change, and the 'Triton' net was penetrated on 13 December 1942 following the capture of material from

U 559 before she sank within the Mediterranean. BdU operations were once more exposed to the scrutiny of the Allied navies.

Oblivious to these developments, and appalled at the devastation wrought against his U-boats during 'Black May', Dönitz finalised plans for his attack deep into the Indian Ocean and against the Arabian Sea. In an operation codenamed '*Monsun*', eleven combat boats, supported by a Type XIV *Milchkuh*, were prepared for departure in mid-June, their arrival and commencement of operations scheduled for September 1943 as the rainy season diminished.

A number of unique factors come together within the Indian Ocean to make that region's monsoon north of the Equator the most intense in the world. The area is surrounded by the largest land mass on Earth, and the differential heating that this produces within the humid atmosphere creates fierce winds and blinding torrents of rain. Between June and September the prevailing south-westerly winds push the obliterating rainfall across the ocean into the Arabian Sea and on to the Indian subcontinent, where its life-giving moisture slaked the often parched landscape. In the southern hemisphere the monsoon winds are generally milder, but severe summer storms near Mauritius would have made U-boat operations difficult. When the winds change towards the end of September and a new, predictable weather pattern brings strong north-easterlies for the remainder of the year, cyclones sometimes strike the shores of the Arabian Sea and the Bay of Bengal. It was into this natural maelstrom that Dönitz's U-boat men would bring their own lethal and destructive force in an effort to hamper Allied shipping that had seen little German pressure after nearly four years of war.

The *Monsun* group were not the first to depart Europe with the intention of reaching Penang. Responding to Japanese requests that a pair of Type IXC U-boats be transferred for evaluation and possible copying, Hitler had finally decided that a single example should indeed be granted in partial payment for some of Germany's imported rubber, tin and other raw materials that had already arrived by surface blockade-runner. Despite Dönitz's misgivings that the Imperial Japanese Navy would be unable to build such boats on a scale sufficient to influence the war, *U 511*, a veteran of Caribbean and Atlantic operations, was prepared for the journey to Japan as '*Marco Polo I*'. *U 511* had led an interesting career even before her July 1942 assignment to combat with the 10th U-

Flotilla at Lorient. Commissioned on 8 December 1941 by ex-merchant seaman *Kapitänleutnant* Friedrich Steinhoff, she had gone through the traditional gruelling working-up within the Baltic, spending the week from 31 May to 5 June involved in rocket trials in Peenemünde. The head of the German rocket programme, *Dr* Werner von Braun, was given the use of *U 511*, then still attached to the 4th U-Training Flotilla, to experiment with the launching of rockets from a submerged U-boat. It was no coincidence that Steinhoff's boat was chosen—he was the brother of Ernst Steinhoff, a scientist at the rocket research establishment at Peenemünde and colleague of von Braun's.

In these trials, codenamed Project '*Ursel*', six solid-fuel rockets were installed on the deck of *U 511* in wire traps in a similar fashion to the Army's half-track mounted Nebelwerfer. The rockets were set at a 45-degree angle and an electrical charge provided the impulse for launching. However, the 30cm *Wurfkörper 42* projectiles later proved to be almost impossible to aim with sufficient precision to be used for anything other than blanket shore bombardment. The notion of bombarding the American coast with these weapons was also found to be impractical from the point of view of seaworthiness: although Steinhoff stated that he could launch the rockets at a shore target with some hope of success, the boat handled very poorly while submerged and with rockets mounted on deck. There was not enough room to accommodate the weapons inside the boat and a completely new design was therefore called for. Despite satisfactory test firings, the project was, needless to say, cancelled.

The boat's second war patrol into the Western Atlantic had been curtailed owing to an illness suffered by Steinhoff while at sea. After returning to Lorient he relinquished command to *Kapitänleutnant* Fritz Schneewind, who, following a single Atlantic patrol, was charged with taking the boat to Japan and handing it over to the Imperial Japanese Navy. Schneewind—who was, ironically, born in Padang, Sumatra, in 1917—departed Lorient on 10 May 1943 carrying bottles of mercury, a 3,000hp Daimler Benz engine, blueprints for Type IX U-boats and a human cargo. The last comprised three *Kriegsmarine* engineers, the first of eleven destined for technical missions in Japan, and several dignitaries—Dr Ernest Woermann, the German Ambassador resident in Nanking; *Chujo* Kichisaburo Nomura, chief officer of the Japanese Naval Attaché in Berlin; *Chusa* Sugita; and Spahn, the Nazi Party's representative in Japan.

A Type IXC, *U 511* was compelled to refuel from *U 460* during late May before Schneewind, who had also been given freedom to operate in an anti-shipping role while en route to Malaysia, rounded the Cape of Good Hope and entered the Indian Ocean. During the morning of 27 June *U 511* sighted and attacked the first of two victims, the American cargo steamer SS *Sebastian Ceremeno*. This 7,194-ton ship was travelling from Mombasa, Kenya, to Bahia when, south-east of Madagascar, two torpedoes hit her within seconds of each other. Five lifeboats were quickly launched, and 70 of the 75-strong crew escaped their sinking ship:

> The sub surfaced about quarter of a mile away; light grey and rusted, sloped shark-nosed bow and sloping stern; guns appeared to be in bad condition . . . The sub circled the lifeboats while an officer asked for the captain and chief engineer. The usual questions were then asked and truthful answers given. There were about five or six Germans and one Japanese seen. Commander spoke good English, appeared to be about 45. The Japanese was taking pictures.[7]

A second American, the 7,176-ton Liberty ship SS *Samuel Heintzelmann*, was despatched on 9 July east-south-east of the Chagos Archipelago that lay in the middle of the Indian Ocean. During the final approach to her destination *U 511* underwent the indignity of attack by Japanese sub-hunters, despite being spotted running surfaced with huge swastika and Rising Sun ensigns attached to the conning tower. Under direct shellfire Nomura signalled in Japanese a message that was couched in terms not entirely diplomatic, informing their attackers that their target was not an American submarine but a German one. Finally, on 15 July '*Marco Polo I*' entered Penang harbour, the first German U-boat to do so. Greeted with full ceremony, Schneewind docked his boat and began to unload cargo, weary crew and passengers. Nomura and his colleagues soon departed Penang by aircraft for Tokyo, while *U 511*'s crew re-embarked on their boat, taking aboard a Japanese pilot before transferring from Malaysia to Kobe, where they docked on 15 August. There the *Kriegsmarine* ensign was lowered for the last time, to be replaced by the vivid blood red of the Rising Sun as *U 511* became *RO-500* of the Imperial Japanese Navy.

Schneewind and his men were given ten days of leave at Mount Fujiyama—under Japanese supervision—where they encountered many

German women and children who had been transferred to Japan from the Dutch East Indies after the Japanese invasion. Talking with the civilians, the uneasy crewmen discovered that they held a deep-rooted fear of their Japanese hosts, many claiming (perhaps improbably) to have been 'forcibly separated from husbands and fathers [who] had been murdered while in transit on Japanese vessels.'[8]

At the end of their leave the German crew were transferred to Yokohama, whence they travelled to Kobe and boarded the blockade-runner *Osorno*, bound for Singapore. In due course they planned to travel to Penang in order to form a small pool of spare U-boat crewmen in preparation for the arrival of their comrades from France and Germany. The apparatus for administering the new Eastern bases was already in place and *U 511*'s crew would augment a core of men from various German military and merchant ships that had already formed a logistical hierarchy and a reserve of personnel. In March 1943 *Korvettenkapitän* Wolfgang Erhardt had become commander of all *Kriegsmarine* bases in Malaysia and Singapore as *Leiter des Marinestützpunkt*. He had previously been First Officer aboard the raider *Michel*, which had been sunk after his departure by the US submarine *Tarpon* during the morning of 17 October 1943. *Kapitän zur See* Günther Gumprich's *Michel* was nearing the end of her second combat cruise, having sailed from Yokohama during May and having sunk three ships totalling 27,632 tons, when intercepted by *Tarpon*. The latter had been conducting her ninth war patrol off the coast of Honshu when she sighted what was taken to be a large auxiliary warship in the approaches to Yokohama. Tracking the target until 0156hrs the next morning, *Tarpon* fired four torpedoes, at least three of which impacted and stopped *Michel* dead in the water. However, the German ship managed to regain momentum and headed straight for the enemy submarine, intent on ramming. The American submerged, dashed under the target ship and attacked from the opposite beam with three more torpedoes, one of which hit the stern. Yet another torpedo strike finally ended *Michel*'s death throes, producing a huge explosion and sending the ship under. Gumprich and many crewmen went down with their ship because the Japanese authorities, despite pleas from Berlin, failed to mount an effective search for survivors. Only half of the complement made landfall in Japan, using floats and small rubber dinghies. *Michel* was the first German raider sunk by a US sub-

marine in the Pacific, but her demise marked the end of the German
merchant raiders at large on the world's oceans: their era was over.

NOTES

1. *U 428–U 430, U 746–U 750, U 1161* and *U 1162*, scheduled to be redesignated
    by the Italians *S 1–9*.
2. W. S. Churchill, *The Second World War*, Vol. IV, p. 114.
3. Krug, Hirama, Sander-Nagashima and Niestlé, *Reluctant Allies*, p. 188.
4. See Krug, Hirama, Sander-Nagashima and Niestlé, *passim*.
5. At first the Japanese had also offered Sabang and the Andaman Islands as poten-
    tial U-boat bases, but their lack of port facilities precluded them from practical
    consideration.
6. *Emden* was sunk by Australian cruiser HMAS *Sydney* within two weeks of the
    audacious attack.
7. US Naval Intelligence: Collected Accounts of Survivors (SS *Sebastian Cere-
    meno*).
8. Charles Dana Gibson, 'The Far East Odyssey of the UIT 24' (article based on
    the wartime recollections of Petty Officer Heinz Rehse of *U 511* and *UIT 24*).
    The original quote is Rehse's.

Four

Monsoon

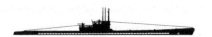

ALTHOUGH both *U 178* and *U 511* had sailed weeks previously, bound ultimately for Malaysia, it was not until 12 June 1943 that the first *Monsun* boat put to sea. The elongated hull of Type IXD2 *U 200* slipped its mooring lines from Kiel's Tirpitz Pier to the familiar strains of martial music played from a scratchy record through the harbour's tannoy system, the days when *Wehrmacht* bandsmen gathered to recite anglophobic battle tunes all but over. A small crowd of fellow *Kriegsmarine* men and family members had congregated and *U 200*'s crew, assembled on the boat's casing, were bedecked with garlands of summer flowers as their boat eased from the military harbour. Atop the conning tower the U-boat's commander, Heinrich Schonder, closely supervised the departure, electric motors purring as the heavy boat glided into the Kieler Förde in company with *U 194* and *U 420*, preparing to enter the Kaiser Wilhelm Canal that bisected Schleswig Holstein and linked the Baltic and North Seas.

Schonder was a veteran seaman. A graduate of the officer's class of 1935, he had served in U-boats since 1938 and had risen steadily through the ranks to take his first combat command two years later. By mid-1943, at the age of 32, Schonder was a holder of the Knight's Cross, awarded to hin the previous year for sinking nine enemy ships—including the escort destroyer HMS *Grove*—within the Mediterranean while in command of the Type VIIC *U 77*. With the launch of *U 200* during August 1942 Schonder had been earmarked as her commander, transferring from *U 77* to oversee the completion of his new boat, which was finally commissioned at the year's end. As *U 200* embarked on her inaugural patrol Schonder was still celebrating both his recent promotion to *Korvettenkapitän* and the successful completion of six months of difficult trials and exercises in the Baltic.

Meanwhile within the Atlantic battleground, in the space of time that it had taken Schonder and the instructors of 4th U-training flotilla to lick *U 200*'s crew into shape, the U-boat war on Allied convoys had finally collapsed, and by the time that Schonder and his crew were readying their boat to sail Dönitz had had his change of heart and endorsed fresh proposals for U-boats to operate in the Indian Ocean and proceed from there to Penang. Schonder's *U 200* led the way and ten other boats were ordered to follow shortly thereafter.

Dönitz, however, had allowed his spearhead *Monsun* boat to take on an extra role. Schonder's crew of 56 had swollen with the addition of five men, all dressed in the traditional U-boat fatigues. Under close examination they may have appeared slightly aloof from the remainder of the crew, because they were members of the elite Brandenburger Special Forces division, detached from the coastal raider (*Küstenjäger*) battalion. *Leutnant* Brügmann and his four men had undergone weeks of intensive training at the battalion's home ground at Langenargen near Lake Constance on the German-Swiss border. There they had been drilled in explosives handling and sailing before being briefed on their forthcoming mission, the target and destination no real surprise to the small group. Brügmann, *Unteroffizier* Bill Fesq, *Feldwebel* Wilfried Moll, *Obergefreiter* Reinhard Schneider and *Obergefreiter* Herbert Bauer were all *Auslandsdeutsche* ('foreign Germans'), born in German South-West and East Africa—colonies lost to the British during the First World War. Their mission was to sabotage the huge Australian-built drydocks in Durban, South Africa, and with support from *Ossewabrandwag* sow as much discord as possible after being landed by Schonder on a deserted stretch of the African coast.

The undertaking did not begin auspiciously. Brügmann's team received orders on 9 June to transfer to Kiel, where Schneider and Bauer were almost immediately hospitalised before sailing, to be replaced by Rudolf Otto and Otto Hand. Undaunted, the team carefully loaded their explosives and small arms aboard *U 200*, taking their place quietly among the crew as the boat sailed from Germany. Once through the Kaiser

Wilhelm Canal, Schonder separated from *U 194* and *U 420* and shaped course for Bergen, where his boat would take on final fuel and whatever fresh supplies could be found in preparation for her impending marathon trek to the Far East.

In Norway, docked away from prying eyes, the Brandenburg team practised their disembarkation, slipping over the side of the high-riding U-boat into small rubber dinghies until they were familiar with the intricacies of their mission. The following day the young crew and their passengers waved goodbye to friendly shores for the last time and *U 200* sailed once again, heading towards the northern passage around Great Britain. Unable to lie idle within the boat during the long voyage, the small team of Brandenburgers had already begun to help with manning the anti-aircraft weapons when the boat was travelling on the surface.

Here, however, Schonder's successful career came to a tragic end. Hoping to make good speed into the Atlantic, he was sailing fully surfaced on diesel power south-west of Iceland when lookouts spotted the unmistakable shape of a Liberator bomber. Above them Australian Flight Lieutenant A. W. Fraser's bomber, from No 120 Squadron, had been on distant escort for convoy ONS.11 when the dull grey hull of the U-boat had been sighted, a strong wake leaving a betraying indicator behind it. Immediately beginning an attack run, Fraser's aircraft was rocked by accurate and sustained flak as the German crew responded with all available anti-aircraft weapons. Balls of tracer flashed past the Liberator, several shells smashing through the port wing and fuselage as Fraser barrelled overhead and released two depth charges. He was unable to launch his planned salvo of four owing to damage to the bomb door's hydraulics from the German fire, but the two that were released straddled the U-boat cleanly and *U 200* was momentarily obliterated in the spume of detonation. With fuel leaking from his damaged wing Fraser pulled his bomber around for a second pass, which again failed when his depth charges refused to budge.

For Schonder, however, the battle was over. The Coastal Command aircrew could plainly see that their victim was sinking and they circled once more as *U 200* submerged for the last time. Fraser and his colleagues watched as oil, debris and fifteen swimming men bobbed to the surface before he was forced to abort his vigil and turn for the flight home to Reykjavik. After informing the nearby convoy of the German survivors, Liberator 'H for Harry' flew away, Fraser nursing his aircraft to safety and making a deliberately tail-heavy landing to protect the bomber's nose wheel, which had also been damaged by German flak. Behind him neither Schonder nor any of the 61 men aboard *U 200* were seen again. The first *Monsun* boat was gone, taking with her the small Brandenburger commando team and their plans for South African sabotage.[1] With such early casualties the *Monsun* operations had got off to a shaky start, but things were shortly to become far worse.

The Type IXD2 U-boat was capable of making the entire journey to Malaya without the necessity to refuel, but only two of these boats had been included in the original *Monsun* group. The remainder were Type IXCs, which would have to take on diesel fuel within the South Atlantic before rounding the Cape and heading into the Indian Ocean. The *Milchkuh U 462* was despatched from Bordeaux to supply the *Monsun* boats in an area 300 miles east of St Paul's Rocks. Thirty-nine-year-old *Kapitänleutnant der Reserve* Bruno Vowe had already undertaken three successful cruises into the North Atlantic since his boat entered front-line service in March 1942. However, as Vowe proceeded, surfaced, through the Bay of Biscay two days later, he had the misfortune to be sighted by four Coastal Command, No 19 Group (Nos 151 and 456 Squadrons) Mosquitos engaged on 'Instep' patrol, aimed at combating the Junkers Ju 88s of the *Luftwaffe*'s KG 40 that also patrolled the Bay of Biscay, albeit with decreasing success. Immediately banking to attack the broad-hulled U-boat, the four Mosquitos strafed their target with machine-gun and cannon fire. The sudden fusillade slashed through the startled bridge watch, killed *Matrosengefreiter* Ferdinand Brunnbaur and wounded four other men. As the bloodied lookouts struggled below, Vowe, his boat damaged, had little alternative other than to abort his mission and return to Bordeaux.

When *U 462* was placed into dock for repairs, however, the damage was judged to be not so serious as to prevent Vowe sailing again for his rendezvous with the eastbound combat boats; and no others had yet left port. Therefore on 28 June, four days after *U 200* had ceased responding to position requests from BdU, Vowe put to sea once again, this time in company with *U 160* bound for the Western Atlantic. Their sailing in tandem was part of a new doctrine advocated by Dönitz to repel the potent threat of enemy aircraft by the use of combined flak weaponry until the opportunity to dive arose. However, ill fortune dogged *U 462*'s voyage yet again when, on 2 July, a No 224 Squadron Liberator from No 19 Group made radar contact during the early afternoon and homed in unerringly on the two surfaced U-boats, which had been sighted at a range of only two miles. Breaking through the cloud cover at an altitude of 1,000ft, WO E. J. J. Spiller brought his Liberator into the attack against the leading U-boat in the face of light flak. As the companion boat began to submerge, the Liberator roared over *U 462*, dropping depth charges wide of the target and pumping machine-gun bullets into the wide flat decking. As *U 160* disappeared Spiller opted for a second attack against her projected location; Vowe took the opportunity to submerge too, and a third attack with ASW bombs and depth charges rocked the escaping *U 462* and caused her severe damage, holing an outboard ballast tank. Fortunately for Vowe and his men there had been confusion aboard Spiller's aircraft and the release of bombs and depth charges had been simultaneous, rocking the aircraft and throwing their aim wide. Nevertheless, enough damage had been caused to force *U 462* to abort her mission once again and return to Bordeaux. *U 160*, having escaped unscathed, continued west.

In the meantime *U 188* had departed Lorient on 30 June as the second of the *Monsun* group, and she was followed on 3 July by *U 168, U 509, U 514, U 532* and *U 183*. Within less than a week of this massed departure, the final three, *U 506, U 533* and *U 516*, were also at sea heading south, *U 533* having suffered a false start as splintered glass was discovered within the grease cap of the periscope mounting. This piece of sabotage forced a return to Lorient, where the offending glass was removed before the boat could sail again. Dönitz faced a thorny dilemma as a result of *U 462*'s inability to break out of Biscay and a complicated alternative refuelling schedule was hastily organised. Another *Milchkuh*, *Oberleutnant der Reserve* Helmut Metz's *U 487*, was already at sea and active within quadrant DF south-west of the Azores. However, Metz had already supplied ten U-boats with fuel and provisions and, although still holding sufficient food supplies, he lacked the diesel required by the *Monsun* boats. Dönitz thus ordered the outbound *U 160* to rendezvous with the tanker and transfer all fuel but that necessary for a return voyage to France aboard *U 487*, leaving that tanker able, in turn, to supply the *Monsun* group with 40 tons of diesel per boat. *U 487* was ordered to proceed south to a point where she could take on provisions from *U 160* and then make the vital *Monsun* rendezvous.

Dönitz's convoluted planning was in vain. As *U 487* and *U 160* converged on one another to begin their fuel transfer, the *Milchkuh* was sighted by an Avenger/Wildcat team from the escort carrier USS *Core* and immediately attacked as the German crew were in the act of pulling apart a bale of cotton that they had retrieved from the sea. While the Wildcat strafed the surfaced U-boat its Avenger partner dropped four depth charges that cleanly straddled the tanker. Severely damaged in the attack, *U 487* began to circle, rudders jammed and with a shimmering trail of oil leaking from damaged tanks. Worse for Metz and his crew, much of the cotton that had been carried into the submarine's interior burst into flames during the bombing, filling the U-boat's interior with dense smoke. Still the German flak crew continued to return fire, and as Lt E. Steiger began a second strafing pass in his Wildcat the aircraft was hit by heavy-calibre anti-aircraft shells and spun out of control into the sea. Steiger was killed during the attack—*Core*'s only combat casualty during the Second World War. A second Avenger/Wildcat team arrived as the flames of Steiger's aircraft died away and a second combined strafing and depth-charge attack ended *U 487*'s chances of survival. The boat lifted from the water at a sharp angle and slid beneath the surface. Metz and 31 of his crewmen went with her to the seabed; 33 others were rescued by the destroyer USS *Barker*.

U 487's fate had been sealed by a combination of clever deduction by Allied intelligence sources and plain misfortune. The rendezvous area that Dönitz had chosen had four US Navy aircraft carriers—*Core*, *Santee*, *Bogue*, and *Card*—in the vicinity, all playing an active anti-U-boat role in American operations. Although 'Ultra' decryption of Enigma messages did not specifically betray *U 487*, they certainly played a major role in the tanker's sinking. Through 'Ultra' it was known that the area south-south-west of the Azores was a favoured location for refuelling operations. The *Monsun* boats themselves were also known to the Allies, intercepted messages having shown that several U-boats had been despatched from France, probably for the Far East. Most damning for Metz, Dönitz's messages ordering *U 487*—known by the Allies to be a U-tanker—to head for that general area had allowed educated guesses to be applied to aircraft patrols, leading to her discovery. Thus even though

Enigma traffic was not at the time being read, past 'Ultra' information had been instrumental in revealing that a large and important refuelling operation was about to take place.

For Dönitz and his *Monsun* boats the implications of this disaster were not clear until five of the group's boats spent days waiting in the rendezvous area for refuelling that would never come. As the BdU War Diary recorded on 18 July, '*U 487* has not reported any more; it must be presumed lost. In order to carry out the *Monsun* task as intended, it is necessary to appoint two more submarines as tankers besides *U 160*.' However, unbeknown to Dönitz, the alternative tanker already on its way, *U 160*, had in turn been sunk the day after Metz's boat, hit by a homing torpedo as she tried to escape the attentions of aircraft from the USS *Santee*. From her crew of 54 there were no survivors.

The refuelling arrangements were not the only part of the *Monsun* plan to run foul of Allied air power: by 17 July, when BdU issued new orders to resume the southward journey, only seven of the original eleven boats remained. *U 200* had been the first of the group to be lost, while on 8 July *U 514* had been destroyed, followed four days later by *U 506*. *Kapitänleutnant* Hans-Jürgen Auffermann's *U 514* had been sighted by Squadron Leader T. M. Bulloch's No 224 Squadron Liberator on 8 July, only five days from port and still north-east of Cape Finisterre. Bulloch was already an experienced ASW pilot and was carrying the newly developed, top secret 'Type 24 Mine'—otherwise known as the 'Fido' homing torpedo. Over calm seas and beneath a brilliant blue, cloudless sky, the Liberator's passenger, weapons specialist Flight Lieutenant C. V. T. Campbell, sighted *U 514* riding on the surface amongst a small fleet of Spanish trawlers. Bulloch roared into the attack at low altitude and showered *U 514* with rockets, several of which were seen to strike the grey hull as machine-gun fire peppered the German bridge watch. *U 514* immediately dived, only to emerge stern-first moments later. As the U-boat submerged once more Bulloch deployed the torpedo, which appeared to miss the target and began streaking along the surface of the sea. Unsure of the identity of the fast-moving object, Bulloch used depth charges to destroy it, reasoning that if it were an escaping U-boat then it was a worthy target and if it were the errant torpedo then the destruction of this highly classified weapon was necessary to forestall its recovery by the enemy. Regardless, *U 514*'s crew of 54 crew died with their boat.

An American Liberator of the USAAF's 1st Antisubmarine Squadron destroyed *Kapitänleutnant* Erich Würdemann's *U 506* west of Vigo on 12 July. Würdemann, a veteran of operations in the Gulf of Mexico and off South Africa, was amongst the 49 men killed as a result of the attack, dying from wounds sustained as he waited in the water for rescue after abandoning ship. Six survivors were later made prisoner. The last of the trilogy of losses during July was that of *U 509*, sunk on 15 July by an Avenger/Wildcat team from the USS *Santee*. The Avenger deployed a 'Fido' against the U-boat as it was crash-diving away from the strafing Wildcat and a huge underwater explosion was observed by the Americans, marking the grave of *Korvettenkapitän* Werner Witte and his 53 crewmen. Since no radio message had been sent before her destruction, *U 509* was presumed lost only after failing to make the reshuffled fuelling rendezvous.

Dönitz faced a grim dilemma. The presumed loss of *U 487* was a potentially crippling blow to the entire operation, and with *U 160* also failing to report her status he was forced to rely on further stop-gap measures. *Korvettenkapitän* Adolph Piening's veteran *U 155* had departed Lorient on 30 June for a central Atlantic patrol, but BdU now directed him to rendezvous with the waiting *Monsun* boats and provide what fuel and provisions he could spare before returning to France. Between 21 and 23 July Piening met *U 168*, *U 183* and *U 188* 600 miles west of the Cape Verde Islands and passed over what supplies and diesel he could—35m³ of diesel fuel to each boat—but, although valuable, these were insufficient for the group as a whole. Rather than abort the mission entirely the *Monsun* boat *U 516* was allocated the task of passing all but necessary fuel and provisions over to *U 532* and *U 533*, *Kapitänleutnant* Hans-Rutger Tillessen then cancelling his own journey to the Indian Ocean and returning to Lorient.

The targeting of Germany's *Milchkuh* force was beginning to have dire consequences for Dönitz. As a direct result of the stationing off the Azores of the four US carriers, eight U-boats had been lost during June and July, two of them U-tankers. Consequently seven other combat boats were used at various times as auxiliary tankers, unable to pursue their planned combat roles. South Atlantic operations suffered considerably, the Type VIIC boats destined for that region being forced to remain in equatorial West African seas for lack of refuelling possibilities. Dönitz also directed all boats to skirt around the danger zone of grid squares CF, DH and DG if possible and proceed with 'special caution' if unable to add the extra miles to their journey for any reason. Reports from a Spanish steamer of a large aircraft carrier in DG 9910 on 11 July had fuelled Dönitz's speculation that the presumed losses of *U 487* and *U 160* were attributable to carrier-borne aircraft reconnaissance, probably followed by attacks from escorting destroyers.

By mid-August the first of the remaining *Monsun* boats was rounding the Cape of Good Hope and preparing to enter the Indian Ocean. Already in action near Mauritius were the six independently sailing Type IXD2s from Bordeaux's 12th U-Flotilla. The seventh U-boat that had departed Germany for the region, the Type IXD1 *U 195*, had already reversed course and begun to trek back towards France: as was the case with sister-ship *U 180*, her diesel engines had proved extremely unreliable. After having sunk two ships while still outbound in the central Atlantic and damaging a third, *Korvettenkapitän* Heinz Buchholz had patrolled off Cape Town, to no further result, and, having taken on board a sick crewman from *U 178* on 8 June, Buchholz headed home, refuelling from *U 480* south-west of the Azores and reaching Bordeaux on 23 July. There *U 195* was taken out of service alongside *U 180* and work was scheduled to commence in November to convert the pair into supply U-boats with the standard propulsion units of a Type IXC.

Each of the remaining cruiser-submarines had departed European shores during March or early April and gradually moved from Madagascar and the Mozambique Channel toward Mauritius from the middle of June, refuelling from the MT *Charlotte Schliemann*, which had sailed from Japan for that purpose. The 7,747-ton Danish-built tanker had been trapped in the neutral port of Las Palmas at the outbreak of war in September 1939. *Kapitän* Dohmen's ship had been loaded with 10,800 tons of fuel oil in Curaçao during the previous August, and as war clouds dimmed Europe's horizon the German naval command issued coded messages to all German merchant ships advising them of their best possible course of action in the event of hostilities. Many were subordinated directly to *Kriegsmarine* control—including *Charlotte Schliemann*. Strategically interned within the Canary Islands, the tanker lay ready for possible use as a covert U-boat refuelling stop, a role shared at Las Palmas with the tanker *Corrientes* and begun with the resupply of *U 69* on 28 June 1941.

On 20 February 1942, when her position as a refuelling stop in the Canary Islands became increasingly untenable on account of British pressure on the Spanish authorities, *Charlotte Schliemmann* broke out of Las Palmas and sailed into the South Atlantic. After supplying the raiders *Schiff 28/Michel* and *Schiff 23/Stier* Dohmen lay course for Japan, arriving at Yokohama on 20 October. There his ship was reprovisioned, was armed with six flak weapons and had 48 new naval personnel added to her regular complement of 42. The new contingent, commanded by an ex-merchant officer, *Oberleutnant der Reserve* Adolf Wimmel, was tasked with maintaining the ship's weapons and aiding in the difficult U-boat supply operations that would ensue. *Charlotte Schliemann* was about to become the most important tanker in the Indian Ocean, her first mission being the supply of the six Madagascar U-cruisers.

On 22 June the great meeting of six rust-streaked U-boats and their tanker took place nearly 700 miles south of Mauritius. During the long humid day and early the next, the U-boats took turns at taking on an extra 200m³ of diesel oil each from the tanker, those unable to provision circling the conglomeration of German vessels serving as picket boats, acutely aware that the arrival of a solitary Allied aircraft or fast warship would mean disaster for them all. The entire German naval presence within the Indian Ocean in June 1943 was clustered together in one small area centred on the *Charlotte Schliemann*. For many officers and crewmen it was a chance to tread the boards of a surface ship after months confined to a submarine, and one by one they savoured a brief but welcome shower aboard the tanker as the refuelling proceeded and the six captains conferred about their future tactics. Lüth's *U 181* also received a new crew member from the tanker, a man named Müller. He replaced Wilhelm Willige, the *Smutje*, who had had his knee shattered by the explosion of the 3.7cm gun barrel on 10 April when Lüth had attacked the SS *Empire Whimbrel* southbound within the Atlantic Ocean.[2] Aboard *U 178* Dommes was unwilling to let too many men aboard the tanker at once, mindful of the fate that had befallen *Atlantis* as she refuelled *U 126* in the South Atlantic when the U-boat's commander, Ernst Bauer, had been stranded aboard the raider during the British attack that sank her.

Dommes had by that time reached the end of his tether. He was suffering from severe stomach cramps, his illness mainly a result of battle fatigue: years of combat in the Mediterranean had worn his nerves to the point of exhaustion. Often he lay in a deep depression as his boat headed east, mumbling to himself that he would never return from this voyage—a sentiment that provoked heated rebukes from Wilhelm Spahr, his IWO, and *Kapitänleutnant* Karl-Heinz Wiebe, the LI. With Dommes' spirits slumping and his stomach pains increasing, Spahr assumed more and more the mantle of command.

Restocking with supplies and the opportunity to set foot on the deck of a surface ship pitching and rolling only fractionally compared to a U-boat were more than welcome to the six U-boat crews, but the food taken aboard was Japanese in origin, and at least one man was distinctly unhappy about it. Lüth recorded in his War Diary: 'Meat and vegetables are particularly meagre, and, taking into account the possible length of this patrol, they won't even last as long as the fuel.'[3] This was later to become a recurrent problem for German submariners in the Eastern theatre, until they were later able to cultivate and prepare enough food within the German bases for their purposes. As Hans-Joachim Krug, later IWO of *U 219*, remembered: 'Japanese food didn't agree with us . . . they lived much more simply than Germans and didn't need the different categories of foodstuffs that our crews needed.'[4]

It was not only the lack of variety in the food that caused trepidation among the crews: there was also a dearth of spare parts for the boats' overworked compressors and for those systems vital for submergence and thus survival. The *Charlotte Schliemann* carried no replacement components for such vital machinery and thus the crews were forced to nurse worn equipment through the remainder of their voyages, limiting practice dives to the bare minimum in order to reduce unnecessary strain on their boats' systems.

The Germans also managed to taken on board more unwelcome passengers. Within the Japanese supplies transferred laboriously aboard the boats were hundreds of cockroaches, and the detested insects swiftly multiplied in the dark humidity of the U-boats' hulls and became a genuine nuisance, disturbing sleeping crewmen and gnawing at damp, flaking skin. However, the war against this new enemy at least provided a focus during the weeks of boredom ahead, as all manner of traps and weapons were deployed against the inexorably growing population.

Once the resupply of the six boats had been completed, the *Charlotte Schliemann* laid course for Japan via Jakarta and Singapore. The first major refuelling within the Indian Ocean had gone without a hitch. While the boats were travelling between Java and the Malayan peninsula, however, warnings of an American submarine within the area were radioed to *Schliemann*'s commander and he commenced to zig-zag, all eyes aboard straining for any sign of tell-tale torpedo tracks. This time there was nothing—the American submarine force was in fact absent from the Strait of Malacca—but it highlighted a problem that would soon grow to lethal proportions for the *Monsun* boats. The *Charlotte Schliemann* docked in Kobe in August in order to take on fresh fuel and provisions for the next wave of inbound U-boats.

The six large submarines continued their operational cruising. Among the interesting technological developments that they used to aid their hunting was one peculiar to the Type IXD2s—the Focke-Achgelis Fa 330, commonly known as the *Bachstelze* (Wagtail), a towed gyrocopter. Germany possessed a pioneer in the field of rotorcraft technology in the shape of Heinrich Focke. He had flown his first helicopter in 1937, and by 1942 the *Kriegsmarine* was engaged in testing another twin-rotor helicopter, the Flettner Fl 282, for a possible ASW role.

Progressing from this initial development, BdU soon began investigating the use of gyrocopters to extend the long-range surveillance capabilities of U-boats in action. Generally U-boats rode so low in the water that the visible horizon lay little more than eight miles distant. A small aircraft offered a novel solution to the problem, though only if the submarine could remain undetected on the surface long enough to launch and recover it. During the First World War several nations had experimented with submarine-based observation aircraft, albeit with discouraging results. In the inter-war years, although the Imperial Japanese Navy continued to develop such submarines and aircraft, German attempts at utilising the collapsible Arado Ar 231 seaplane proved a failure, its handling proving poor at best and its assembly and disassembly times far too time-consuming, exposing the submarine to possible attack.

However, by 1942 *Kriegsmarine* officials had asked Focke-Achgelis to build a rotor kite that could be towed aloft from a moving U-boat. The aircraft had to be capable of reaching an altitude that would boost the U-boat's scouting range yet remain compact and mechanically simple to maintain and operate. The Fa 330 was the result. Easy to produce and quick to assemble, launch and recover, it weighed so little that two men could easily lift the machine on to its small launch pad. The Fa 330 needed no engine: towed through the air, it flew by autorotation, the movement of relative wind through the rotor blades causing them to turn with sufficient speed to generate lift.

The airframe consisted of two 6.35cm diameter steel tubes joined to form an inverted 'T'. The bottom of the 'T' acted as the gyrocopter's fuselage, mounting the pilot's small seat as well as the rear control surfaces. The vertical tube housed the rotor mast. A control stick hung from the hub of the blade that sat atop the mast, and moving the stick allowed accurate pitch and roll control. Foot pedals were provided for the pilot to move the large rudder, controlling the machine's rate of yaw. A simple altimeter, airspeed indicator and tachometer were mounted for the pilot to use.

When the *Bachstelze* was inoperative it was stored in two watertight metal canisters, each nearly 4m long, built on to the conning tower's '*Wintergarten*' platform. One canister housed the blades and tail, the other the fuselage; a third horizontal container held the cable and winch used to tether the kite to the U-boat. In calm seas it took four crewmen three minutes to assemble the rotor kite in preparation for take-off. It was possible to rotate the blades by hand immediately before lift-off, but a rope wrapped around a drum on the rotor hub was also provided to spin the rotor. The Fa 330 rose into the air from a small platform attached to the aft railing of the '*Wintergarten*', taking off and landing on two hollow-tubed skids mounted on the craft's underside. The 300m of towline that extended from the electric winch included a quick-release coupling at the end furthest from the boat.

Once aloft, the pilot communicated with the U-boat via an interphone system, its wire wrapped around the tow cable. When the pilot indicated that he was ready to land, the crew winched him back aboard, the pilot applying a rotor brake upon touchdown before disassembly could begin. However, if the U-boat came under threat and needed to dive, the pilot pulled a large red lever above the seat, activating the quick-release coupling which jettisoned the towline and simultaneously separated the spinning rotor blades from the mast. As the rotors detached and spun away they pulled a cable deploying a parachute for the pilot, who in turn ditched his seat and harness before falling into the sea. In theory, the U-boat would later surface and recover the pilot once clear of any potential danger.

By the middle of 1942 the first Fa 330s had been completed by the Weser-Flugzeugbau in Hoyenkamp and had begun trials aboard the Type IXC *U 523*, engaged in Baltic exercises as part of the 4th U-training Flotilla. Results were judged to be excellent. A wind tunnel at Chalais-Meudon, France, served as a flight simulator to train several crew members from each submarine that would carry an Fa 330, and the gyrocopter was cleared for operational use at the beginning of 1943. Unfortunately the Fa 330's large radar signature made it impractical to deploy the rotor kite in the Atlantic Ocean and it was relegated to use with the Type IXD2s heading for the Indian Ocean, where escorts were considerably less well equipped with radar gear and merchantmen still sailed independently.

Gysae's *U 177* was the first to use this device in action, deploying the Fa 330 on at least 30 occasions, although the only sinking that resulted was that of the Greek steamer SS *Efthalia Mari*, which was sighted and successfully attacked on 5 August east of Madagascar. The time taken to launch and retrieve the device on other occasions often allowed vital minutes to slip by before the U-boat was able to give chase, her prey making good its escape.

Indeed the period of action that followed the refuelling of the six U-cruisers reaped a much higher harvest. Once again Lüth reopened the scoring, sinking the British SS *Hoihow* north of Réunion on 2 July with two torpedoes and leaving four men stranded on the Indian ocean swell aboard a small liferaft, having provisioned them with water. Four days later Lüth missed with a two-torpedo shot as he stalked another freighter, prompting a brief, humorous notation within his KTB (an unusual thing for Lüth to make amongst his generally dry reports) after he observed the ship following his attempted attack: 'A lot of men out of open hatchways, one after another, as though something had disturbed their sleep—the noise of a torpedo having passed under their keel, for example.'

The six boats were given freedom of movement once again by BdU and independently prowled the waters south and east of Madagascar. Their toll steadily mounted through July and into August, when, towards the latter half of that month, the six cruiser U-boats began their trek towards France.

Aboard *U 178* there was jubilation over the imminent end of the voyage. On 16 July Dommes had sunk the SS *City of Canton* north-west of Madagascar, although suffering from further erratic torpedo performance during the submerged attack.[5] Left with only one 'eel', *U 178* sailed southwards, preparing to round the Cape of Good Hope and enter the Atlantic once again.

On 1 August at 1330hrs Dommes received an unusual refuelling instruction from BdU. *U 178* was ordered to refuel the outbound *Aquila* boat *Luigi Torelli*, which was en route for Malaysia. *Torelli* had departed Bordeaux on 14 June under the command of TV Enrico Gropalli, carrying a cargo of mercury, steel, 800 Mauser MG 151/20 aircraft cannon, a 500kg SG 500 bomb and spare torpedoes for the Penang base still in establishment at that time. Her passengers included Colonel Satake Kinjo, a telecommunications officer returning to Japan after extensive training in Germany, a radar engineer, Heinrich Foders of Telefunken, who had a set of *Würzburg* AA radar blueprints, and two civilian mechanics. However, in the weeks since the Italian boat had sailed from Bordeaux, disaster had finally engulfed Mussolini's fragile grip on power within Fascist Italy. Tired of war against an increasingly potent enemy that had landed in Sicily on 10 July and was making inexorable headway towards the 'boot' of Italy, on Saturday 24 July the Italian Fascist Grand Council passed a motion to place the King of Italy at the head of Italian forces, deposing Mussolini. The dictator's fall from power was completed when he resigned and was arrested the following day, Marshall Badoglio becoming Prime Minister and excluding all Fascists from his emergency cabinet.

While confusion reigned in her homeland *Torelli* continued east, weathering an air attack in the Atlantic and facing the possibility of a fuel shortage as the boat entered the Indian Ocean. Dommes was ordered to refuel the Italian, and the two boats successfully made their rendezvous on 12 August after their first meeting on 7 August had been aborted when the Italian failed to appear:

> The refuelling proved to be quite a problem because we had only about 40 to 50 metres of fire hose, and the weather was hardly encouraging for such complicated manoeuvre. In the end it became necessary to transfer our Engineering Officer to *Torelli* to help make a coupling device to join each other's hoses. Even so, the distance between the two boats was still too short for comfort and, to make matters worse, the rough seas prevented us from getting Wiebe back.[6]

The two boats sailed in company for several days as the weather prevented Wiebe from returning to *U 178*. As Dommes and Gropalli battled through the steep seas yet another radio message was received aboard the U-boat from BdU, and this one hit the crew like a bombshell. Labelled 'Officers Only' and double-enciphered, it enquired whether Dommes considered *U 178* capable of reaching Penang rather than returning to France. Dommes revealed the contents of the message to his officers and the matter was discussed freely. On the one hand the Far East held images of exotic splendour and the lure of the mysterious; on the other it was far from France, let alone Germany. The boat had already endured nearly four months at sea and Dommes was uncertain that the men would be capable of restaging in Penang, where unknown facilities awaited them. He replied to Dönitz that although the majority of his crew were generally in good shape, as was he himself, some had fallen ill, and if hospital care could not be provided for them he could not guarantee their ability to crew an operational U-boat effectively for combat missions. His reply was accepted in Berlin with assurances of health care in Penang, and thus *U 178* turned east and, in company with *Torelli*, headed towards her new station. On 26 August 1943 the two boats arrived off the coast of Sabang, Sumatra, and three days later they docked in Penang. *U 178* had been at sea for one day short of five months.

While the drama was over for Dommes and his weary crew, it still had time to run for Enrico Gropalli and his Italians. *Torelli* was compelled to move on from Penang, where there was no docking facility, to Singapore, where the rust-streaked boat could be stripped of her carefully stored cargo. On 31 August *Torelli* arrived at the erstwhile British naval base to be placed into drydock by the *Kriegsmarine* personnel available there. A little over a week later the collapse of Italy became complete as the unconditional surrender of Italian troops, secretly signed on 3 September, was announced to a stunned world. Immediately after news of the armistice, signed by representatives of one of the Tripartite countries, Tokyo advised the capture of all Italian personnel within Japanese ports and *Chujo* Hiraoka Kumeichi, commander of the 9th Imperial Japanese Navy Base Unit at Sabang, ordered that Gropalli and his crew be taken prisoner at Singapore. Surrendering without resistance, they were transferred to a camp, where they joined the crews of the *Reginaldo Giuliani* and the *Comandante Alfredo Cappellini*.

Above: The end of Axis power in East Africa: the Italian armed merchant cruiser *Ramb 1* is sunk by HMNZS *Leander* in the Indian Ocean, 27 February 1941. *(Tim Watson)*

Right: Survivors from *Ramb 1* are herded on to *Leander*'s deck. Italy's loss of her African empire was complete by November 1941. Italian naval power had already departed from the Indian Ocean, either retreating to Europe or destroyed. *(Tim Watson)*

Below left: U-boat operations in the South Atlantic and Indian Oceans were aided by the development of *Milchkühe*—U-boat tankers. Here a baker aboard one such submarine tests his freshly made rye bread before it is issued to a combat boat as new rations.

Below right: When *U 180* sailed from Kiel in February 1943 she carried two important passengers. At left, in the *Wehrmacht* cap, is Subhas Chandra Bose, at right his Arab adjutant Dr Habid Hassan.

Above: On 27 April *U 180* rendezvoused with the Japanese submarine *I-29* to transfer Bose and Hassan in exchange for Japanese passengers and equipment bound for Europe. Here a torpedo is floated across toward *U 180* (right).

Left, upper: Among the Japanese passengers taken aboard *U 180* was the submarine design specialist *Shosa* Hideo Tomonaga (centre). Tomonaga would later attempt to return to Japan in 1945 aboard *U 234*, but he committed suicide when the U-boat was forced to surrender at the end of the war in Europe.

Left, lower: Wearing the pith helmet more familiar to members of the *Wehrmacht*'s *Afrika Korps*, a lookout aboard *U 177* sweeps the horizon for targets.

Opposite, top: The exchange of material between Germany and Japan involved the Japanese *Yanagi* transport missions to Europe. Here *I-30*, the first Japanese submarine to dock in France, departs Lorient on 22 August 1942 for her return to the East. *I-30* successfully reached Singapore on 13 October but was then sunk in a defensive minefield en route for Japan. (U-Boot Archiv)

Right: *U 511* enters Penang's Georgetown harbour on 15 July 1943, the first U-boat to do so. Designated *Marco Polo 1*, *U 511* was a gift to the Japanese from Adolf Hitler, as well as partial payment for goods shipped aboard *I-30*.

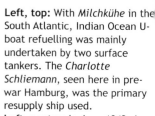

Left, top: With *Milchkühe* in the South Atlantic, Indian Ocean U-boat refuelling was mainly undertaken by two surface tankers. The *Charlotte Schliemann*, seen here in pre-war Hamburg, was the primary resupply ship used.

Left, centre: In June 1943 six Type IXD2s gathered around the *Charlotte Schliemann* to refuel and replenish 700 miles south of Mauritius.

Left, bottom: Of the epic voyages of the six Type IXD2s that survived their Indian Ocean foray, *U 181*'s was the most successful. The boat is pictured here returning to Bordeaux on 14 October 1943. Her long patrol marked the end of Wolfgang Lüth's combat career and had also seen him awarded the prestigious Diamonds to the Swords and Oak Leaves of the Knight's Cross.

Below: The first *Monsun* U-boat to sail was *U 200* on 12 June 1943. Aboard were five extra men—commandos of the elite Brandenburger unit, tasked with a sabotage mission in South Africa. Here their commander, *Leutnant* Brügmann, practices disembarkation from *U 200*.

Above: *U 200* was never to reach the Indian Ocean: she was sunk during this attack by a No 120 Squadron Liberator bomber on 24 June near Iceland.
Right: German U-boat deployment in the Indian Ocean was trumpeted within the pages of propaganda magazines, as in this article in *Die Kriegsmarine* entitled 'The Indian Ocean as an Arena of War'.

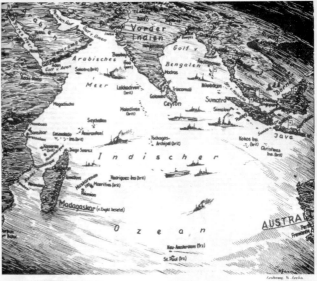

Der Indische Ozean als Kriegsschauplatz

Von Konteradmiral a. D. Brüninghaus

Die erstmalige Ernennung eines Soldaten des Feldmarschalls Wavell zum Vizekönig von Indien ließ bereits darauf schließen, daß man im Lager der Alliierten in irgendeiner Form auf eine Aktivierung des Indischen Ozeans und seiner Anliegerstaaten hinarbeitet. Noch stärker wird die Bedeutung des Indischen Seeraums, den englische Überheblichkeit oft mit „Englischer Ozean" bezeichnet, hervorgehoben durch die Berufung des Admirals Lord Mountbatten, des früheren Prinzen Ludwig Battenberg, dessen Name im ersten Weltkriege höchst geschmacklos in Mountbatten anglisiert wurde, zum Höchstkommandierenden der alliierten Streitkräfte im südostpazifischen Raum. Ob allerdings auch über etwaige amerikanische Seestreitkräfte, scheint nicht ohne weiteres sicher zu sein. Der USA-Marineminister Knox äußerte sich jedenfalls in der Öffentlichkeit in ablehnendem Sinne. Es erscheint keineswegs ausgeschlossen, daß die Ernennung von Mountbatten mit der behaupteten Entsendung einiger Schlachtschiffe aus dem Mittelmeer in den Indischen Ozean zusammenhängt. Trifft diese Nachricht zu, so erhöht sich wahrscheinlich die Zahl der den Alliierten im Indischen Ozean zur Verfügung stehenden englischen Schlachtschiffe auf 5—6, mithin auf ein Geschwader, dessen Kampfkraft von Japan sicher nicht unterschätzt wird. Die Verwendung eines starken Geschwaders, das außer den Schlachtschiffen zur Durchführung von Operationen auch über Flugzeugträger, Kreuzer, Zerstörer und den nötigen Troß verfügen muß, ist, sowohl strategisch als auch taktisch, außerordentlich abhängig von dem Besitz von Stützpunkten. Da zeigt sich der ungeheure Verlust, auch an Seemacht, den unsere Gegner durch den Übergang Singapurs in japanische Hände erlitten haben. Im engeren Indischen Ozean gibt es keinen Stützpunkt erster Klasse, in dem größere Schiffe docken und reparieren können. Diego Suarez auf Madagaskar ist zwar ein guter Naturhafen, besitzt aber keine Reparaturmöglichkeiten für schwere Einheiten. Es bleiben daher für das ganze Kriegsgebiet nur Durban an der Südostküste Afrikas und die weitentfernten australischen Häfen als Stützpunkte zur Verfügung. Ob und inwieweit die australischen Häfen als Operationsbasen herangezogen

Deutsches U-Boot gegen die See anstampfend

PK-Aufn.: Marine-Kriegsberichter Prokop, Sch

133

Left, upper and lower: The sheer size of the Type IXD2—and the number of crew needed aboard—can be judged from these two photographs taken during *U 861*'s commissioning ceremony, on 2 September 1943 in Bremen. (Jürgen Oesten)

Right, top: By 1943 U-boats were equipped with an array of radar detection equipment. In the foreground aboard this U-boat in the Indian Ocean can be seen the flimsy *Metox* 'Biscay Cross' while at right is the boat's dipolar antenna. (Jürgen Oesten)

Right, centre: Upon arrival in the East, German submariners were often unpleasantly surprised by the inadequacy of Japanese escort vessels that met them: the protection they offered from enemy submarine attack was negligible at best. (Jürgen Oesten)

Right, bottom: For many of the German crews this was their first experience of the Far East, and an air of mystery pervaded everything that surrounded them. (Jürgen Oesten)

Above: Georgetown pictured from the conning tower of a U-boat during the approach to the docking station. (Jürgen Oesten)
Left: Swettenham Pier, the myriad small Japanese and Malaysian craft kept clear of the submarine's intended berth. (Jürgen Oesten)
Below: The welcoming party on Swettenham Pier. To right can be seen the workshops established by Japanese occupation and used by *Kriegsmarine* personnel as well. The figure fifth from the left in this photograph is *Fregattenkapitän* Wilhelm Dommes. (Jürgen Oesten)

Right, top: The first *Monsun* boats began to arrive in Penang on 30 October 1943. In the foreground is *U 183*, while behind are *U 188* and *U 532*. In the background a Japanese submarine can be seen moored offshore.

Right, centre: Pictured later, in 1944, crewmen of *U 861* while away the time with coffee and cake on deck. (Jürgen Oesten)

Right, bottom: *Korvettenkapitän* Wolfgang Erhardt (left) and *Fregattenkapitän* Wilhelm Dommes. These men were responsible for the smooth running of the Far Eastern U-boat installations in Penang and Singapore. (U-Boot Archiv)

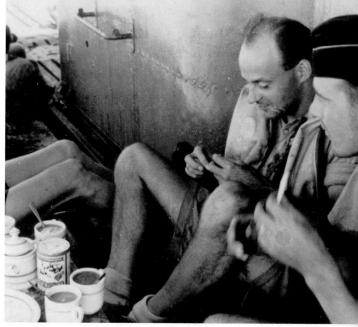

Left, top: Once ashore, U-boat crews were billeted in beautiful surroundings, with Malaysian staff on hand to provide every comfort. (Jürgen Oesten)

Left, centre: Sports events, often between German and Japanese as seen here, were actively encouraged to keep the men fit and away from 'less wholesome' pastimes. (Jürgen Oesten)

Left, bottom: While the tide of war turned in Europe and the quality of life in the *Reich* deteriorated, conditions in Malaysia were very opulent for visiting Germans. (Jürgen Oesten)

Above: This view over Penang, taken by a German war correspondent from the *Kriegsmarine* rest areas in the hills, faces south-east and shows the small island of Pulau Jerejak in the distance. (Jürgen Oesten)

Right, upper: Among the delights to be found in Malaysia for the U-boat men were beautiful local girls, often hired by the *Kriegsmarine* staff as dancing partners, and sometimes more, for visiting servicemen. (Jürgen Oesten)

Right, lower: The mile-long funicular railway that stretched between Penang Hill and Georgetown had been opened in October 1923 to allow access to the cooler climates of the highlands for European colonists who desired rest during the sweltering heat of the day. During the years of German presence the cable-drawn cars were used as shuttles to reach the *U-Boot Weide*, where the crews could relax in the manner envisaged by the railway's designers. (Jürgen Oesten)

Left, top: The difference in Oriental and Occidental cultures did not always throw insurmountable barriers in the way of genuine collaboration between the two navies. On the ground in Penang and elsewhere men were often capable of the successful interaction that was lacking at strategic levels.

Left, centre: German propaganda expended a great deal of energy promoting the closeness of the two allied countries. While servicemen did manage to overcome the racial divide, there still often lurked a Western suspicion of Japanese inscrutability, while extremely generous conditions for *Kriegsmarine* sailors often caused resentment amongst the less well-catered for Japanese.

Opposite page, bottom: The Imperial Japanese Army occasionally showed less good-will towards the *Kriegsmarine* than this photo would suggest—an extension of their often bitter and strained relationship with the Imperial Japanese Navy. (Jürgen Oesten)

Right: Activities were arranged for relaxing crewmen at all of the German installations. Here two crewmen from *U 861* try their hand at touring by pony. (Jürgen Oesten)

Below: In Europe, Japanese officers were frequently hosted within the U-boat bases. In this photograph Karl Dönitz (seated, centre) listens as a Japanese naval officer addresses an assembly in Lorient via a German translator.

Left: *Kapitanleutnant* Konrad Hoppe and two of his Japanese naval staff.
Below: U-boats at rendezvous during their return from the East. Refuelling between combat submarines was a way of enabling U-boats to complete their long voyages if a dedicated tanker were not available.

Right, top: The platform that the two stern-facing men are sitting on was provided for the launch of the *Bachstelze* rotor-kite from the Type IXD2 U-boat. In front of the platform are the two vertical waterproof containers that housed the stored *Bachstelze*, flanked on either side by twin-barrel 2cm flak weapons. (Jürgen Oesten)

Right, centre: Another view of the *Bachstelze* platform and two containers, seen from the lower '*Wintergarten*'. (Jürgen Oesten)

Right, bottom: The *Bachstelze* stowed within one of the upright canisters

Left, upper: Manning the *Naxos* radar alarm atop *U 861*'s conning tower. (Jürgen Oesten)
Left, lower: War correspondent *Leutnant (PK)* Hermann Kiefer's watercolour painting within *U 861*'s guest book of his time as Naxos operator: 'There is definitely a broken cable!' (Jürgen Oesten)

Da ist bestimmt das Kabel gebrochen!

Als Naxosdreher

The latter two Italian submarines—*Aquila II* and *Aquila III*—had also managed to traverse the Atlantic and Indian Oceans successfully, carrying between them nearly 300 tons of cargo, including specialised armaments and munitions, mercury, aluminium, machine parts and steel for Japanese use or study as well as torpedoes and spare parts for the U-boats in Penang. Escorted from Sabang to Singapore by the gunboat *Eritrea*, *Cappellini* had made fast at her final destination on 13 July, the first Italian to arrive safely in Malaysia, after suffering minor damage from heavy seas in the 'Roaring Forties'. *Giuliani* followed two weeks later, on 1 August. Of the remaining *Aquila* boats that had departed Bordeaux there was no trace: *Enrico Tozzoli* (*Aquila I*) had disappeared in the Gulf of Gascogne shortly after sailing from France and *Barbarigo* (*Aquila V*) had vanished in the same region, both to causes unknown (though possibly enemy mines).

On the announcement of the Italian armistice the Japanese seized both the other Italian submarines within their harbours. *Cappellini* was in Sabang, where she was preparing to begin her return journey to France carrying 156 tons of materials, including zinc, tungsten, quinine, opium, spices and 92 tons of rubber. Walter Auconi's boat had been delayed in sailing on her return leg by a request from the *Kriegsmarine* that *Cappellini* await the preparation of *Giuliani* for her own return journey; the latter was still being unloaded at Singapore. *Cappellini*'s crew unanimously decided to continue to fight alongside Germany and Japan and so sailed to Singapore with assurances from the Japanese that their wishes would be respected. However, once she had arrived at Singapore (under Japanese escort), the submarine was captured by armed troops and the crew imprisoned with their comrades, initially within 'open' camps. Ultimately, many of the Italians would eventually be transferred to Changi Prison, where they would endure the same inhuman conditions that Allied prisoners had suffered since the fall of Singapore. In Bordeaux itself, the two *Aquila* boats that had not departed for the East—*Giuseppe Finzi* and *Alpino Bagnolini*—were also seized as they lay at the Italian *Betasom* base at Bacalan, this time by German personnel, alerted by the issuing of the prearranged codeword '*Achse*' from Hitler's headquarters in Berlin.

Confusion reigned within Italian ranks, both in Europe and in Malaysia. The *Betasom* commander, *Capitano di Vascello* Enzo Grossi, described accurately by the distinguished Italian military historian Alberto Santoni as a 'fat and unimpressive officer', opted to remain allied to the *Kriegsmarine* at first, before later absconding to Spain with a large sum of money.[7] There he was arrested and returned to Italy for trial. Meanwhile, on 23 September 1943 in Salò, Italy, Mussolini, recently freed from captivity in the Gran Sasso mountain retreat by Otto Skorzeny's daring combined *Waffen-SS* and *Fallschirmjäger* rescue mission, founded the new *Repubblica Sociale Italiana* (RSI), a puppet fascist regime controlled by the Germans. The RSI maintained control over central and northern Italy as well as Grossi's *Betasom* command. Opinion within the ranks of the Italian Navy was divided. Many elected to remain loyal to Mussolini's new Republic and fight alongside the *Kriegsmarine* while others immediately surrendered. The last of the *Betasom* boats still in action and unaccounted for was the attack submarine *Cagni*, at sea in the Indian Ocean and destined for Penang when news of the Italian surrender reached it. *Capitano di Corvetta* Giuseppe Roselli Lorenzini promptly laid course for Durban, where he surrendered his boat to Allied forces on 9 September. Likewise, the gunboat *Eritrea* was sailing between Singapore and Sabang in support of *Cappellini* when it received an official notice from Reuters at 0200hrs (local time) on 8 September which announced the Italian surrender. *Eritrea* immediately changed course and evaded Japanese pursuing forces, eventually docking at the British base at Colombo, Ceylon.

In Singapore and Sabang the Japanese authorities suddenly found themselves the owners of three large Italian submarines. With no available crews to men them and unsure of their value anyway, the Japanese began talks with von Zatorski in Singapore about handing the Italian boats over to German crews. By coincidence the crew of *U 511* were on the point of arriving in Singapore aboard the *Osorno* when the Italian boats were seized, and after a brief conference with Wenneker, and thus with OKM and BdU, it was agreed that the three interned boats be transferred to *Kriegsmarine* control. Rearmed with the addition of deck guns and anti-aircraft weapons, *Giuliani* thus became *UIT 23*, *Cappellini* became *UIT 24* and *Torelli* was redesignated *UIT 25*. In Bordeaux the same procedure was repeated with the two Italian boats captured there, *Finzi* becoming *UIT 21* and *Bagnolini* becoming *UIT 22*. Volunteers from among those men willing to continue within the Italian Fascist Navy were retained aboard ship by the Germans, a sprinkling of *Kriegsmarine* personnel filling out the ranks.

In Singapore, however, there was also an acute shortage of German manpower: even the 49 trained submariners from *U 511* would have been unable to man all three boats successfully since the minimum crew requirement for each was considered to be 35. With the permission of the Japanese, the Germans appealed for volunteers from the interned Italians to return to their boats and continue in the service of Mussolini's RSI. These, supplemented with German civilians from the region, bolstered the small number of trained men, who assumed the roles assigned to Petty Officer upwards. Both senior watch officers from *U 511* became commanders, *Oberleutnant zur See* Heinrich Pahls of *UIT 24* and *Oberleutnant zur See* Johannes-Werner Striegler of *UIT 25*. *UIT 23* remained without a captain until the arrival of a suitably experienced man from Germany aboard one of the incoming *Monsun* boats.

This drama was being played out on land and it was not until September that the first of the *Monsun* boats made her presence felt within the Indian Ocean hunting ground. Junker's *U 532* made the first successful attack of the group past the Atlantic boundary when, on 19 September, he torpedoed the SS *Fort Longueuil* deep within the Indian Ocean, southwest of the Chago Archipelago. It was Junker's first combat success— and a disaster for the crew of the British steamer. The SS *Fort Longueuil* had left Barry docks in Wales on 16 July carrying holds full of government stores that included ammunition destined for Alexandria. Having safely unloaded in Egypt on 8 August, she sailed through the Suez Canal bound for Aden, where she docked in order to bunker. On 9 September she left for Australia after loading a cargo of phosphate. She was ten days from harbour when Master George Cardno Edward's unescorted ship was torpedoed by *U 532*, going down rapidly as the crew scrambled to abandon ship. The vessel was not reported missing until 15 October, her sinking so swift that there had been no time for a distress message to be transmitted. Of the 49 crewmen and ten British gunners only two Indian crewmen, Thakar Miah and Mohamed Aftab, survived on a raft, becoming Japanese prisoners on 1 February 1944 when the raft drifted ashore on Sumatra after 134 days at sea.

On 21 September Lüdden's *U 188* added her own weight to the *Monsun* arrival in her fresh hunting ground. After pausing to reconnoitre the

Mauritian harbour of Port Louis, Lüdden sailed into the Gulf of Oman where, east of Mogadishu, he torpedoed and sank the American Liberty ship SS *Cornelia P. Spencer*. It was Lüdden's first victory after nearly three months at sea. Like Junker's victim, Master Elmer H. Kirwan's *Cornelia P. Spencer* was travelling unescorted and on an arrow-straight course when a single torpedo from *U 188* impacted against her port side at No 5 hold, blowing the hatch cover high into the air and flooding it The ship's propeller shaft was sheared in two and she began to drift out of control as the water engulfed the cavernous cargo stowage area. Lüdden brought *U 188* to the surface, but at a range of only 100yds the merchantman's gunners fired nearly 75 3in rounds, forcing *U 188* back under lest her precious pressure hull be damaged. Thirty minutes later Lüdden fired a second torpedo which again struck the port hull, this time at the after peak, igniting ammunition stowed within the ship's magazine and killing two crewmen as the stern gun was blown off the ship. The blast also swept away the rudder and propeller and *Cornelia P. Spencer* began to settle rapidly by the stern. Kirwan ordered her abandoned and the surviving men of the crew of eight officers, 32 men, one Royal Navy radio operator and 27 gunners left the ship in four lifeboats and two rafts. A third torpedo struck the ailing vessel amidships on the port side and ten minutes later *Cornelia P. Spencer* was gone.[8]

The *Monsun* group had passed the Cape of Good Hope, each boat operating independently of its comrades. There had been few successes for them and their original number of ten combat boats had been whittled down to five by September, when they finally swung into action. After the early loss of *U 200* near Iceland in June, *U 506*, *U 514* and *U 509* had all succumbed to aerial attack during their voyage south into the Atlantic in July. The fifth disaster was the destruction of *U 847*, a late departure from Bergen for the Indian Ocean on 29 July and scheduled to act as an emergency tanker before continuing to Penang. Knight's Cross holder *Kapitänleutnant* Herbert Kuppisch had taken the new Type IXD2 *U 847* from Kiel on 6 July but his boat had suffered damage in a collision with an iceberg in the Denmark Strait, forcing him to return to Bergen, where repairs could be undertaken. By the time the boat was ready to sail once more calamity had overtaken the U-boat tankers sent into the South Atlantic to refuel the *Monsun* boats and those returning from action off West Africa and the Americas. Kuppisch's boat was pushed into the breach and he sailed with tanks brimming in order to refuel the homebound boats of the 2nd and 10th U-Flotillas. While bound for the central Atlantic, Kuppisch was directed to deal primarily with those scheduled to take diesel from the Type XB auxiliary tanker *U 117*, which had been sunk on 7 August by air attack.

The first to rendezvous with Kuppisch was Carl Emmermann's *U 172*, returning from action off South America. Emmermann surfaced near *U 847*, his gun crews manning every available flak weapon and alarmed at the apparent nonchalance aboard *U 847*: 'He [Kuppisch] was from the earlier times, when aircraft were not a great threat. He had not been to sea in almost two whole years.'[9] Emmermann was correct. Kuppisch was a veteran submariner, a graduate from the officers' crew of 1933 and a successful captain of three wartime boats before taking command of *U 847*. He had spent the latter half of 1942 and early 1943 as a staff officer attached to BdU, but there, especially, he should have become aware of the increased threat of enemy air attack as more and more boats failed to report at sea. Possibly he failed to make the vital connection and still underestimated the growing threat that U-boats now faced—that of American carrier-borne aircraft, in particular within the central Atlantic. As Emmermann refuelled, nearby an Avenger/Wildcat team from the USS *Core* sank *U 185* as the latter attempted to close the distance with Kuppisch and take on board fuel. However, *U 847* successfully supplied five homebound Type VIICs and *U 508*, a Type IXC, the group of boats a tempting and vulnerable target as they awaited the chance to take on diesel. One of those replenished by Kuppisch was *U 230*, whose IWO, Herbert Werner, later related their meeting:

> Knowing that we were helpless while taking the heavy oil into our tanks, our boys manned the guns and stood ready to cut the hoses instantly. Not so the crew of the supply boat: they simply stood around the large superstructure like street corner idlers. In disgust I yelled to the Exec of *U 847* through the megaphone, 'What's the matter with you people? Don't you have any respect for aircraft?'
>
> 'We haven't seen any since we passed Greenland,' he shouted back.
>
> Two hours after our departure the supply boat broke radio silence and reported that she had completed the refuelling of all four [*sic*] boats. By sending that message *U 847* not only jeopardised the four boats she had supplied but also sealed her own fate.[10]

Werner was correct: almost inevitably, the signal provided an HF/DF fix upon which Allied forces could converge. On 27 August *U 847* was

located, surfaced, by an Avenger and two escorting Wildcats from the
USS *Card* and Kuppisch's boat was subjected to severe and prolonged
strafing until forced to dive. Once the boat had submerged, Lieutenant
Ralph W. Long deployed a 'Fido' homing torpedo from his Avenger
immediately ahead of the swirl left by the disappearing craft. The resultant explosion marked the end of Kuppisch and his 61 crewmen:
'That afternoon I heard the reverberation of many bombs some 60 miles
astern, and I knew that *U 847* had died a needless death.'[11] BdU's sum-
mary of the loss of *U 847* that was presented to SKL was even more
succinct: '*U 847*: First cruise, old commander. Last message 9.9 when
SE of Greenland. Probably sunk by plane.'

Aircraft had indeed become the prime enemy of the U-boats, an issue
compounded by the failure of the Germans fully to grasp the effective-
ness of Allied HF/DF and their discovery that the *Metox* radar radiated
detectable impulses of its own. Experiments by German aircraft with
Metox sets on the French coast had confirmed suspicions that this system indeed radiated and could be picked up by aerial radars, but it was
an off-the-cuff remark made by a captured British airman in early August to the effect that the radiation received allowed aircraft to pinpoint
U-boats and attack them undetected that caused sudden panic within
BdU: 'Special importance must be attached to this statement by the
English pilot in view of the most recent results of experiments and the
events of losses in the Atlantic during recent months.'[12] Although Dönitz
acknowledged that he could have been 'deliberately attempting to mislead', he felt the risk too great and the following order was immediately
transmitted to all boats: 'The use of *Metox* and *Grandin* receivers is
now forbidden in all sea areas as it is thought that [the] enemy makes
use of the receiver radiation to approach the U-boat from a great distance without himself using location gear. All previous orders to the
contrary are cancelled.'[13]

Meanwhile the remaining five *Monsun* boats had replenished once
more on 11 September, this time from the German tanker *Brake* that
had been despatched from Penang specifically for the purpose. BdU's
War Diary for 1 September recorded:

> The *Monsun* boats *U 168*, *183*, *188*, *532* and *533* have a rendezvous with the
> German tanker *Brake* on 8.9 in KS 4792. Boats will replenish and then pro-
> ceed north to their operational areas in the Arabian Ocean after these have been
> decided.

As the Japanese have already fought in this area, attack will be sanctioned once the boats have replenished. This is contrary to the operational order issued.[14]

The five U-boats originally met with *Brake* on the day that Italy had capitulated and had been expecting the Italian *Ammiraglio Cagni* to join them. However, after the Italian failed to appear all six vessels made full speed from the area for fear of their rendezvous having been compromised. Three days later the refuelling commenced several hundred miles to the south. From there the *Monsun* boats separated and sailed to their individual patrol areas as directed by BdU, sanctioned to begin attacks after having refuelled and having headed north in search of enemy shipping. The boats were directed to the following areas:

U 533—Gulf of Aden, *U 188*—Gulf of Oman, *U 168*—Gulf of Cambay, *U 532*—southern tip of peninsular India, *U 183* off Mombasa.

Boats have a free hand in this area according to the defenses and shipping. *U 533* may penetrate as far west as the entrance to the Red Sea at her own discretion. Surprisingly large successes may be possible there.[15]

A single proviso followed on 15 September after Japanese requests for the group to pass no further northward than 17° south latitude because of IJN submarines operating within that area, but, unwilling to accommodate the Japanese requirements, Dönitz compromised by ordering no attacks against submarines for fear of a possible 'friendly-fire' incident. To encourage his men in their long-distance battle, Dönitz radioed on 17 September: 'You will reach your operational area after a particularly long passage, for which extensive preparations have been necessary. This operation will only be worth all this if you utilise all your opportunities. I expect each one of you to make a great success of this undertaking.'

After his successful sinking of SS *Cornelia P. Spencer*, *Kapitän-leutnant* Lüdden took *U 188* further north, into the Arabian Sea, where the conditions he encountered, and noted within his boat's War Diary, were typical of the frustrations aboard the other four boats as well. A hazy mist often obscured the horizon, making it difficult for lookouts to distinguish sea from sky, and an extremely bright phosphorescent effect within the dead calm sea made Lüdden constantly anxious of detection, both of the boat herself and of the torpedoes that left sparkling silver trails behind them when they were fired. The heat played havoc with the crew and machinery, the overworked diesels suffering from excessive exhaust temperatures that required large quantities of lubricating oil as a result. Constant attention by the engine-room crew in temperatures that soared almost above endurance was required in order to nurse the engines during the voyage. Finally, and crucially, the now familiar problems of battery degradation caused the torpedoes loaded at Lorient to run erratically.

On 27 September Lüdden's lookouts sighted a convoy of ten ships, seven of them tankers, near Masirah Bay and heading for Aden. After sixteen hours of pursuit Lüdden was infuriated at having to break off the chase when both diesels failed under the stress. The following day *U 188* found another small convoy sailing parallel to the Somalian coast. The boat was well placed for an attack and Lüdden launched a full bow and stern salvo of six torpedoes, each of which was heard to explode after eight to ten minutes—not on target but as the result of presumed 'end of run' detonations. Frustrated, Lüdden was forced under and away by the appearance of a twin-engine enemy aircraft and the convoy made good its escape. Unbeknown to the German *Monsun* crews, their presence within the Indian Ocean was being closely followed by Allied codebreakers, decrypting the messages that flashed to Berlin and redirecting merchant traffic as often as possible out of harm's way.

U 188 cruised northwards, entering the Gulf of Oman in anticipation of tanker traffic plying the route to and from the oil port of Abadan on the Persian-Iraqi border. Lüdden was not to be disappointed by what lay before him—four tankers were sighted within six days. However, his results were spectacularly unsuccessful because three of four separate attacks were thwarted by torpedo failure. His initial attempt on 1 October resulted in the following disgusted entry in the ship's War Diary: 'Electric torpedo exploded after 8 minutes 26 seconds—attacking distance 800 meters.'

Harassed by the presence of enemy aircraft and patrolling naval forces, Lüdden did not manage another attempt until four days later, when he actually hit the 9,977-ton Norwegian MT *Britannia*. Claiming her as sunk, Lüdden's crew were finally given cause to celebrate, although their celebration was short-lived because they were fired upon by the ship's gunners and compelled to beat a hasty retreat. Captain Johan Karsten Hallén's *Britannia,* which had left Durban in ballast on 17 September, took the torpedo hit between Nos 8 and 9 oil storage tanks and was badly holed, but because the ship was high riding and empty the flooding was brought swiftly under control. The tanker reached Bandar Abbas during the evening of 6 October, where Hallén examined the damage before announcing that the *Britannia* was 'saved'. The Norwegian crew 'wired' the two halves together, Hallén earning the sobriquet 'the crazy Norwegian' from the British naval authorities after they had inspected the improvised repairs that involved various lengths of wire and chains.

Lüdden's next two attacks resulted in dismal failure, the strong phosphorescence present in the water betraying his torpedo tracks; moreover, the weapons' batteries had deteriorated to the point at which they travelled too slowly to impact anyway. A radioed appreciation of his experiences thus far was transmitted to BdU, which summarised Lüdden's report:

> Convoy traffic on courses of 35 degrees and 215 degrees from MF 8635 to 8865 and further 30 miles off along the 200-metre line. Surface escort untrained and weak, twin-engine aircraft by day. Convoy assembly and dispersal point believed to be in MK 2929. Spasmodic heavy single-ship traffic at night from there to the inner Gulf, course 310 degrees. Numerous sailing vessels in inner Gulf. Aircraft only observed in MF 2272, except for convoys. Radar suspected. No night air activity . . .
> Since 25.8 electric torpedo acid level around zero millimetres . . . altogether 10 end-of-run detonations.[16]

Finally the German crew's torment was ended when Lüdden was ordered to break off on 8 October and head directly for Penang so that repairs could be made to the troublesome diesels. His place in the Gulf of Oman was to be taken by *U 533*, which had thus far experienced no success at all.

Kapitänleutnant Helmut Hennig was on his second war patrol as captain of the 10th U-Flotilla Type IXC/40 *U 533*. His previous journey into the North Atlantic, where he took part in the 'wolfpack' operation '*Star*', had yielded nothing but the near-disaster of being rammed by the corvette HMS *Sunflower*. The voyage into the Indian Ocean had also tested Hennig's and his crew's mettle to the limits. Their boat suffered mechanical plagues similar to those which had afflicted Lüdden's, the crankshaft bearing in particular giving repeated trouble—perhaps, once more, as a result of sabotage within Lorient's dockyard. During the replenishing rendezvous with *Brake* Hennig took the opportunity to have one of the troublesome bearings remetalled by mechanics aboard the tanker; their workshops were far more extensive than that aboard any U-boat.

After sailing into the Gulf of Aden in loose company with Lüth's *U 181*, Hennig was dismayed to find not the expected independent sailing ships but small convoys, one of which *U 533* attacked, claiming an unconfirmed freighter sunk. However, retaliation from escorting Indian sloops had so damaged the boat's torpedo tubes that Hennig was forced to break away and make repairs. For *U 533* there was greater woe ahead. While Hennig was travelling surfaced in the Gulf on 16 October a twin-engine Blenheim Mk V (Bisley) light bomber piloted by L. Chapman of No 244 Squadron and based at the RAF airfield on the northern tip of Jazirat Masirah off the coast of Oman sighted the grey hull and immediately swooped to attack. Without delay Hennig ordered his boat into a crash dive, but as the hull cleaved slowly through the water the detonation of bombs from Chapman's aircraft rocked the boat and ruptured the thick pressure hull. The bilge pump clattered into action as hydroplanes were reported inoperative. As water gushed unchecked into the control room Hennig ordered all tanks blown, but even this emergency measure was unable to arrest his boat's downward descent and Hennig shouted for his men to don their escape gear.

Leutnant zur See Paaschen and seaman Günther Schmidt were both immediately beneath the conning tower hatch as the water level inexorably rose within their boat. Paaschen climbed into the tower above and, as Schmidt climbed to help him, used all of his strength to try and open the outer hatch. As *U 533* slipped lower into the sea the outside water pressure grew and the hatch at first refused to budge. It was not until the U-boat was virtually flooded and the interior and exterior pressures equalised that the hatch abruptly sprung open, the gush of trapped air nearly dragging the men to the surface. Clinging to the open hatch, both sailors waited for the turbulence to subside, breathing from their *Tauchretter* escape gear. Paaschen motioned for Schmidt to lead the way and the young submariner released his hold on the sinking boat, arcing upwards to the surface as the air trapped within his escape gear expended. Bursting free of the water, he sucked a lungful of air and waited for Paaschen to appear. Only moments passed before the officer also reached the glassy surface, although he appeared unconscious, hanging motionless in the water. Schmidt swam to help him, supporting his inert body for 30 minutes before finally acknowledging that he was dead. Paaschen had made the fatal mistake of holding his breath as he ascended, the trapped air expanding and bursting his lungs. Around him there were no others as Chapman circled above: Schmidt was the sole survivors from the crew of 53.

As Chapman finally flew away from the scene another sensation gripped Schmidt—fear. He had seen many sharks within the warm tropical seas and he immediately began to swim towards the setting sun, where he knew eventually land must be. As night fell he carried on, guided by the Southern Cross, his escape gear providing buoyancy as he relentlessly swam to the west. The following day he was rewarded with his first glimpse of a low coastline, partially obscured by the haze of the Arabian heat. Finally, after swimming for 28 hours, he was washed ashore at Khor-Fakkam on Somalia's Muscat coast, where he immediately collapsed. Found by local Arabs, Schmidt was cared for until a British patrol of men from No 244 Squadron arrived and took him prisoner, later removing him to Basra in Iraq and from there to Cairo.

By the end of October the *Monsun* group had been reduced to four operational boats. Their few successes represented a humiliating failure for the German U-Boat Service: in months of alternately monotonous and perilous patrolling they had managed to sink an aggregate total of six ships and six small sailing vessels. On 30 October the first three *Monsun* boats docked in Penang, escorted into harbour by small Japanese patrol vessels after rendezvousing at 6° 10' N, 94° 50' E. *U 183*, *U 188* and *U 532* arrived at their destination port of Georgetown to an enthusiastic reception from dockside German sailors, Dommes at their head, and immaculately uniformed Japanese naval personnel.

Despite the high expectations of a fresh slaughter of unsuspecting merchant ships within the Indian Ocean, *Kapitänleutnant* Heinrich Schäfer's *U 183* had sunk nothing during her seventeen weeks at sea. After successfully refuelling from *Brake* on 11 September near Mauritius *U 183* had cruised the waters between the Seychelles and Kenya. Eight faulty electric torpedoes spoiled the few attacks that had been mounted by Schäfer by missing their targets completely, failing to detonate or prematurely exploding. To add further insult BdU also reprimanded Schäfer for extraneous communication after a long-winded radio report relating to an unsuccessful chase of a single freighter in stormy seas was tersely rebuked as 'superfluous and incorrect to transmit . . . [and] dealing with unimportant matters. All three boats' banks of batteries had suffered from the humidity and heat—built to withstand relatively clement climates, they had shown premature deterioration—while the diesels also appeared badly worn and in need of thorough overhaul. After ten days of cruising near Mombasa, Schäfer had sighted nothing but two small patrol vessels and a destroyer and requested that he be allowed to head for Penang and repair damage suffered by boat, crew and weapons. BdU acquiesced, though prompting Schäfer to take any possible offensive action that came his way by chance during his crossing 'at high speed' of the Indian Ocean. His state of mind was at such low ebb, however, that the decision was taken on 8 October by BdU to replace him upon arrival. Tropical rashes and skin infections were rampant among many of the crew as *U 183* finally eased into Georgetown, the heavily bearded Germans reeling as they took their first steps on *terra firma* for several months and needing help from their welcoming committee in making the adjustment from sea legs to land. The frustrating voyage had been too much for Schäfer and he was transferred from the boat's command into a local personnel reserve pool, to be replaced by Schneewind from *U 511*. Schäfer later was placed in command of the commandeered Italian boat *Reginaldo Guiliani*, renamed *UIT 23* by the *Kriegsmarine*, but he died of natural causes on 8 January 1944.

Schäfer's was the only complete failure among the four surviving boats. *U 188*'s meagre success was displayed in a pair of pennants fluttering from the extended periscope as she sailed into port alongside the other two boats. *U 532*'s *Kapitänleutnant* Ottoheinrich Junker had experienced the greatest success, having despatched four freighters (one of which, the MV *Tahsinia*, was incorrectly assumed to be an auxiliary warship with nets and magnetic gear aboard) during his voyage by combined torpedo and gun attacks, reporting 'lively single-ship and convoy traffic' inshore along the Indian coast. Meanwhile the group's final arrival, *Kapitänleutnant* Helmut Pich's *U 168*, had sunk a single confirmed 2,183-ton British freighter near Bombay by torpedo and six sailing cargo boats with his gun in the same region before docking in Penang on 11 November. Pich had also been on the receiving end of a brief but uncomfortably close depth-charging from an unidentified Catalina as he attempted to close a convoy, driving him under and losing him contact.

The idea that the *Monsun* boats would open a full-scale offensive within the Arabian Sea while en route to Malaysia had never fully materialised, and the lack of success was not solely attributable to faulty weaponry. Allied intelligence had monitored their progress as they passed South Africa, Enigma decrypts providing a virtual step-by-step track chart of the German submarines. Convoys had largely been diverted away from the cruising threat, minimising what little impact they could have had. The 'Triton' ('Shark') Enigma net in use by U-boats had been cracked at the end of 1942. While the different code net used by supply ships and U-boats stationed in the Far East, known as 'Sunfish' to the Allies (its correct designation was 'Tibet'), had been in use since September 1941, it too was broken and read by the Allies—albeit intermittently—from August 1943 until the war's end. Finally 'Bertok', the code network that was used for communication between OKM and Tokyo's German Naval Attaché, was also broken, laying bare German strategic decisions in the Far East.

NOTES

1. Fraser, awarded the Bar to his DFC, outlived *U 200* by a little over a year. He was killed in a flying accident on 4 July 1944.
2. Williger's left leg had been amputated under primitive conditions inside the boat but the unfortunate man perished from a loss of blood.
3. Vause, *Lone Wolf*, p. 170.
4. Interview with Hans-Joachim Krug, 3 May 2003.
5. The ship's Second Officer, Reginald Harry Broadbent, was recovered from a lifeboat and taken prisoner. Readily adapting to U-boat life—despite complaints about the lack of cigarettes—he was even eventually allowed to take part in lookout duty atop the conning tower.
6. Showell, *Wolfpacks at War*, p. 102.
7. *The Battle of the Atlantic: The 50th International Naval Conference*, Naval Institute Press, p. 331.
8. Thirty-four survivors were picked up from two lifeboats by the British destroyer HMS *Relentless* the following afternoon. Another sixteen were rescued by the British steamer SS *Sandown Castle* and the remaining sixteen were landed on the coast of Somalia fifteen days after Lüdden's attack.
9. Clay Blair, *Hitler's U-Boat War*, Vol. 2, p. 394.
10. Herbert Werner, *Iron Coffins*, pp. 154–5.
11. *Ibid.*, p. 155.
12. BdU KTB, 14 August 1943.
13. *Ibid.*
14. BdU KTB, 1 September 1943, National Archives Microfilm, PG30331, Roll No 4065.
15. BdU KTB, 7 September 1943.
16. BdU KTB, 7 October 1943, National Archives Microfilm, PG30333, Roll No 4065.

Five

Germany in Asia

T HE GERMAN command structure in place within South-East
Asia during the war's early years was tangled by an influx of
officers from various raiders and U-boats, either destroyed or
under changed captaincy. Admiral Paul Wenneker, the German Naval
Attaché in Tokyo, continued to co-ordinate all *Kriegsmarine* activity
within the region after the arrival of combat U-boats. Assisted from
1942 by a newly transferred Chief of Staff, *Kapitän zur See* Werner
Vermehren, Wenneker found his tasks expanded to include all logistical
matters pertaining to U-boats stationed in Asia, particularly with regard
to the co-ordination of matters concerning maintenance or operational
activity with the Japanese authorities.[1] However, he had no active control over the deploymentof the U-boats: that duty was still handled thousands of miles away by BdU in Germany. From March 1943 *Korvettenkapitän* Wolfgang Erhardt, lately of the sunken raider *Michel*, had become commander of all German bases in Malaysia and Singapore as
Leiter des Marinestützpunkte, exercising his office from Singapore.

In April 1943 the German installation at Penang (*Stützpunkt Paul*)
and during August that at Singapore (*Stützpunkt Siegfried*) received new
commanders—still subject to Erhardt's and, ultimately, Wenneker's command structure—when *Kapitänleutnant* Konrad Hoppe, an aerial observer from the seaplane aboard *Michel*, and *Kapitänleutnant* Walther
von Zatorski, the captain of the tanker *Uckermark* that had been destroyed in an explosion within Yokohama harbour on 30 November 1942,
arrived at those respective destinations.[2] The work in Penang was aided

by *Kapitänleutnant* Waldemar Grützmacher, formerly the minelaying officer aboard *Doggerbank*, who acted as adjutant for the base continuously from October 1942 through to the end of the war. In Jakarta *Korvettenkapitän Dr* Hermann Kandeler, the artillery officer aboard the raider *Thor*, which had been consumed by flames from the *Uckermark* explosion along with the prize capture *Leuthen*, commanded the *Kriegsmarine* harbour there, and its facilities, from its establishment as a German post for loading raw materials in September 1943, although he moved to take Penang over from Hoppe in January 1944. Hoppe in turn departed to become IWO aboard *U 168* for seven months before returning to a staff position as German commander at the newly established base at Surabaya, the ex-Dutch facility which hosted the U-boats owing to overcrowding within Singapore's dockyards. The Dutch port had already seen submarines during its colonial days, the Royal Dutch East Indies Navy (*Nederlands-Indië Marine*) having based a flotilla headquarters for fifteen submarines there under the command of Lt-Cdr A. J. Bussemaker within the base. Finally in January 1945 Kandeler left Penang to return to command at Jakarta. Days later a new installation at Kobe for the replacement of U-boat batteries was established under the command of *Kapitänleutnant* Karl-Friedrich Kentrat, formerly of *U 196*. This was in fact the second German command post to be established in Japan: during March 1944 *Kapitänleutnant* Walther von Zatorski had moved from Singapore, leaving the port directly controlled by Erhardt, and established an office at Yokohama, officially titled as the Naval Station Chief and Shipping Agent.

Amongst this tangled web Dommes occupied a *de facto* flotilla command post in Penang from March 1944. There he received orders directly from BdU regarding the disposition of operational U-boats, passing them on to the boats in harbour. For all other matters he deferred to Wenneker, via either Kandeler or Erhardt. In December 1944 Dommes was named *Chef in Südraum* and assumed control of all *Kriegsmarine* bases in the south Orient, exercising his new command from Singapore. He was promoted to *Fregattenkapitän* during January 1945. Despite his grandiose title he continued to work through Wenneker, using the divided and unwieldy chain of command that existed in the Far East.

The lack of an officer of flag rank directly concerned with U-boat warfare in the Far East had a distinctly adverse effect on Dommes' and other local commanders' authority amongst the Japanese. He found himself in the peculiar position of working alongside *Taisho* Uzumi and his staff, many of whom also held higher rank and authority than he. For the Imperial Japanese Navy, let alone the Army, which thrived on a strictly enforced hierarchy, this was an unthinkable situation and caused friction that could have been avoided had Dönitz either promoted Dommes further or despatched a man of higher rank as *Chef in Südraum*. The same situation later faced Hoppe in Surabaya when he dealt with *Taisho* Hoshino and Zatorski in Singapore dealing with *Taisho* Nakamura. Interestingly for the combat U-boats, Dommes' inability to implement operational decisions of his own on account of orders that he defer to Wenneker or Dönitz actually allowed a certain freedom of movement for German commanders on the ground. Because of the time lapse involved in communicating with either Berlin or Tokyo the Germans managed to maintain a wider margin for decisions than if Dommes had had to react directly to events.

In fact the Japanese maintained formal control over the main radio transmitting station in Penang, despite the fact that it had been erected by mainly German personnel and was staffed by German servicemen. They objected to any foreign wireless transmitters within their territory and refused to relinquish control of it. In Singapore and Jakarta they allowed the Germans the use of their own transmitting equipment at dedicated times allocated for the *Kriegsmarine*. The transmitter situated near Jakarta, established originally by the Dutch at Bandoeng, remained the largest radio station operated by the Japanese—larger even than the home station at Nagasaki. From there messages were transmitted at up to 80kW to Germany and Japan, as was propaganda aimed at Australia and New Zealand. Thus messages from Berlin were often routed either through Tokyo itself or via the ponderous chain of Japanese and then German command:

> They did not allow us to run our own radio service and we didn't want to trust Japan with our Foreign Service network and codes and we wanted our own equipment. We could make our own messages and encode them, but we still had to use their transmitters. We received from Dönitz directly, but not the other way around.[3]

Another peculiarity of the Japanese bases within conquered South-East Asia was that the branch of service that had taken a port tended to be the same that administered it. Thus the Imperial Japanese Army held authority over Jakarta and Singapore (except for the naval base at Selatar) while the Navy controlled Penang and Surabaya. There had been a long-standing rivalry between the Imperial Japanese Navy and Army that dated back to the mid-1930, with a web of intrigue, plotting and attempted military *coups* staged by predominantly Army factions. With the battle for resources between the two services a continuing affair, political manoeuvring and discrimination on both sides became commonplace. While German military departments also suffered from the effects of high-level intrigue and conspiracy in their struggle for dominance in Hitler's military court, it remained largely confined to that level and the experience in the Far East was the first time that many U-boat personnel had come across such barely hidden antipathy between two services. In those ports controlled by the Japanese Army a *Kriegsmarine* officer would first have to liaise with his opposite Japanese number, who in turn would be forced to appeal for assistance to the regional Army commander, facing all of the petty feuding that had developed between the branches of service. For example, although the Japanese Navy held sway over the Singapore naval station at Selatar, if U-boats were forced to use the Keppel Harbour docks because of overcrowding elsewhere German personnel were forbidden to enter technical workshops or store houses controlled by the Army. As if the tangled German command structure were not enough to deal with, the Japanese added their own peculiar layers of difficulty. The results were often characterised by incredible inflexibility:

> During our loading *U 196* arrived in a tropical downpour. The docking manoeuvre in the powerful current took a long time . . . Finally the boat got a line ashore, which one of our men picked up and put around a bollard about a hundred yards ahead of where we stood.
>
> But to our surprise we saw a Japanese Army soldier go calmly to the bollard and unhook the line. The Japanese Admiral didn't react. We were disturbed, since it took another hour for *Kaptlt.* Kentrat to get his boat docked at the place reserved for him.
>
> The other pier had belonged to the Army and it did not in the least interest the soldier that the high-ranking naval officers of his own country were waiting and that the arriving boat was friendly ally and guest.[4]

In Penang, although there were no drydocking facilities available, the mooring space at Georgetown's Swettenham Pier, beneath the parapets of Fort Cornwallis, was largely turned over to German use. The Japa-

nese built 26 sheds housing various workshops on the esplanade adjacent to Fort Cornwallis, blocked from the gaze of civilians by a six-foot
wall. The 300,200 square feet of machine shops and maintenance areas
was linked by railway track to Swettenham Pier. The facility was able
to accommodate up to five U-boats at a time alongside the wooden py-
lons, and as there was initially little fear of an Allied air attack the Germans did not hesitate to leave their boats tied up in a position that would
be considered dangerously exposed in the increasingly bombed French
ports. At Swettenham Pier they quickly established a torpedo balancing
station within the established Japanese balancing workshop as well as
maintenance facilities where diesel repairs could be undertaken. A
mobile torpedo balancing unit was later established aboard the Japanese supply ship *Quito*.

Owing to a lack of skilled workers U-boat crewmen were compelled
to undertake the majority of maintenance themselves, adding to their
workload between operational patrols. Whatever parts were required
were shipped from Germany, or else samples were produced so that the
Japanese could copy them and produce high-quality replicas, despite
the fact that many Japanese replacement parts not based on German
specifications lacked the quality finish of the European spares. Likewise, welding and general hull maintenance did not match the high standards set within European shipyards. Unfortunately the major problem
encountered by German machinery stationed in the East could not be so
easily solved by a mere replication of parts. The issue revolved not around
machinery but rather around the lubricating oils used by U-boats. German engines required a much higher set of specifications than Japanese
units, which called for lubricating oils of correspondingly higher quality. This vital material could not be sourced, and thus wear on U-boat
machinery was much more severe than anticipated.

A small unit of two German Arado Ar 196 seaplanes was based at the
former Imperial Airways station beneath the command of *Oberleutnant*
Horn, he and his men being accommodated in the Elysee Hotel at the
junction of Farquhar and Leith Street in downtown Penang.[5] Taken from
the AMC raider *Michel* before she had been sunk and operated by the
raider's pilots, the Arados were incongruously painted with *hinomaru*
(Japanese national) markings and provided at least a token escort and
ASW presence for incoming U-boats. In fact the difference in mechani-

cal tolerances between Japanese and German equipment can be demonstrated by the experience of Japanese pilot Hiroshi Yasunaga, who operated a three-seater E13A Aichi reconnaissance floatplane in Malaysia. He came across one of the two light-blue painted German Arados as it arrived at the Japanese seaplane base for repair:

> They said they were here to change the floats, so moved the German plane to the hangar and our maintenance crew brought out the pair of floats, struts, and the wires. The floats were smaller than those of our Type O, and I felt a bit superior since they looked stubbier and less refined than the floats on my mount. However, the feeling didn't last long as the big-handed pilot started giving instructions to our ground crew who held up the floats.
>
> '*Choi ue, mou choi ue* (Up, a bit more up),' the pilot instructed in Japanese. But that was as far as his Japanese went. The instructions to left and right were given in German and gestures. When the fittings on the end of the struts and the fittings on the bottom of the fuselage were matched, our crew swiftly inserted the bolts . . . and, in no time, the pair of brand new floats were mounted on the airframe.
>
> The maintenance crew at Singapore were used to this, and performed all this matter-of-factly, but the fleet crew, pilots, and officers were all very much surprised. The time it took to change the floats was about a tenth of the time it would take to do the same for our Type O. And the German officer did this by commanding a band of our crew mostly by gestures only!
>
> Curiosity took the better of me. I stepped forward to the workbench between the two floats, took the spanner from the maintenance man's hand, and touched the brand new bolt that he was tightening. My guess was, there was considerable 'play' between the bolt and the bolt hole for it to go in that smoothly. However, the bolt was securely inserted without any play. There was not even a tenth of a millimetre nor even a hundredth of a millimetre of space between the hole and the bolt. It was amazingly precise. Utterly unthinkable from experience. And the material of the bolt was high-grade steel with a beautiful gleam. I was no expert on steel, but the difference of material was obvious.
>
> When we changed floats, it was a much more of a major operation . . . The holes on the three fittings do not match, so the bolts do not go in. The fittings are filed, and the bolts are sometimes hammered in. The banging of the hammer kills my nerves. If all that hammering creates unseen cracks on the fittings, maybe the floats will collapse when landing on rough sea. The filing was also depressing to the pilot as each second of filing lowered the strength of the fittings and, consequently, the safety margin on emergencies. Sometimes the bolts go through really smooth, but then I have to worry that the bolt is loose.
>
> The sad fact was there was a world of difference in the precision of our products, as well as in the quality of material.[6]

The Portuguese, Dutch and British had left their own indelible imprints within the city of Georgetown, the colonial bastion also absorbing the influence of the many Chinese and Indians who had immigrated to Penang to work in the tin mines and rubber plantations. In fact during September 1942 the Japanese conducted a census of Georgetown, and this concluded that the majority (70 per cent) of the 167,370 inhabitants were of Chinese extraction, considered moderately pro-British and distinctly anti-Japanese; only 16 per cent were Indian and a little over 10 per cent native Malay.[7]

Within the palm-fringed streets the Japanese provided several fully equipped houses for the German crews. The *Stützpunkt* operated a main service building on Northam Road that ran past the British colonial Penang Club, parallel to the waterfront of the North Channel. Further offices and accommodation were provided within the elegant Elysee Hotel (accommodation for enlisted men as well as the few *Kriegsmarine* airmen in Penang) and in a requisitioned villa on Bell Road, and an officer's home was provided on Rose Road. Recreational facilities in Georgetown included the swimming pools at the Spring Tide Hotel and the Penang Swimming Club, and Sakura Park with its Chinese and Malaysian theatres and three cinemas, although the last showed predominantly Japanese films. Possibly the most memorable venue for many German submariners was the Shanghai Hotel, which had been established to cater for what might euphemistically be described as their more basic needs.

The lack of medical facilities in Penang ensured that the German authorities lectured their men on the importance of avoiding local prostitutes, all of whom were to be viewed as potentially riddled with venereal disease: 'Without use of a contraceptive and the compulsory protection treatment an illness is sure!!!'[8] However, knowing full well that even the direst warnings would not deter all of their men from sampling the delights of Asia, they established an alternative facility:

When we [the crew of *U 861*] got to Penang, I went to the Japanese Admiral and said 'I want a "hotel" for my boys', and we were given the Shanghai Hotel, which had been requisitioned. I had a crew of youngsters, the youngest born in 1924 I think, and of course it was their first time in the tropics, their first time abroad at all. I didn't want the possibility that they could catch any venereal disease. So we started this hotel and we engaged nice girls that were checked by our own medical officers. We made contracts with these girls that if they only wanted to dance then okay, they got a certain kind of flower to wear, but if they were willing to sleep with the boys then they wore a different kind of flower as a signal. We also arranged with them that while they were under contract with us they had to stay at this hotel so that they didn't get any disease elsewhere. So by taking this precaution I succeeded in my aim, in that none of my crew ever suffered from venereal disease. There were some other boats that spent perhaps two months maybe in Jakarta or Surabaya, and half of the boats caught syphilis, the crews wandering into the Chinese brothels.[9]

Once German sailors had begun to disembark in numbers at Penang, Erhardt organised an informational booklet and distributed it among the new arrivals. As well as historical background and a directory of services, within its ten pages were the following instructions for the U-boat men in order that they might successfully interact with the Japanese at some level, avoiding the problems that could have followed them since they were the only white men at liberty within the occupied areas:

> Behaviour towards the Japanese, especially Japanese sailors:
> Between the Japanese and German soldiers, there is a cordial and comradely relationship. The Japanese soldier feels as a host in Penang, and likes to extend invitations to German soldiers. Such invitations can safely be assumed to come genuinely from the heart.
> The German soldier must uphold this comradeship; one expects restraint and adaptation from him. Their behaviour must always carry the thought that Japan is our single most strongest and loyal ally, exactly as Germany is Japan's single most valuable and strong ally.
> Dress within Penang's city is always civilian clothes. A special walking-out uniform (white) is made available from the German service department. To make yourself recognisable to the Police Department, each German must carry a pin of the black, white, yellow cockade.[10]

Eating from roadside stalls was strictly forbidden, for fear of contracting typhus or cholera, as was the consumption of locally produced alcohol—with the exception of beer.

Outside the actual facilities within Georgetown the *Kriegsmarine* established rest and recreational facilities in the highlands, both on the island and opposite on the mainland, where portions of U-boat crews could go in rotation in order to relax. The most spectacular of these was accessed by the funicular railway that ran 830m (2,722ft) up Penang Hill above Georgetown, providing cool relief from the sweltering heat below. There, with views stretching over the town and across to the Malay peninsula, the crews could relax in spacious bungalows and villas requisitioned for the purpose, staffed with Malaysian and Chinese waiters and cooks and many boasting swimming pools, tennis courts and extensive gardens—a hangover from colonial grandeur. The keen horticulturists were encouraged to plant vegetable gardens in order to augment the supply of food that could be eaten immediately or stored for future U-boat operations. As Otto Giese remembered, 'Only a small number of our men could be sent on leave up to the beautiful resort, Penang Hill . . . With nearly unlimited freedom, they felt as if they were in paradise.[11]

Out of view on the Malaysian mainland further stations were established on Fraser's Hill and in the Cameron Highlands that ran in a ridge along the centre of the peninsula, comprising a series of hills rising to altitudes of between 1,500 and 1,800m (5,000–6,000ft). This fertile area, the centre of Malaysia's tea industry, was dotted with English colonial houses, plantations and inns and once again provided the Germans with the chance to relax in colonial surroundings while escaping the heat of the plains below. Again the opportunity was taken to keep animals and grow whatever vegetables and fruit could be provided for the German palate in Asia.

Owing to the different ration needs of the German troops, several facilities were put into high production in order to service requirements. Bakeries were established to make the rye bread so beloved of the German nation, fruit and vegetables (in particular potatoes) were grown within a huge plantation handed over for German use as well as within smaller plots tended by sailors using the highland rest areas, while a local German butchery plant provided both fresh and preserved meat. The supply of such items was aided considerably by the capture by the raider *Thor* in May 1942 of the refrigerated steamer SS *Nanking*, travelling fully loaded from Australia to Burma. Within the ship's cavernous holds and cold-storage chambers were 42,000 cases of canned meat, 28,000 cases of fruit and vegetables and 800 tons of flour, as well as fresh butter, meat and bacon. The *Nanking* spent the rest of the war tied up in Penang harbour, where she provided a welcome food storehouse. The production of tins for the provision of preserves aboard homebound U-boats was a greater obstacle at first, not least because of a lack of metal sheeting. A small cannery was eventually found that could supply the requisite number of containers, manufactured from pure tin. Thus once the contents had been used each can was hammered flat and put into storage to augment the cargo of tin being carried to Germany. The sole disadvantage to this technique was that now the submariner's food tasted for once not of diesel but of tin instead.

The other German bases within Malaysia and Java featured similar standards of working and living for the U-boat men. Jakarta and Surabaya both had differing degrees of shipyard facilities. Jakarta had been known as Batavia for more than three centuries after Dutch settlers constructed a commercial and military centre at the mouth of the Ciliwung river on the site of an ancient Muslim port that had borne the original name. The Japanese resurrected the name Jakarta in early 1943 as German sailors began using the port, the port of Tanjong Priok featuring only a single floating dock that was capable of accommodating a U-boat for the required maintenance work. Therefore, for heavier repair work Surabaya and its ex-Dutch naval base was the next nearest facility. However, by 1944 and the time of high German U-boat concentration within the region, the Japanese had suffered a great deal of battle damage as a result of their bitter Pacific naval campaigns and were using most of the services available themselves, to prepare major surface units for action again. German U-boats as a result found it very difficult to obtain the necessary dock space for maintenance and refitting.

Probably the most efficient—and certainly the largest—naval station used by U-boats was the ex-British naval station at Singapore, or 'Shonan' as the Japanese had renamed it. Close to the causeway that linked the island to the Malaysian mainland, the facilities there included the King George VI Graving Dock, rated at the time as one of the world's best floating drydocks. However, even within that great naval base, with all its excellent amenities, space was largely taken up with priority Japanese work, and waiting times for U-boat repair were lengthened with every new Japanese casualty. The majority of U-boats arriving after the first wave of *Monsun* boats carried weight in their keels which had to be removed. This job and others, such as shaft and propeller repairs, could only be done within drydock, leading to a backlog of work as demand outstripped availability.

The living conditions in all areas mirrored those provided in Penang. In Java the Selpentana and Tjikobo resorts (the latter a 4,400-acre tea plantation), were made available to German personnel, along with their swimming pools, tennis courts and such like:

> For us, Jakarta was tremendous. We came from a country with curfews and so on, even a ban on dancing, and in the East we lived as if at peacetime. There was very nearly no white population left there when we arrived; the Japanese had put everybody in camps. The mixed-race people could decide if they wanted to talk Dutch or not, so the only people we had contact with were either pure Indonesian or mixed race.
>
> In Jakarta we had villas; the Japanese had taken most of the housing so we were allocated our areas. So we had one whole street for enlisted men and POs, and the CPOs and officers lived in separate houses, mostly two or three to a house.[12]

Likewise, within the centre of the conglomeration of sprawling streets that comprised Singapore the *Kriegsmarine* occupied three large buildings on Gilstead Road, No 39 (the radio transmitting station) and another two streets away that housed Wolfgang Erhardt's office as Malaysian Chief at 23 Newton Road. The centre of gravity for the *Kriegsmarine* services within Singapore was in the Union Building. A larger compound, Lager Pasir Panjang, comprised several buildings near a sweeping beach, all leased from the Japanese occupation authorities and rivalling even the extensive rest areas that had been established by the *Kriegsmarine* in occupied France—Lager I (Sack Lager), Lager II (Maerz Lager), *Werftkommando* Lager, *Haus Lagerkommandant* (*Kapitänleutnant* Meckmann) and the naval engineering office, *Offizierhaus*, *Soldatenheim* and the officer's nightclub *Tigerhaus*:

> The hall was frequented by beautiful Eurasian girls who waited to be invited by the German officers to drink or dance. The Tiger Club was run by a former Japanese dance star of the Takarazuka Ballet, Mrs Kadowaki, who, it was said, worked for the Japanese *Kempeitai* Secret Police. Our men were not forgotten: we turned a bungalow into a most comfortable haven for them, with all the amenities afforded officers. It was called the Jungle Club.[13]

However, not everything was idyllic for the Germans. Malaria soon became rife within the ranks of the U-boat crews and at one point 25 per cent of all sailors stationed within the region were affected. Working conditions for those men not on rotation to the *U-Bootweide* were arduous in the extreme. Heat and humidity sapped the strength of men who in European harbours would normally have handed over the major portion of maintenance duties to shipyard personnel. The waiting times between patrols increased correspondingly. In Penang, on average it would require over 50 days to prepare a recently arrived U-boat for sea, the time estimated being divided thus: cleaning the boat—3 days; urgent maintenance—20 days; docking in Singapore drydock—3 days; cleaning and maintenance of the boat's outer plating—14 days; replenishing with diesel, provisions, ammunition, crew recreation, trial runs—14 days; and then diving tests. Plainly, the slightest delay in finding allocated time within the crowded Singapore dockyard available to German U-boats would throw even this schedule into chaos. Jakarta possessed only the single floating dock—hence the decision to open Surabaya as another alternative loading and maintenance depot in July 1944.

Another potential problem concerned the intrinsic differences between the Germans and Japanese themselves. Several times German passengers aboard Japanese submarines running the gauntlet from West to East reacted badly to the food, the standards of discipline and the apparently relaxed attitude towards homosexual behaviour amongst some crewmen. Complaints from several Germans who had endured the long voyages reached the highest echelons of OKM but were discreetly ignored.

Japan's war on European dominance within Asia and the Pacific—for the 'liberation' of oppressed native people under colonial rule—virtually amounted to a 'race war'. The Japanese sought to eliminate all traces of Western influence from within their domain. Shortly after their capture of Singapore in 1942 a writer for the Japanese-controlled *Shonan Times* reported that 'One of the first imperatives . . . is the breaking down of the habit and custom left behind by the haughty and cunning British . . . Side by side [with this] . . . must proceed the work of reviving Oriental culture based on moral spiritual principles.'

In Java many greeted with great enthusiasm the removal of Dutch colonial power, although Japanese promises of Indonesian independence never reached full fruition. The internment of the Dutch and other Europeans heralded an opportunity for many Indonesians to line the roadside verges, spitting and hurling abuse at the internees on their way to camps. In the former Dutch East Indies, as in Penang and Singapore, the myth of European invincibility had been profoundly shattered. Thus the presence of Germans within the 'Greater East Asia Co-Prosperity Sphere', in which all traces of European dominance were being removed, was often fraught with its own problems as regards their relationship with the Japanese. The memories of men who served aboard the Eastern U-boats provide an interesting insight into their impressions and experiences while mixing with Japanese Allies. For example, Jürgen Oesten, commander of *U 861* remembered that

> Wartime conditions in Malaysia under Japanese occupation were quite interesting as this was a racial war as far as Japanese propaganda was concerned and we were the only white people running around free. The economy was in the hands of the Chinese, and everything in short supply was channelled through the black market. The Japanese could not afford to requisition any stores, in that case all the rest . . . vanished.[14]

Another aspect of potential conflict occurred when U-boat personnel came into contact with the Japanese treatment of Allied prisoners-of-war. Held in appalling conditions, malnourished and worked often to the point of death, they made a pitiful sight for the Germans:

> It caused problems on one occasion. Our crew, when they saw these British prisoners put to work by the Japanese, well, they gave them cigarettes and so on, which I don't think the Japanese liked. And then something else happened when one of our submariners was sitting on the pier in Singapore. A Japanese soldier came along with his gun and he thought that the man was a prisoner-of-war, so he tried to attack him with his rifle, but the German was quicker than the Japanese soldier and threw him in the water. Later on the Japanese apologised for this action, but things like that happened. The relations [between us] were a little reluctant up to a certain extent, there is no doubt, but the Japanese came aboard our boat once to visit, although all the work was done by our own people; we had no Japanese people working on it."[15]

Hans-Joachim Krug, the IWO on board *U 219*, remembers similar impressions of his time at Jakarta as his boat lay in dock awaiting vital maintenance:

> The Japanese were very harsh with their own people. We were not used to that, and many of our men were quite upset at first. They tried to treat us that way, but we didn't accept it. To slap a subordinate was quite normal for them. To us it would be unacceptable, but this poor chap would get up salute and thank his officer for the treatment.
>
> We mixed with the local population very much. But the Japanese did not always treat them very politely. If there was a guard, they had to bow to him no matter who they were, but with us they didn't have to do any of that. Initially there was some trouble with the Japanese and our boys, but in the end we always got away with it.
>
> The Japanese were very keen on security. They were not so sure if these whites [the Germans] were the right partners for them. For example, they had an advertisement, a billboard, with a large picture of a big round blue eye and under it the slogan 'watch for the eyes of the enemy'. So we approached them and said, 'But most of us have blue eyes too; you can't do that to us,' so they took them down, but immediately after we had lost the war the placards came back again.[16]

Perhaps the final word on the German impression of the Japanese can be found within the pages of Otto Giese's autobiography of his time as IWO aboard *U 181*: 'The Japanese attitude towards us was cautiously friendly. It was tolerant, occasionally arrogant, and, loosened by liquor, it could become aggressive . . . How strange these people were, we thought—intelligent, traditional, ceremonial, but cruel and dangerous at the same time.[17]

Of course it was not only the Germans who held a certain reserve when relating with the Japanese: the same could be said of the other side. Shortly after conquering Singapore, *Taisho* Yamashita delivered a

speech to local Chinese delegates gathered together to pay virtual ex-
tortion money in order to survive the terrible Japanese purges. Within
his hour-long monologue he mentioned the 'fact' that the Japanese were
descended from Gods (*Tenno*) while Europeans were the descendents
of monkeys, as proved by Charles Darwin. Thus there could be but one
outcome to any war between Gods and monkeys. This view of Europeans is also once again demonstrated in the memoirs of the Japanese
pilot Hiroshi Yasunaga. However, the Japanese perspective of Europeans as uncultured and clumsy barbarians was tested by their encounters
with German servicemen:

> Just before lunch yesterday, a two-seat floatplane of the German Navy paid a
> visit to our base. The plane was a twin-float, low-wing monoplane . . . that
> belonged to the submarine fleet command stationed in Penang. It touched down
> gently on the sea about 200 metres off the command post. It was a beautiful
> touchdown. The plane killed its speed way low, pulled up near stall, and touched
> down quietly from the rear end of the floats. It was a surprise for me, who
> firmly believed that we Japanese are much superior than the white people at
> such a delicate operation as bringing a floatplane down.
>   . . . The two German Navy officers appeared at the command post. The pilot
> was a tough looking man, at least ten years older than I was. He put out his big
> clumsy looking hand out to our commander, and I wondered how that hand
> could make such a delicate and gentle landing manoeuvre.[18]

The strange clash of cultures that occurred between the two major
Axis partners was in fact least obstructive when encountered on the
ground in Malaysia. Far away in Berlin, German national arrogance
when dealing with the Japanese, and an inherent distrust of its oriental
partners, deprived the *Kriegsmarine* of potentially war winning weaponry. Working examples of the superb Japanese 'Long-Lance' destroyer
torpedo, the Type 93, and its smaller submarine version, the Type 95,
had been transported to Germany by blockade-runner, but they lay undisturbed within Eckernförde's *Torpedoversuchsansalt* (TVA) institute,
ignored by German technicians who were trying in vain to make the
Walther hydrogen-peroxide propulsion system safe for torpedo use.
While German G7a steam torpedoes were capable of travelling 4,000m
at a speed of 40kts, the electric G7e was limited to 3,500m at 28kts. Of
course, the thermal propulsion unit of the G7a left a betraying wake of
disturbed water behind it, making it really only suitable at night . The
oxygen-propelled Japanese Type 95 submarine torpedo model, however, could travel 20,000m at the exceptional speed of 50kts, or accu-

rately cover 37,000m at a reduced speed of 36kts, leaving no visible wake as it travelled towards its target. At a time when German torpedoes continued to be plagued with erratic performance—and not only within tropical waters—the adaptation of the Japanese model could have provided a simple, cost-effective solution. Ironically, and fortunately for the Allies, it was largely defeated by German conceit, the *Kriegsmarine*'s experts being unwilling to acknowledge Japanese superiority in that particular field of development. The Walther system never saw action.

Certain elements of the exchanged technological information were, however, absorbed into German plans, although by and large the primary interest in the exchanges between the countries remained with the raw materials shipped from the East. In Japan there was a greater willingness to use German ideas as a basis of their own weapons development programmes, although Dönitz was ultimately proved correct about his assumptions regarding Japan's inability or unwillingness to copy the Type IXC *U 511*. Since the boat was never seriously studied or used. Officially the reason given for this by the Japanese was that the Type IXC was too small for their needs, although many of their earlier model submarines were of a comparable size and indeed had been developed during the inter-war years by German designers. In other fields, though, the Japanese were willing students. In fact at one stage German technicians became alarmed at the speed with which Japan adapted plans for the Me 163 rocket fighter, lest they introduce the weapon into combat in advance of the *Luftwaffe*, while also beginning to experience the sensation that they were providing more information to the Japanese than was being received:

> The Japanese were very interested in German technological developments. They sent many specialists to Germany all the time, since the twenties, to look on and gather technical information. But they did not deliver anything the other way around except for the 'Long Lance'. Of their other developments, we got very very little. On the other hand, we were very high-handed and didn't care to try too hard to get anything, and probably wouldn't have used it anyway. The Japanese did the same. We sent many specialists to Japan, and they put them into their factories or development plants, where they talked about what these men had to offer, and when they had finished these talks they moved them out. From then onwards they just sat around and had nothing to do.[19]

So despite formal declarations of combined ambitions for the outcome of the war, the gulf between Oriental and Occidental remained wide throughout the sometimes turbulent relationship. German sailors received rations, pay and accommodation within the Malaysian and Indonesian bases that greatly outclassed anything on offer to Japanese servicemen, causing some measure of resentment and hostility to creep into the dealings between the enlisted men from the two navies. Officers tended to develop closer working relationships and friendships with their Allies, although frequent references in U-boat records to frustration at the 'Japanese mentality' belie complete harmony. The Japanese, correspondingly, often viewed their European allies with disdain for their 'barbarian' ways and also harboured the suspicion that they themselves were being treated with a certain level of condescension when in the company of Europeans.

However, racially motivated distrust between Occidental and Oriental nations, as well as the more obvious elements of racism, were nothing new to the world by the time *Wehrmacht* forces arrived in Malaysia and the Dutch East Indies. This was no more evident than in those two countries, former European colonies where the 'yellow man' remained subservient to the white man. Indeed, as the Japanese invaded Malaysia in 1942, Penang's magistrate, Lim Khoon Teck, arrived at the ferry landing bound for Butterworth and away from the Japanese invaders late at night on 13 December but the British authorities prevented him and his family from taking the boat to possible freedom: it was reserved for whites only.

As German soldiers arrived in the Far East they no doubt brought a certain amount of institutionalised racism with them, as much as they suffered it from the Japanese who had developed their tenet of *Hakko Ichiu*, meaning 'the whole world under one rule' (i.e., that of Nippon). From the German perspective, even Heinrich Himmler's SS theorists devoted much time and effort to research in order to prove that the Japanese, too, were Aryan—a theory never fully endorsed by the *Führer*. However, while in distant Berlin Hitler may have consigned the Japanese to the 'primitive' classification of the 'yellow man', the experience of German submariners in the East rather reflects the inevitable result of two alien cultures thrust together unexpectedly, neither fully comprehending the attitudes and beliefs of the other. This is an attitude still prevalent in most societies 60 years after the end of the Second World War.

NOTES

1. Vermehren, born in El Paso, Texas, in 1890, had been *OKM/Abw. Ausl. IV Referent* between 1934 and April 1942 (Naval Intelligence).
2. Zatorski later moved to Yokohama to look after *Kriegsmarine* interests there.
3. Interview with Hans-Joachim Krug, 3 May 2003.
4. Otto Geise, *Shooting the War*, p. 201.
5. A third Arado had been destroyed by an accidental fire.
6. Hiroshi Yasunaga, Shito no Suiteitai, Asahi Sonorama, 1994. Selected text quoted on http://www.j-aircraft.com/research/stories/yasunaga1.html.
7. According to the *Penang Daily News* (September 2002, reprinted from 1942), Georgetown comprised at that time 117,484 Chinese, 27,852 Indians, 17,521 Malaysians, 2,145 Eurasians, 1,564 Indonesians, 326 Thais, 162 Ceylonese, 137 Filipinos, 73 Jews, 63 Burmese and 43 Europeans. The Jews were among those listed by the Japanese as 'enemies of the state' and were forced to wear red-and-white striped tags for identification. They were also forbidden to approach within half a mile of Penang's shoreline.
8. *Kriegsmarine* Handbook: Penang, OKM Berlin, 1944. Original emphasis.
9. Interview with Jürgen Oesten, 8 March 2003.
10. *Penang*, OKM Berlin, 1944.
11. Geise, *op. cit.*, p. 200.
12. Interview with Hans-Joachim Krug, 3 May 2003.
13. Geise, *op. cit.*, p. 207.
14. Interview with Jürgen Oesten, Hamburg, 8 March 2003.
15. *Ibid.*
16. Interview with Hans-Joachim Krug, Wolfratshausen, 3 May 2003.
17. Geise, *op. cit.*, pp. 201–2.
18. Yasunaga, *op. cit.*
19. Interview with Hans-Joachim Krug.

Six

Reinforcements to the Far East

IN BORDEAUX during September and October 1943, the four long-range Type IXD2s that had accompanied Dommes' *U 178* into the Indian Ocean began to arrive home. Following the group's successful refuelling from the *Charlotte Schliemann* around 22 July they had once again sailed northwards, operating independently of one another off Madagascar. Their successes slowly mounted—individual sinkings achieved sporadically among the Allied merchantmen that continued to run the new gauntlet of German steel.

As the toll gradually accumulated the boats began to run short of ammunition and provisions once again until they headed westward in the last days of August, *U 178* parting company and sailing for Penang. Aboard *U 181* in particular there was jubilation during August. On 9 August Lüth received notification of a fresh award for him following the boat's hard-won Indian Ocean success: he had been granted the Diamonds to the Swords and Oak Leaves of the Knight's Cross. This incredibly prestigious award was the highest that Germany could offer; it was awarded to just one other member of the *Kriegsmarine* throughout the war, and at the time that Lüth received it there were only six recipients in total.[1]

The fifth of their number, *U 197*, had joined the ranks of the casualties after being found and sunk by aircraft on 20 August off South Africa. *Kapitänleutnant* Robert Bartels had made his final sinking on 17 August when he torpedoed the SS *Empire Stanley*, having been ordered to rendezvous with Lüth's *U 181* two days previously so that he could pass over the Enigma settings—'Bellatrix'—needed for the remainder of Lüth's journey. As the *Empire Stanley* was being attacked Lüth waited impatiently at the rendezvous point, low on fuel and food and, because of a lack of torpedoes, unable to attack several steamers that were sighted. A new rendezvous was arranged and two days later the boats met, Lüth telling Bartels of the ships he had sighted and departing in good spirits for the homeward trek. Bartels, still holding supplies and ammunition having sunk only three ships and damaged a fourth, elected to remain within the area and hunt for Lüth's steamers. It was a fatal mistake.

Efficient Allied HF/DF had picked up a transmission from *U 181* as Lüth awaited Bartels' arrival and had despatched a Catalina to investigate. By remaining within the region *U 197* lay vulnerable to discovery, and on 20 August Bartels was spotted by a Catalina of No 259 Squadron operating from Saint Lucia, Natal, as *U 197* cruised, surfaced, southeast of South Africa for the rounding of the Cape. A little after noon Flying Officer Eccles, the Catalina's 2nd Pilot, spotted the long wake of the large submarine and alerted Flt Lt L. O. Barnett, who immediately put his Catalina into a diving attack. Six depth charges were dropped as the aircraft flew low over Bartels' boat, machine-gun fire peppering the exposed conning tower. Aboard *U 197* the alert lookouts had spotted their attacker, and by the time Barnett roared overhead the flak crews were on station and returning fire.

Bartels swung his boat through 90 degrees as the depth charges tumbled down, slightly throwing off Barnett's aim. Nonetheless the six detonations had caused considerable damage and, as the spray subsided, the circling Catalina could see that *U 197* was listing to port, her speed reduced. Accurate flak continued to buffet the aircraft as Barnett shadowed the damaged U-boat, the supply of depth charges exhausted. Aboard *U 197* the Chief Engineer estimated that the boat would be able to submerge despite her wounds. A rapid message was radioed from *U 197*: 'FL. FL. Aircraft has attacked with bombs. Marginally able to dive. [Position] KQ 87. *U 197*.'

At 1245hrs Bartels took *U 197* below. Water soon began to enter the cracked hull and the crippled boat started to trail a thick slick of oil from damaged bunkers. The Catalina dropped smoke floats over the suspected position, although the shimmering rainbow trail rendered *U 197*'s position visible. Within 40 minutes Bartels had resurfaced, his flak weapons manned and ready once more. He ordered a second quick radio message sent: 'Aircraft has attacked with bombs. Unable to dive. [Position] KQ 52. *U 197*.'

The distress signals were relayed to BdU by Werner Hartmann's *U 198* and Dönitz deliberated briefly over what to do to aid the imperilled boat. At 2240hrs he ordered the nearest U-boats—*U 181* and Kentrat's *U 196*, recently together so that Lüth could pass on the 'Bellatrix' key to his comrade—to race to the aid of Bartels. However, in his desperation Bartels or his radio operators had made one more crucial error— transmitting co-ordinates that were 250 miles apart. Lüth and Kentrat, monitoring the transmission of three more appeals for help, decided to use the latter, KQ 52, and both ordered course laid to assist, Kentrat receiving a stern rebuke from BdU after having initially withdrawn to the south away from *U 197*.

Above *U 197* Barnett continued to shadow the limping German until reinforcement arrived in the form of another No 265 Squadron Catalina piloted by Canadian Fg Off. C. E. Robin:

> When we arrived, C/259 [Barnett] was circling the area and the sub was on the surface, making about ten knots in a southerly direction. My first reaction was to set the D/Cs and head right in, but my crew had a better thought, and although the sub was firing at us and had longer range and better guns, the crew thought that we should try to silence them first, which we did by circling close and using our .5s.

Both Catalinas began to hose their machine-gun fire over the German flak crews, cutting down a number of men until the remainder were left with no option but to retreat to the shelter of the conning tower. *U 197* now lay defenceless. Robin continued:

> I made a run at the U-boat and the German skipper . . . turned about 90 degrees just when I was ready to press the button . . . so another pass and we were out-manoeuvred again. However, the third time, by which time I was getting a lot of 'flak' from my crew, the German made his mistake and turned straight along our path and I hit the button. I recall we were very low and had to lift up to avoid the conning tower and masts [*sic*].[2]

Robin's patience spelt doom for Bartels and his men. The six shallow-set depth charges were perfectly on target, three straddling the boat and landing next to the hull and one hitting the deck where it lay malevolently. The ensuing explosions hurled debris into the air, and as *U 197* reeled over and submerged for her final dive, the last depth charge still on deck exploded and a huge upwelling of oil gushing to the surface signalled the end of Bartels and his 66 men. At 1830hrs transmissions from *U 197* ceased, and aboard *U 181* and *U 196* the men were in little doubt as to the likely cause. Two days were spent searching for survivors within grid square KQ before both boats headed east to round the Cape of Good Hope.

All four remaining boats arrived at their new home port of Bordeaux during September and October. Werner Hartmann's *U 198* was first, docking on 25 September, *U 177* followed on 1 October, *U 181* on 14 October and finally *U 196* on 23 October. The homecoming of the four boats broke records of endurance set by combat submarines: the shortest of their voyages was made by Robert Gysae's *U 177*, which had been at sea for 184 days, and the longest was that by Kentrat's *U 196*, which had been on patrol for a total of 225 days (or nearly eight months)—a record that would remain unbroken during the Second World War.

The men were heavily bearded and unsteady on their feet as they disembarked from the steel tube that had been their home for so long at sea. They were greeted by FdU West, Hans Rudolf Rösing, and flotilla commander Klaus Scholtz and whatever reception committee could be gathered. Victory banquets fêted the returning heroes, each U-boat flying victory pennants marking their latest patrols. Lüth outdid everybody else by displaying 48 in total—the number of claimed sinkings made by *U 181* with him in command. For Lüth it marked the end of his operational career as he was transferred to the post of Commander of Gotenhafen's 22nd U-Training Flotilla. Werner Hartmann also departed his command, transferring to Aix-en-Provence as FdU *Mittelmeer*, while Robert Gysae became head of the 25th U-Training Flotilla. Kentrat was the sole captain to remain with his boat after their epic voyages, his men less than pleased with that unexpected development as Kentrat's threats at sea bore fruit on land: 'From day one some of our men were thrown into the brig, and many had to appear at courts-martial. Our watch engineer was sent to Paris to a mental hospital and torpedo mechanic Boost had a terrible case of nerves.'[3]

Despite the awards and propaganda coverage that greeted the four boats and their crews, their results had been less than had been hoped for. Between them they had destroyed 25 ships (claiming 36), the lion's share of ten sunk by Lüth while the arrogant though record-breaking

Kentrat achieved a miserable two victories (albeit claiming three). On balance it was not much to show after so long at sea, and the boats were not considered seaworthy again until the beginning of the following year. However, elsewhere U-boat successes had been even slimmer, and although the relatively poor showing by the long-distance boats in the Indian Ocean caused some doubts as to the wisdom of pursuing such operations, a further five boats had either already departed or been scheduled for despatch by Dönitz to augment the Eastern presence, their ultimate destination planned as Penang. Named unofficially (by themselves) *Monsun II*, they were led from Germany by *U 848*, which departed Kiel on 18 September. *U 849* and *U 510* soon followed, by which time *U 848* was already approaching trouble west-south-west of Ascension Island.

U 848's captain, *Korvettenkapitän* Wilhelm Rollmann, continued the pattern of experienced commanders taking charge of newly commissioned Type IXD2 boats, having won the Knight's Cross for a successful captaincy of *U 34*, when he had sunk 22 ships totalling 100,838 tons during 1939 and 1940. Returned to active duty after serving as an officer of the 2nd U-Boat Training Division, he oversaw the construction of *U 848* within Bremen's A. G. Weser shipyard before beginning the five months training necessary before entering the ranks of the 12th U-Flotilla.

Rollmann's voyage began successfully when he torpedoed and sank the British freighter SS *Baron Semple* on 2 November north-west of Ascension but his luck quickly deserted him. During the morning three days later *U 848* was spotted, surfaced, by a US Navy Liberator of the Ascension-based VP-107. Lt C. A. Baldwin immediately attacked the U-boat, straddling it with six depth charges that apparently inflicted enough damage to prevent Rollmann submerging. Amidst heavy return flak a second Liberator arrived and managed to inflict further damage on *U 848* but was unable to cripple her or silence the flak. A third Liberator attempted a similar attack but suffered such severe anti-aircraft damage that her pilot, Lt W. E. Hill, was forced to return to Ascension with one engine disabled.

That afternoon two B-25 Mitchell bombers from Brig.-Gen. Robert Charlwood Richardson III's 1st Composite Squadron, which had arrived on Ascension during August, proceeded to make a level bombing run from 4,000ft that failed to have any effect on the frantically manoeuvring Rollmann. It was not until Baldwin returned, refuelled, rearmed and accompanied by another Liberator, that *U 848* was finally sent down, the two Liberators roaring low overhead as gunners sprayed the flak positions and dropping perfect straddles of depth charges on their hapless victim. Camera equipment aboard Baldwin's Liberator recorded the attack and show the gun crews, in steel helmets, crouching behind whatever cover was available as the depth charges began to detonate. The U-boat's hull was fatally ruptured and *U 848* rapidly sank. About twenty survivors were seen in the water, the Liberators dropping liferafts and radioing for naval units to rescue them before returning to base. However, it was not until 28 days later that a single delirious survivor, *Oberbootsmannsmaat* Hans Schade, was picked up by the light cruiser USS *Marblehead*. He died two days later.

It was a harbinger of things to come for the boats of *Monsun II* as *U 850* and *U 172* also put to sea during November from Kiel and St-Nazaire, heading for Penang. By the year's end only one was left. *Kapitänleutnant* Heinz-Otto Schultz's *U 849* had been destroyed on 25 November by a clean depth-charge straddle delivered by another Liberator of VP-107 east-north-east of Ascension; none of the floating survivors from the 63-man German crew was ever found. *U 172* had been sunk on 13 December after being surprised whilst she was refuelling from the Type XB auxiliary tanker *U 219* the previous day after Allied forces had been alerted to the rendezvous by intelligence interceptions of radio traffic.

Although the tanker escaped, *U 172*, now commanded by *Oberleutnant zur See* Hermann Hoffmann after Carl Emmermann had rotated ashore, was damaged by aircraft from the escort carrier USS *Bogue*, detached from escort duty for convoy GUS.23. Hunted into the following day, Hoffmann was depth-charged by destroyers from the carrier group and forced to the surface, where, after a brief gun battle during which Hoffmann himself manned a machine gun and killed an American sailor, the German crew abandoned ship. Hoffmann and 45 survivors were rescued, the remaining fourteen having been lost during the action. The last of the quartet to be destroyed was veteran *Fregattenkapitän* Klaus Ewerth's *U 850* after she had been attacked by several Avengers and Wildcats of US *Bogue*'s VC-19 on 20 December, driven under and hit with a 'Fido' homing torpedo. None of the 66 men aboard survived, and

American destroyers later recovered debris and body parts from a large pool of floating oil.[4]

In total the group had lost four boats and 207 men during its transit of the Atlantic, none of the four even reaching the Cape of Good Hope. It was a disaster for Dönitz and a severe blow to his hopes of continuing the Indian Ocean campaign. The American aircraft on Ascension Island and the *Bogue* carrier group had been on high alert searching for possible inbound blockade-runners from Japan and the four U-boats had fallen foul of their attentions.

The sole survivor also came under pressure from the American presence but she managed to make good her escape. *Kapitänleutnant* Alfred Eick's Type IXC *U 510* refuelled successfully from *U 219* on 24 November west of the Cape Verde Islands but attracted unwanted attention after Eick had radioed a sighting report of the blockade-runner *Osorno* to BdU on 10 December. Spotted by a Liberator of VP-107, *U 510* became the subject of an extended hunt by warships of Task Groups 41.1 and 41.3 that lasted for the best part of three days before Eick managed to slip free of the net.

Rounding the Cape of Good Hope during mid-January, *U 510* refuelled once more, this time from the *Charlotte Schliemann*, before heading north towards the Gulf of Aden. There Eick experienced greater success. On 22 February 1944 *U 510* attacked convoy PA.69 sailing from the Persian Gulf to Aden and, in the course of two separate attacks, sank the British tanker MV *San Alvaro* and the American freighter SS *E. G. Seubert*, also damaging the Norwegian tanker MV *Erling Brövig*. The last, already a veteran of war damage after having been struck by Japanese aircraft during the evacuation of the Dutch East Indies, was hit by a single torpedo and broken in half, although the two floating sections were later beached and repaired. Eick claimed a further ship sunk and another damaged, but Allied records show no trace of these vessels.

During March *U 510* roved the Arabian Sea and managed to destroy Captain Hans Bjønness's MV *Tarifa* east of Socotra on the 7th. Travelling from Suez to Aden with 8,000 tons of phosphate and 500 bags of mail, and with 102 British soldiers aboard, the Norwegian motor ship was hit by two torpedoes, the first between Nos 1 and 2 hatches and the second at the stern . Within ten minutes she was gone, one crewman killed by the initial blast and a second crushed between a lifeboat and raft on the stern deck.

The American Liberty ship SS *John A. Poor* was sunk by Eick on 19 March north-west of the Laccadive Islands. A small sailing vessel was sunk by his artillery fire before his final victory on 27 March, when he sank the 249-ton minesweeper HMS *Maaløy*. This small auxiliary was in fact the Norwegian whaler *Globe VI*, built in 1935, hired by Royal Navy during April 1941 for use as a minesweeper, renamed and crewed by Norwegians. She was torpedoed near Ceylon, and her destruction signalled the end of *U 510*'s patrol as shortly thereafter, on 5 April, Eick entered Penang, earning the award of the first Knight's Cross bestowed in Penang and several of his men the Iron Cross First Class.

Eick's reception by the Japanese was enthusiastic, not least because they felt that he would possess knowledge, and perhaps a working example, of the *Zaunkönig* acoustic torpedo. However, Eick was under firm instructions from BdU not to reveal details of this much-vaunted weapon that Dönitz fervently (and, as it transpired, vainly) hoped would provide an antidote to destroyer attack.[5] Indeed the desire for secrecy was so intense that Eick had been ordered to ditch overboard any working example of the torpedo before entering harbour, much to his bewilderment and disbelief. This strange order once more belies the façade of technological co-operation between Japan and Germany, at least in the higher echelons of power. The Japanese had learned of the new torpedo from the American Press and immediately asked Eick about the weapon during the greeting ceremony on Swettenham Pier.

'Eick San,' said the Japanese admiral after entering Penang and when gathered in a small circle following the welcoming ceremony, 'where have you stored the new torpedoes?'

'I don't understand,' replied the commander of *U 510* with practised composure. 'What torpedoes do you mean *Herr Admiral*? Those with magnetic fuses? They are already old, however.'

'Oh no, *Herr Kapitänleutnant*, I mean an entirely new thing . . . those that follow screw sounds.'

'But I know nothing about that.'

'But we do, *Herr Kapitänleutnant*.' The translator repeats the Admiral's final words as he rises, still speaking.[6]

Eick's boat had suffered from the effects of her long voyage and was forced to relocate to Singapore for an extensive overhaul. The interminable heat and humidity left their mark on both machinery and crew.

After two months in the Singapore shipyard *U 510* sailed to Kobe, Japan, where the *Kriegsmarine* had established a small yard after facilities within the Japanese Kawasaki Shipbuilding Company's docks had been placed at the disposal of U-boats requiring extended drydocking, most commonly for the replacement of worn batteries. The *Kriegsmarine* had already established a small unit at Yokohama, commanded by Zatorski (late of the Singapore shipyard) and ostensibly concerned with supplies for blockade-running, but the new outpost at Kobe not officially placed under the command of Kentrat until January 1945.

By mid-1943 the war had deteriorated for both Axis partners and during September, having suffered reverses within the Pacific Ocean, the Japanese authorities had revised their plans: instead of expansion towards the west, Japan would consolidate her own defensive position against American advances, defining an 'Absolute Defence Zone' that contained the Kurile and Ogasawara Islands, New Guinea, Sunda and Burma—a supposed 'ring of steel' that was considered defensible by the overstretched Imperial forces. Thus Japanese submarine strength was gradually diverted to the Pacific, boats being withdrawn from the Indian Ocean until, by April 1944, there remained only four Japanese submarines active within the region. The end of 1943 and the beginning of 1944 found U-boat operations within the Atlantic riddled with extreme difficulty in the face of improved Allied detection and weapons technologies augmenting an already fearsome aerial and naval strength.

The Type IXD2s that had been constructed continued to be directed towards Malaysia, where hopes remained for effective Indian Ocean operations despite the relatively poor precedents. Coupled with the offensive factor and the presumed virtue of tying down enemy ASW forces in an area removed from the Atlantic, the outbound boats carried equipment, spare parts and supplies for the Penang base. Correspondingly, in the East the first of the *Monsun* boats began her return voyage to France on 27 November 1943 when *Kapitänleutnant* Wilhelm Spahr took his new command, *U 178*, from Penang, bound for Bordeaux.

Spahr had relieved Dommes of his command of the boat officially two days before her departure, although he had effectively occupied the post since the U-boat's arrival in Malaysia. The War Correspondent, *Leutnant zur See* Walther Schöppe, accompanied the boat on her homeward journey, along with the first load of raw materials bound for Europe to be carried by U-boat. A total cargo of 139 tons, comprising 107 tons of tin ingots, two tons of tungsten and 30 of crude rubber, was packed within the bilge, living quarters and superstructure of the boat.

The boat was not tasked solely to return with her cargo to France. Dönitz was always loath to have combat U-boats assigned to non-combatant duties and double-tasked virtually all such submarines within the Far East. Despite the cramped conditions aboard and the nagging problems with torpedoes caused by the inclement climatic conditions, Spahr was ordered to operate against shipping off the Indian sub-continent before heading for home. For the first half of December *U 178* was assigned the eastern coast of India, transferring to the western area during the latter half of the month.

The patrol began with the anticlimactic scouring of empty seas until, on 27 December, Spahr sighted and attacked the American Liberty ship SS *José Navarro* 200 miles west of Trivandrum. It was to be the voyage's sole success, and scant solace in a voyage otherwise dogged with mis-fortune, albeit related to the other U-boats and shipping with which Spahr was to co-ordinate his activities.

On 4 January 1944 *U 532* slipped from Penang harbour to begin a patrol also planned to hunt the waters off southern India before ending in France. The boat was packed with tin, quinine, rubber, opium and wolfram concentrate sealed into tin pots within the keel as well as a full weapon load. The Penang 'flotilla' as it stood at the beginning of 1944 could barely support itself. Dockyard capacity remained limited to five U-boats and, as the *Monsun* boats were extremely short of torpedoes, *U 532*, *U 168*, *U 188* and *U 183* were ordered to embark strategic mate-rials needed in France and cruise home via patrol areas in the Indian Ocean. It was to be another period of disaster for the U-boats.

Kapitänleutnant Ottoheinrich Junker took *U 532* straight towards Ceylon, his crew sweating below decks and above in the tropical humid-ity. After a week of sailing Junker attacked and damaged the British freighter SS *Triona* south of Ceylon and on 26 January sank the Liberty ship SS *Walter Camp*. He then proceeded towards the position in which he was to take on fuel from the tanker *Charlotte Schliemann*. There was no way in which the Type IXC could make it to France on the fuel that it carried itself, and Junker was dependent upon refuelling before con-tinuing his lengthy voyage.

Siegfried Lüdden followed the next day in *U 188*, taking his boat from Penang with 11½ tons of crude rubber wedged within the boat's superstructure, 117 tons of tin and tungsten within the keel and nearly three quarters of a ton of quinine, wolfram and opium aboard in sacks and chests. Lüdden had spent two weeks during December in Singapore's dockyard where the side plates of the boat's keel had been unscrewed and filled with the heaviest cargo items, tin and tungsten. Penang was unable to offer drydocking facilities for such a time-consuming task and, as with all other such cargo carriers, the expansive yards at Singapore were used.

In what the Admiralty's Anti-Submarine Warfare Reports attributed to the 'benefits of acclimatisation', Lüdden and his crew would achieve far greater success on their return cruise than the outbound voyage. Assigned to hunt the waters east of Aden, Lüdden opened his account with the successful torpedoing, a little before midnight on 20 January, of the British steamer SS *Fort Buckingham*, which was travelling in ballast from Bombay to Durban. A second victim followed five nights later when Lüdden attacked the SS *Fort La Maune* bound from Aden to Cochin with a cargo of 8,130 tons of military stores. Hit in the port side by a single torpedo a little after 1920hrs local time, the steamer took 40 minutes to sink by the head as repeated distress calls were broadcast from the radio shack. After the ship had finally gone under, Lüdden approached the survivors and questioned them regarding their ship's identity and cargo, leading to some interesting speculation amongst the survivors as to their attacker's identity—as revealed by the subsequent interrogation of all 56 crewmen by Allied naval officers after their rescue by the corvette HMS *Nigella*:

The lifeboat in the charge of the Third Officer was hailed by a man in the conning tower and the following conversation in English ensued:
　'What is the nationality of the ship?'
　'Spanish'
　'What is the ship's name?'
　'Maria'
　'Where are you from?'
　'Port Said'
　'Come alongside and tell the truth or I shall shoot you!'
Four men then appeared on the sub's deck with boat hooks. The lifeboat was again hailed and the officer asked the survivors if their ship was a big fast one they were waiting for in London. They replied 'No' [apparently this was the SS *Port Adelaide* due to sail from Aden shortly afterwards]. The officer in the U-

boat talking was Japanese and he said 'That is not our information; our information is that you are a new ship out from London!'

The Third Officer thought that the sub was German, manned by a Japanese crew with a German commander.[7]

Lüdden's warning that he was prepared to open fire on the survivors remained an empty threat, although subsequent events in the Indian Ocean would show the tragic possibility of such an action if allowed to occur. His War Diary entry reveals his version of the incident:

> I went up to the larger lifeboat. From my question I first heard the name '*Marie Espaniol*'. From my threat, said the correct name '*Fort La Maune*' from Port Said to Colombo—but we are sure this is still not the name of the ship. Its appearance is like a ship of the '*Port Adelaide*' type, 8,422grt.[8]

U 188 continued her run of sinkings with three more ships destroyed by the month's end. Lüdden's boat was again identified, this time by survivors of the British SS *Surada*, as 'a Japanese I-4 type' after the boat surfaced to question them and distribute water; moreover, they were fended off the U-boat's casing by 'two Japanese crewmen'. The scrutiny of repeated flying-boat sightings and Allied escort groups attracted by the sudden flurry of attacks resulted in a brief lull until 4 February, when *U 188* sank the Chinese freighter SS *Chung Cheng* en route to Aden. Lüdden's next victories were rather less spectacular—the destruction of four cotton-carrying Arab dhows by a combination of 2cm gunfire and ramming during 7 February.

As Lüdden was engaging the small Arab sailing vessels, *U 168*, under *Kapitänleutnant* Helmuth Pich, was putting to sea, again with a cargo of valuable supplies for Germany. The boat had made a false start when sailing from Penang on 28 January, being forced to abort this mission only days later when the IWO, Hans-Georg Stenger, developed appendicitis and had to be returned for hospitalisation. His place was taken aboard *U 168* by the erstwhile commander of *Stützpunkt* Penang, Konrad Hoppe, whose place was in turn taken by Kandeler, transferring from Jakarta. Like Junker's *U 532*, Pich's boat carried a full cargo of goods for unloading in France. Ingots of tin had been stored within the keel and 29 tons of tungsten within the pressure hull. As well as the heavy metals carried aboard, a load of quinine, opium and vitamins was crated and distributed throughout the boat's living area.

Pich was ordered to patrol south-west of India before taking on fuel from the tanker *Charlotte Schliemann* and continuing home to France.

Three days after *U 168* put to sea for the second time *U 183* also sailed from Penang harbour, for operations south and south-west of mainland India. *Kapitänleutnant* Fritz Schneewind took his large boat into the humid Indian Ocean for what would amount to a little over five weeks, his voyage planned to end in France, where the cargo of tin, tungsten, rubber, quinine and opium could be added to the incoming blockade-running stockpile.

The departure of so many U-boats bound for France had entailed another refuelling schedule with the tankers *Charlotte Schliemann* and *Brake*. These ships had spent the previous Christmas at Singapore, sharing the harbour with two Italian gunboats, *Lepanto* and *Carlotto*, seized by the Japanese, along with the ex-Italian submarines *UIT 23*, *UIT 24* and *UIT 25*. The tankers sailed for their supply positions in early February, passing through the Sunda Strait and heading for the Indian Ocean once more. The first U-boat first to refuel was Spahr's *U 178*, which took on diesel from *Charlotte Schliemann* in late January.

As *U 168*, suffering a multitude of engine problems in the heat, and *U 183* arrived at their patrol stations and began their hunt around India, *Kapitänleutnant* Junker's *U 532* was in position and preparing to refuel from the *Charlotte Schliemann*. Junker had damaged the British steamer SS *Triona* south of Ceylon during early January and made a single sinking on 26 January west of South Island, Lakshadweep, when he destroyed the American Liberty Ship SS *Walter Camp* with torpedoes. Weeks later, and with no further successful attacks, Junker prepared for his journey to France, the Type IXC-40 U-boat dependent on resupply from the German tanker as its range was insufficient to make the journey unaided.

The two vessels met on 11 February but bad weather prevented the refuelling operation and they sailed southward to a rearranged rendezvous 600 nautical miles distant in search of calmer seas so that the transfer could be completed within the ensuing 72 hours. Apparently Junker communicated his intention to remain surfaced and accompany and repulse any potential attackers from the air during their voyage, but in the periodic blinding squalls that swept across the ocean Junkers lost sight of *Kapitän* Dohmen's *Charlotte Schliemann*.

Unfortunately for Dohmen and his crew a Catalina aircraft sighted their boat, his own lookouts tracking the aircraft and the *Charlotte*

Schliemann altering course to attempt to throw off the pursuit. Aboard *U 532* Junker's lookouts sighted two distant Catalina aircraft, leading the commander to suspect that their rendezvous had been compromised. He radioed his feelings to BdU and received orders to make for a second alternative rendezvous point, where he found no trace of the tanker. Dönitz ordered the revised co-ordinates transmitted to *Charlotte Schliemann* but, ominously, received no reply.

Aboard the tanker a second Catalina sighting had brought all gun crews to readiness as Dohmen manoeuvred once more to attempt to rid himself of the enemy aircraft that remained out of flak range. Ultimately it was to no avail, and during the evening of 11 February *Charlotte Schliemann* was intercepted by a two-ship Royal Navy hunting group sent specifically to attack the tanker network. The destroyer HMS *Relentless* and the cruiser HMS *Newcastle* had been vectored to the meeting point following 'Ultra' decryption of the initial instructions radioed to *U 532*. With seven Catalina aircraft from Mauritius screening them the two warships opened fire, forcing the German tanker to scuttle herself at 0100hrs the next morning by igniting 80kg of stored dynamite. There then followed a test of endurance for the 42 survivors of the shipwrecked crew, as revealed by the recollection of radio officer Alfred Moer:

We wake up between 5.50 and 6.00 a.m. and see in the bright sunshine pieces of wreckage everywhere. A short distance away is a second lifeboat, which is turned upside down with four men sitting on it. The seas wash large quantities of gas oil over me, and already my eyes are burning horribly. I feel I cannot stand this for much longer.

My God! I am sitting in water up to my waist, our own boat is leaking, but we must struggle on and try to get closer to the other upturned boat. Suddenly I jump over and scramble on to its keel. A quick inspection and it looks OK, so we jump into the cold water and attempt to turn the boat over. It isn't easy, but we struggle on and in the end we just manage it. Thank God we find there is some food and a little drinking water left in one of its lockers. Not much, but with rationing it will keep us going for a few days.

We also find a bottle of red wine and we open this to celebrate our success. We sort out the mast and sails and set a course north-north-west, hoping to find one of the Mauritius or Réunion islands. With good winds, we should be able to make it in about fourteen days.

By day we follow the compass and by night we follow the stars. The First Officer, the only mariner on board, becomes the pilot. He sets the watches and gives out the food rations. The men who cannot row because of their injuries have to bail water . . . There are ten men in our lifeboat and someone is constantly on watch. We all hope that, sometime soon, something will show up. Suddenly someone gives a shout, saying he has seen a submarine. The excitement is great and everyone looks in the direction he is pointing, but it's only a piece of wreckage and everyone is distraught.

The terrible heat goes on and on, and our ordeal becomes greater and greater. Our thirst is almost unmanageable, but we dare not distribute any more of our precious water. Our mouths, tongues and lips are covered with a thick crust and we can hardly eat. Our mouths are so dry that when we try to eat a little bread we cannot swallow. To moisten our mouths, we gargle with a little sea-water and then chew the bread quickly and force it down. Sometimes the temptation is too great and I swallow seawater. This brings some relief, but then the thirst comes back stronger than ever.

Then it happens. A wave dashes our helmsman against the tiller and throws him overboard. At the last minute he holds on, and we just manage to pull him back into the boat. Now the sail begins to tear, and we wonder how much longer it will last. We don't care any more, as we are consumed by thirst and there is no room for other feelings.

We don't know any more which is worse, the daytime with the hot sun or the night time when our thin bodies are exposed to the cold. At night, the water which soaks us and the cold feel doubly unpleasant. It is similar when it's raining. On the one hand we are happy because of the additional drinking water, and on the other we start to shiver in the cold.

During the afternoon of the twenty-sixth day, we can hardly stand it any longer. Our limbs are maddeningly painful and our heads feel like they want to break apart. Our last food is handed out, consisting of a small handful of hard breadcrumbs soaked in salt water.

Suddenly someone shouts 'Land ahoy', but nobody believes it. Everyone moans at him and tells him to shut up, even though they would like to believe it. But now, someone else claims to have seen it, and this time our attention is held, our hopes raised. Can it be true?

We are all watching intently . . . there *is* a coastline . . . nobody speaks. Cramp and pain disappear. In this moment, we have even forgotten about our thirst. We are getting closer and closer. Soon we are able to recognise mountains and trees, and in front of them the high surf. Even houses are visible standing above the beach.[9]

The lifeboat had reached the eastern coast of Madagascar, although the survivors believed that they were probably in neutral Portuguese East Africa. Lying at anchor close inshore was the British steamer SS *African Prince*, and at first the Germans were reluctant to take the help offered to them by signalling merchant seamen aboard the steamer, preferring to land in a neutral country if possible rather than become prisoners. However, after finding their access to the beach blocked by strong surf the German survivors clambered painfully aboard the freighter, helped by the British crew and glad to have not attempted the dangerous landing, particularly after discovering that they had reached Allied-occupied Madagascar:

The British had noticed us for some time before we had seen them, and realised we were German, because of our white sail—British lifeboats have red sails—

and had prepared for our arrival. Our eyes grow wide when we see what they have prepared for our reception. On deck are canisters of biscuits and pot after pot of tea and coffee . . . They bring us fresh water and soap and help clean our aching bodies. This is not easy because the sun has burnt the dirt into our skin. We are given a mirror, and my own reflection frightens me. I cannot recognise myself with sunken eyes and body burnt by the sun and gas oil, surrounded by a wild growth of hair. Can this be me?

The British Captain, K. L. [Lt-Cdr] Koile, arrives to see us, and his first words are 'as long as you are on board my ship, you will be treated as ship-wrecked sailors and not POWs.' We are very grateful for this. Our cook and one sailor have fist-sized holes in their backs and are totally exhausted, so they are sent to the ship's hospital for treatment.[10]

A second boat carrying twelve other survivors took four days longer to reach safety before it too landed on Madagascar. Eleven of the men survived the ordeal, one later dying of exhaustion. Two further lifeboats carrying twenty men between them had drifted from sight soon after the sinking and were never seen again

By the time that the second rendezvous had expired, BdU concurred with Junker that the ship had been lost and redirected him to the only other German refuelling ship, *Brake*, which had been hurriedly des-patched to replace *Charlotte Schliemann*. The meeting was set for 11 March at the earliest. Junker himself became the focus of the hunting group, which were vectoring on his radio transmission with their HF/DF—a system still underrated by the German submariners.

On 12 March *U 532* made contact with *Brake*, loaded with fuel, lu-bricating oil and provisions from Singapore, alongside *U 168* and *U 188*. All three boats were eager to refuel and fade away into the expanse of the ocean for their journeys to France. The supply ship's master, *Kapitän* Koelschenbach, was noted by the U-boat commanders as being obvi-ously nervous, unsettled by the surprise sinking of the *Charlotte Schliemann*. His air of uneasy tension pervaded the rendezvous, and soon the crews of all three 'Grey Wolves' were themselves jumpy.

The first to refuel was Lüdden on 11 March, obtaining fuel and sup-plies despite the seas becoming rough enough to cause wastage into the water separating two vessels. *U 188* had been plagued by overheating diesels during the previous weeks and she required considerable quan-tities of lubricating oils from *Brake*. Lüdden had made his final signifi-cant sinking over a month previously, when he torpedoed the 3,798-ton Norwegian SS *Viva*. This attack used the last of the new torpedoes that he had loaded at Penang, and the only 'eels' now remaining aboard

U 188 had originally been taken on board in Lorient some seven months previously and had suffered the predictable degradation by heat and humidity. On 11 February Lüdden was rewarded for his tenacity within the Indian Ocean with the award of the Knight's Cross, receiving notification by radio from Berlin.

The day after receiving his award Lüdden sank three more dhows by ramming. There followed three weeks of uneventful patrolling of the Arabian Sea, broken by *U 188* heading for *Brake*'s position to replenish for the journey westward around the Cape of Good Hope and the perilous crossing of the Atlantic to France.

U 188 departed, her tanks brimming, and the two 2nd U-Flotilla boats took on some of their needed supply before *Brake*'s captain halted the meeting and instructed the two boats to rendezvous a second time in a different location. While *U 532* had taken on all the fuel it needed, it still remained short of lubricating oil. Both boats complied, and it was while beginning their second resupply stop that aircraft from the escort carrier HMS *Battler* sighted the three vessels, their position again betrayed by 'Ultra'. The carrier, supported by the cruisers HMS *Suffolk* and *Newcastle* and destroyers HMS *Roebuck* and *Quadrant*, had been despatched by the Admiralty as 'Cruiser Squadron 4' on Operation 'Covered' to sink the supply ship, risking the discovery of the 'Ultra' breakthrough by again using Enigma codebreaking to achieve tactical advantage. Seven Catalina aircraft from Nos 259 and 265 Squadrons augmented the hunting group, although ultimately it was the carrier's Swordfish aircraft that finally made contact.

Cruiser Squadron 4 had departed Mauritius on 6 March into the face of the same severe weather that was hampering the German resupply operation. The move to the south by *Brake* had been accurately predicted by meteorological staff aboard HMS *Battler*, and the subsequent sighting of the tanker with its U-boat charges in company brought orders for HMS *Roebuck*, the nearest destroyer, to engage. Guided to the enemy by Swordfish aircraft dropping messages aboard the destroyer's deck, *Roebuck* sighted *Brake* at 1116hrs at a range of thirteen miles.

Ten minutes later the British destroyer opened fire. As shells from *Roebuck* began falling on and around her, the German ship's crew scuttled *Brake* while both U-boats dived to safety. Lüdden, some miles distant, recorded the drama in his War Diary:

12/3
1056   Aircraft on port beam.
1128   Two more aircraft on port beam.
1135   Flying boat on starboard quarter.
1210   Smoke cloud bearing 140°. Two aircraft above it.
1219   Gunfire from direction of smoke cloud.
1320   *Brake* sunk.
2358   After *Brake*'s crew taken over by Pich, return passage continued
        according to orders.[11]

Immediately after sinking *Brake*, HMS *Roebuck* retired from the scene and, once the skies and horizon seemed to be free from the British, *Kapitänleutnant* Pich's *U 168* surfaced to begin the rescue of all 135 German crewmen. However, she was chased under by aircraft during the rescue and the U-boat had to plummet like a rock as the LI struggled to maintain trim with so many extra men aboard. A strange scratching noise, as if something had impacted the outer hull, was heard by the sweating crewmen, but other than that they remained unmolested. *U 168* cautiously resurfaced beneath the veil of darkness, hydrophones detecting the clear signature of the enemy destroyers nearby, and, hideously overcrowded, began the return journey with *U 532* to Jakarta. The destruction of the German eastern tankers virtually ensured that neither submarine would ever see France again.

Now even Dönitz could no longer ignore the probability that Enigma had been compromised: two separate but vital ships had been found and sunk within the vastness of the Indian Ocean. As Günter Hessler later wrote, 'Treason, compromise of the U-boat codes or interception of radio traffic to Japan may have been contributory causes, but nothing definite could be established.'[12] Urged by his commanders at sea, Dönitz immediately issued instructions for the current code keys to be discarded as of 13 March and for the 'emergency procedure' of every boat to set the Enigma rotors to match the first letters of the addresses, Christian names and surnames of the boats' chief radio operator and IIIWO (*Obersteuermann*). In Whitehall Churchill was furious that the Enigma secret had been wielded so clumsily by the Royal Navy, although because of the destruction of the two Indian Ocean refuellers the return of three U-boats laden with cargo had been thwarted. The Type IXC-40 *U 183* had also been forced to return, to Penang, for lack of resupply.

On 21 March the first of the three 2nd U-Flotilla boats put into port, *U 183* docking in Penang on that date having sunk a single British ship and damaged a second within the Indian Ocean. *U 168* entered Jakarta three days later, her engines misfiring badly and having consumed every last drop of lubricating oil. She disgorged her passengers from the *Brake* on to the quayside before she underwent repairs to her worn machinery. It was while docked at Tanjung Priok, Jakarta's port, that a massive dent was discovered in the submarine's outer hull—the result of an unexploded depth charge hitting the outer casing.

Fritz Schneewind's meagre run of successes aboard *U 183* had begun with the successful torpedoing of the British MV *Palma*, of the Royal Mail Line, off Galle, Ceylon, on 29 February and continued with another attack on an anchored hulk at Abbu Atoll, south-west of Ceylon. This second target was in fact the floating hulk of the British tanker SS *British Loyalty* that had been damaged by the Japanese midget attack on Diego Suarez in May 1942 and used as storage since October of that year. Schneewind's torpedo attack sank the tanker to the shallow bottom, from where she was later raised and declared a total loss.

NOTES

1. Albrecht Brandi was also awarded the Diamonds in November 1944, although his actual combat achievements had been modest.
2. Norman Franks, *Search, Find and Kill*, pp. 259–61.
3. Wiggins, p. 223, quoted from Peter Marl.
4. Ewerth was almost legendary within the *Kriegsmarine*, an experienced sailor from the Crew of 33 and commander of the *Kriegsmarine*'s first U-boat, *U 1*, during 1935. The attack that sealed his fate came only 25 minutes after a congratulatory radio message from Dönitz informing Ewerth that his wife had just safely been delivered of their fifth child in Germany.
5. The *Zaunkönig* had an acoustic sensor that was designed to home on to the pitch generated by a warship's screws in the water—considerably higher and faster than the low, rhythmic sound of merchant shipping.
6. Brennecke, *Haie im Paradies*, p. 117.
7. US Naval Intelligence collection of survivor's accounts, p. 71.
8. U 188 KTB, 25 January 1944, National Archives Microfilm, PG30175, Roll No 2886.
9. Written account of Alfred Moer; translated by Arthur Binning; sourced at: http://scotland.users.ftech.net/u188p3.htm. Original from Als U-Boot Versorger im Indischen Ozean, SOS, Nr 68, 1955, Arthur Moewig Verlag, München.
10. *Ibid.*
11. U188 KTB, 12 March 1944, National Archives Microfilm, PG30175, Roll No 2886.
12. Günter Hessler, *The U-boat War in the Atlantic*, Vol. III, p. 61.

Seven

The Atlantic Cordon Tightens

T HE CURTAILMENT of all but one of the four U-boat voyages to France with raw materials was an unexpected blow for Dönitz's blockade-running plans. A fifth vessel had also been earmarked for the journey, *UIT 24* departing Penang for France on 8 February 1944. Collectively BdU had redesignated the Italian submarines that were now serving beneath the *Kriegsmarine* flag—both in Malaysia and at Bordeaux—under the codename '*Merkator*', issuing pages of detailed instructions during December 1943 for the perilous scheduled journeys and hammering home the need for discreet communications and secrecy, perhaps having in mind of the relatively junior ranks of many '*Merkator*' officers:

> The most important task is the safe passage of the boat to her port of destination. The following are, therefore, necessary:
>
> Avoid contact with the enemy as much as possible;
>
> Proceed outside the operational areas of our own boats and groups;
>
> Bypass areas with increased enemy sea and air reconnaissance as far as possible, without deviating from route too much;
>
> Deviate from any enemy forces reported.
>
> . . . Always consider when sending messages:
>
> a. How far is Control informed of the situation?
>
> b. What will Control learn from my new situation?
>
> c. Will sending my message prove a disadvantage to other boats here and now? If so, is my message so important that I must take the risk?

    d. What is most important to Control if I decide to make a radio message for special reasons, e.g., short weather report, fuel situation and condition of boat?

    e. After sending my message, have I expressed myself as briefly, and, especially, as clearly as possible, or can I be misunderstood considering what the others know or do not know?[1]

UIT 24 was the first '*Merkator*' boat to attempt to sail from East to West. *Oberleutnant zur See* Heinrich Pahls, ex-IWO of *U 511*, departed Singapore on 2 February loaded with 55 tons of tin as well as an assorted cargo of ten extra tons stowed throughout the boat (and within the torpedo tubes). He sailed first to Penang for a five-day layover while his boat was fitted out and her superstructure packed with 115 tons of rubber, then sailed onwards into the Indian Ocean. The long-range, single-hulled *Marcello* class submarine possessed a range of only 7,500 miles at economical cruising speed and was thus reliant on a scheduled refuelling from *Brake* during March. However, once she was at sea, the disastrous sinking of both surface tankers combined with recurring engine problems aboard *UIT 24* led to her mission being scrubbed as the boat circled in deteriorating weather awaiting beacon messages from first *Charlotte Schliemann* and then *Brake*. The fierce seas battered *UIT 24*, at one point tearing deck planking from the hull and sweeping away the radio antennae, requiring a swiftly rigged replacement in order to receive the expected beacon.

    News of the sinking of both tankers caused great anxiety to Pahls: his boat was dangerously short of fuel and unable either to return or to continue west. Emergency messages from BdU were relayed to *UIT 24* to the effect that refuelling should be made from the similarly aborted *U 532*: the rendezvous was scheduled for 18 March and was met only because the engine-room crew aboard the Italian boat alternated electric and diesel engines in order to extend their range. The two boats met as planned, rigging canvas water hoses through which *U 532* could pass over diesel into the *UIT 24*'s virtually empty tanks. Sharks circled the flimsy hoses that slapped the sea surface, causing the German sailors to shoot some dead in order to distract the others from the canvas. Despite still worsening weather 40 tons of diesel was transferred through the hose, which broke apart more than once, requiring every ounce of skill from the engineers to be sufficiently patched. Both boats then headed east and returned to Penang, where they arrived on 3 April.

Pahls' was the sole Italian boat to begin a crossing from Malaysia to Europe, although in Bordeaux *UIT 22* had put to sea on 26 January bound for the Far East, an earlier sailing on 19 January having been aborted on account of mechanical problems. Commanded by *Oberleutnant der Reserve* Karl Wunderlich, the ex-*Alpino Bagnolini* was a *Liuzzi* class, long-range, double-hulled cruiser, capable of an impressive 13,000-mile sortie—ideal for Dönitz's requirements for a transport submarine to Penang. His was also the only '*Merkator*' boat to remain operational in Bordeaux, the *Calvi* class *UIT 21* having been declared unfit for service and decommissioned in port.[2] Laden with ammunition, *Naxos* radar detector receivers, Enigma keys and spare machine parts for the distant base, *UIT 22* slipped through the escalating level of enemy patrol activity in Biscay and sailed for the Cape of Good Hope, intent on following the suggested sailing route that passed through grid squares CF 67, DG 56, DS 68, FL 19, JJ 45 and KS 35. It was while passing Ascension Island that Wunderlich's good fortune deserted him: his boat was sighted and attacked by an American B-24 Liberator aircraft from VB-107 based on the island. In three separate attack runs the aircraft released six depth charges which splashed into the water alongside and caused severe damage to the Italian boat. One man was killed during the attacks by machine-gun fire from the bomber, a periscope was wrecked and, crucially, a fuel tank was ruptured. Wunderlich reported his damage to BdU, although he assured the authorities that even though his boat had shed 32 tons of fuel into the ocean from the punctured tank he could still reach Penang unaided.

The cruise continued. Wunderlich was ordered to pass over one of his *Naxos* radar detectors to Wilhelm Spahr's inbound *U 178* on or about 11 March as *UIT 22* expected to round the Cape of Good Hope. However, once again the Allies' penetration of the Enigma code net allowed a trap to be set for the two rendezvousing U-boats at their prospective meeting point 600 miles south of Cape Town. *UIT 22* reached the allocated grid co-ordinates on 11 March as planned but soon ran foul of enemy aircraft. As Wunderlich cruised slowly on the surface awaiting Spahr, transmitting position reports to BdU (and thus also, unwittingly, to Bletchley Park) to ensure that the rendezvous was successful, he was sighted by a Catalina of No 262 Squadron which immediately went on to the attack:

The first Cat, under Flt Lt F. T. Roddick, attacked and straddled the vessel twice with depth charges and also fired all guns. The U-boat returned fire, damaging the Cat, which marked the datum with a smoke float. The sub listed to starboard and submerged after twelve minutes. After Flt Lt E. S. S. 'Gar' Nash arrived [in a second Catalina], he patrolled the area in formation with the Cat of Flt Lt A. H. Surridge. Suddenly he sighted the white wash of a U-boat's conning tower breaking the surface one mile ahead. He attacked at once, dropped a stick of six DCs and fired all guns. The sub was straddled, the DCs exploded, and it disappeared. Oil and wreckage came up immediately and spread.

About ten minutes later a mushroom of darker oil welled up and spread. The U-boat did not reappear.[3]

Wunderlich and his entire crew of 42 were lost in the attack, *U 178* reaching the rendezvous fifteen hours later and finding the huge pool of floating oil—the last trace of the Italian-built submarine.

With *UIT 21* decommissioned in Bordeaux and *UIT 22* sunk, the '*Merkator*' group was reduced to three boats, all stationed in the East. *UIT 23*, another *Liuzzi* class boat, was loaded in Singapore during February with cargo destined for Europe, sailing for Penang on 14 February and a final fitting-out with provisions, flak ammunition and fuel for her voyage. (As with the other '*Merkator*' boats, no offensive torpedo armament was carried.) The ex-Italian was under the temporary command of *Oberleutnant zur See* Johannes-Werner Striegler after her previous commander, the unfortunate Heinrich Schäfer, had died in Singapore of a heart attack. Striegler had transferred aboard from *UIT 25*, although he had still not relinquished the previous command for what amounted to a mere transit voyage. It was after one day at sea, and as the boat approached Penang, that disaster struck in the shape of a submerged HMS *Tally Ho!* approaching from the distance. The crew of submariners, largely from *U 511*, had been augmented by men from *Brake* and the raider *Michel* and were scattered across the deck plating as part of standard operational procedure. Enemy submarines had become a plague within the narrow Malaysian waterways, choke-points through which all naval traffic proceeded. With the bare minimum of men below decks, the remainder were relaxing topside wearing life preservers when a single torpedo impacted slightly forward of the conning tower, engulfing the boat in sheets of blinding spray and sending her rapidly, nose-first, to the bottom.

Those blown from the casing struggled through thick upwelling oil as *Tally Ho!*, still submerged, departed. In Penang there was considerable consternation amongst the assembled staff as to the whereabouts of the overdue submarine. Dommes, on the point of officially beginning his tenure as *U-Stützpunkt Leiter* and Penang 'Flotilla Chief' (scheduled to begin in March), conferred with Penang's commander, Kandeler, and the pair quickly ordered one of the Arado 196 aircraft out from Penang in search of *UIT 23*. It did not take long for the struggling survivors to be found in the expanding pool of oil, debris and human remains.

Fourteen men, including Striegler, who had been atop the conning tower at the time, were clustered together as the Arado circled low overhead, landing nearby as the German pilot hatched an improvised plan of rescue. The aircraft could not accommodate all fourteen men—in fact there was no room at all for any passengers aboard the small floatplane— and so five men at a time lashed themselves securely to the aircraft's floats and the Arado, soon joined by another, began shuttling them to Penang. Unorthodox though this was, all fourteen men reached the base safely, though 31 others were entombed in their boat below the waters of the Malacca Strait.

The remaining two '*Merkator*' boats would see little action after February 1944, *UIT 24* and *UIT 25* having been relegated to the unsung, though vital, task of shuttling supplies between Japan and South-East Asia for the remainder of the war.[4] An agreement had been reached between Germany and Japan whereby the two boats would carry food from the abundant plantations of South-East Asia to Japan to provide for European nationals both stranded and stationed there and return to Singapore with war *matériel* from the mainland for primarily Japanese use. Striegler immediately resumed command of *UIT 25*. He and his engineering crew struggled to keep the boat in operational trim, on one occasion becoming stranded for hours drifting off Java with a pair of blown cylinder-head gaskets before makeshift repairs enabled the boat to return to Singapore.

From Europe further departures of supply and combat boats had been made from harbours in both France and Germany. The unusual Type VIIF *U 1062*, commanded by *Oberleutnant zur See* Karl Albrecht, had slipped from Kiel on the first leg of her inaugural patrol on 18 December 1943. The elongated hull of the Type VIIF housed 31 torpedoes destined for the Penang base, including ten of the new TV *Zaunkönig* acoustic torpedoes. Albrecht had worked his way up from the ranks to take command of the new boat, having begun his U-boat career as

Steuermann aboard *U 19* during 1936, thirteen years after joining the Navy.

The issue of supply at sea had once again proved crucial to German decision-making. During 1941 Germany's naval supply network had first been devastated by the Royal Navy in the wake of the *Bismarck* sinking after the location of the surface tankers had been betrayed by broken Enigma messages and careless radio chatter, allowing HF/DF to pinpoint the vital ships. Dönitz had then frantically ordered supply submarines to be constructed, to enable his U-boats to spend longer at sea in action or to extend their patrol radii. While the new Type XIV supply boat could provide fuel, food and other basic supplies to combat U-boats, the large *Milchkuh* had enough storage only for four extra torpedoes, causing Dönitz to in turn demand a new boat to carry the ammunition necessary for total resupply at sea. He decided to use the trusted Type VIIC basic design, which followed the example of the VIID minelayer by adding a 10.5m section aft of the conning tower. Inside this new area would be enough stowage space for 24 extra torpedoes to be carried, stacked in six columns of four, three columns each side of the boat's centreline. An additional torpedo loading hatch abaft the stowage space allowed access to the weapons for loading and removal. Like the Type VIID, the VIIF benefited from the additional room by having two extra bunks and a pair of refrigerated food lockers; again as in the VIID, there was additional fuel and ballast bunkerage within the extended saddle tanks and main hull.

Four VIIFs (*U 1059–U 1062*) had been ordered from *Germaniawerft* on 22 August 1941 and the first, *U 1059*, was launched on 12 March 1943. However, by this stage of the war the U-boats had lost their advantage and the idea of tortuously long surface transfers of torpedoes was unrealistic in the face of Allied air power, which was smothering virtually the entire Atlantic. The VIIF retained the original weaponry of the Type VIIC and was soon put to work on long-range supply missions. Its performance was improved over the Type VIID as the boat's beam had been increased to match the extra length, raising her seaworthiness.

Originally two of the boats that had been put into service—*U 1060* and *U 1061*—were used to run supplies around Norway before three of the four (*U 1059*, *U 1060* and *U 1062*) were earmarked during 1943 and 1944 for torpedo transport missions to Penang to supply the large Type IXC/40 and Type IXD2s stationed there.[5] By the time *U 1062* had left Germany as the first of the trio destined for Malaysia it had already endured the attentions of enemy aircraft.

On 14 May 1943 the American Eighth Air Force launched a major daylight raid directed at the U-boat industry, attacking Kiel's Deutsche Werke and Germaniawerft shipyards with 126 bombers. Within the latter yards there was considerable damage, two U-boats being sunk and the conning tower of *U 1061* suffering a direct hit. The adjacent *U 1062*, launched only six days previously, also sustained bomb damage. Delivery of the new boats was thus delayed and *U 1062* was not commissioned until 19 June.

As Albrecht took his boat north toward Norway he once again fell foul of enemy aircraft, coming under fire from eight Beaufighters of Nos 144 and 404 Squadrons. Four of the formidable aircraft from No 144 Squadron carried torpedoes, the remaining four being armed as antiflak protection. At 1132hrs on 22 December *U 1062* was sighted sailing on the surface in the wake of a destroyer escort by the aircraft that were flying a 'Rover' patrol at low altitude above a rough sea. Beaufighter 'B', piloted by Fg Off. S. R. Cooke, made the first torpedo attack on *U 1062*, dropping the weapon at a range of 800yds and peppering the conning tower with heavy-calibre cannon fire. Albrecht managed to evade the torpedo as his gun crews put up a heavy fire against their attackers, joined by flak weapons aboard the destroyer and also on the nearby Norwegian coast. Two more aircraft dived into the attack, again hosing cannon fire on to the struggling U-boat, which killed one man and seriously wounded two others. Then No 404 Squadron aircraft 'H' was hit and spiralled straight into the sea. Another Beaufighter, 'F', was also hit and was seen to crash headlong into the waves, although Albrecht claimed only one 'kill'. Buffeted by the fierce gunfire, the remaining Beaufighters broke off their attack and *U 1062* was left to limp into Bergen for repair.

Albrecht sailed again on 3 January 1944, successfully making the crossing without serious impediment and arriving at Penang on 19 April, 29 torpedoes intact within the rust-streaked hull. Only hours from port, however, he had been ordered to jettison the ten *Zaunkönig* torpedoes from his cargo rather than allow the Japanese to see them, once again confusing the German sailors as to the trustworthiness of their Oriental allies. It was only a matter of two weeks later that Dönitz rescinded this peculiar order and allowed the *Zaunkönig* to be taken into port.

Worryingly, Albrecht reported constant enemy aerial activity over grid squares LO and LP 50 to the west of Malaysia, a development that threatened potential handicaps to future operations within the Indian Ocean. Reinforced by reports of strong enemy air patrols within the region, BdU ordered a new approach routed for Penang effective as of 14 July 1944, and similar new approach channels to Jakarta were established five days later.

Albrecht's was the only one of four U-boats that put to sea for the East during January 1944 to reach port unscathed. *UIT 22* was sunk in March, by which time *U 177*, which had sailed from La Pallice on 2 January, had also been destroyed. Robert Gysae was no longer at the helm when *U 177* put to sea for the Indian Ocean once more; instead *Korvettenkapitän* Heinz Buchholz, formerly with *U 195*, was in command and his style of leadership differed enormously. Whereas Gysae had demonstrated an affinity for both the complexities of effective seamanship and leadership of men, Buchholz appears to have relied more heavily on harsh discipline to instil loyalty within his men. Buchholz was no stranger to command, having held the post of Flotilla Chief for Brest's 1st U-Flotilla for five months during 1942 before taking on *U 195*. However, his constant gun drills and heavy practice routine stoked great resentment within his boat, the inharmonious relationship dividing the crew between officers and seamen. Unfortunately for *U 177* the daily emergency gun drills appeared to have dulled the senses of the lookouts and flak crew and *U 177* was surprised on 6 February by an American B-24 Liberator bomber of Ascension Island's VB-107, which had been able to get within a mile of the surfaced boat in good visibility before being spotted. As the alarm klaxons shrilled through *U 177* and Buchholz was making his way hastily to the bridge, his boat was bracketed by accurate depth charges, the explosions fracturing the hull and sending the veteran submarine slowly underwater. The majority of the crew went down with her: of the 60 men aboard, only ten were later rescued and made prisoners-of-war.

On 18 January 1944 another new Type IXD2 put out from Kiel, soon to sail into probably the most infamous and controversial U-boat confrontation with a merchant ship of the Second World War. *Kapitän-leutnant* Heinz-Wilhelm Eck, a 27-year-old native of Hamburg, took *U 852* into action for her inaugural patrol after nearly ten years of naval service. He had entered the *Reichsmarine* on 8 April 1934, receiving his commission as a *Leutnant zur See* a week short of three years later. His voluntary U-boat service had begun in 1942 when he was assigned as a commander-in-training aboard *U 124*, the 2nd U-Flotilla boat commanded by a classmate of the Crew of 34, Joachim Mohr, who took up his own captaincy of *U 852* during June 1942 as his vessel was in construction. *U 852* was commissioned into the *Kriegsmarine* on 15 June 1943, gruelling months of shakedown trials and exercises following before the boat was cleared for operations, transferred to the combat roster of the 12th U-Flotilla and sailed for Penang.

It was while undergoing briefings for his forthcoming voyage that Eck received repeated warnings of the perils of enemy air power, particularly within the narrow 'waist' of the Atlantic between Freetown and Natal—an area increasingly dominated by aircraft based on Ascension Island. The first to brief Eck was *Korvettenkapitän* Adalbert 'Adi' Schnee, erstwhile 'ace' commander of *U 201*, crewmate of Eck's and holder of the Knight's Cross with Oak Leaves. Schnee drummed home the message that the Type IXD2 was the most cumbersome and slowest-diving boat in service and thus particularly vulnerable to air attack, a fact borne out by knowledge that the previous four such U-boats that had sailed into this region had been lost. He warned him of the perils near Ascension and that wreckage could remain on the surface and be recognised as traces of U-boat attack 'for the next few days' following any sinking. This message was reinforced by a similar briefing from another 'ace' ashore, *Fregattenkapitän* Günter Hessler, and last of all by *Korvettenkapitän* Karl-Heinz Moehle. The latter also reminded Eck of Dönitz's instructions regarding the 17 September 1942 so-called 'Laconia Order' and of what had happened to Hartenstein's *U 156* during the tragic sinking and its aftermath.

Eck sailed from Germany acutely aware of the dangers of his passage to the Indian Ocean and took nearly two months to reach the Equator after travelling mainly submerged and surfacing only at night to recharge depleted batteries. It was during the evening of 13 March 1944 while undertaking one such surface run that lookouts aboard *U 852* sighted a steamer ahead and to starboard. The U-boat approached to within 500 miles north of Ascension Island and Eck ordered course laid to pursue the distant target. Two and a half hours later Eck launched a surfaced torpedo attack, two 'eels' striking the doomed ship with what Eck recorded as 'very impressive' detonations.

The target was the Greek steamer SS *Peleus*, bound in ballast from Freetown to the River Plate under charter by the British War Transportation Commission. The 6,659-ton ship staggered under the dual impacts in No 2 and immediately abaft No 3 holds and straightaway began to sink, many of the 35 crewmen being unable to escape in time. Among the scattered survivors was Chief Officer Antonios Liossis, who had been knocked unconscious by the blast and hurled from the bridge into the sea and was then revived by the cool water and managed to swim towards a raft alongside seaman Dimitrios Konstantinides. Another survivor, Rocco Said, later stated that it was 'clear [that] the ship would sink immediately'. Few of the swimming survivors had time to don lifebelts, instead clinging to pieces of floating wreckage and what few liferafts had drifted clear of the sinking wreck.

Eck nosed *U 852* amongst the scattered debris and ordered his LI, *Kapitänleutnant (Ing.)* Heinz Lenz, to the bridge to interrogate survivors. Lenz spoke English and correspondingly walked to the U-boat's bow to ask their victim's name, cargo and destination, for confirmation within the KTB. By this stage the Officer of the Watch, IWO *Oberleutnant zur See* George Colditz, two enlisted lookouts and Eck had been joined atop the conning tower by the IIWO, *Leutnant zur See* August Hoffmann, and the ship's Medical Officer, *Oberstabsarzt* Walter Weisspfennig, who merely wanted to see what was happening. Lenz called to a nearby raft that held four men—the *Peleus*'s Third Officer, Agis Kephalas, a greaser named Stavros Sogias, a Russian seaman by the distinctly un-Russian name of Pierre Neuman and an unidentified Chinese seaman. Lenz beckoned the Greek Third Officer to come aboard *U 852*, where he was asked the routine questions. Kephalas giving truthful replies to Lenz, who by now had been joined by Hoffmann—who also spoke English. Kephalas also volunteered the information that another, slower ship was following and Lenz helped him back aboard the liferaft, informing the four men that they would no doubt be rescued by the British the following day. Lenz reported his findings to Eck as *U 852* cruised slowly away, his captain dismissing claims of a second steamer as 'too much of a good thing'. A discussion now ensued amongst Eck, Lenz and Colditz about their immediate course of action, the other pair of officers standing nearby but not partaking in the conversation. Eck stated that he was concerned at the amount of betraying wreckage that remained at the site of the sinking, mindful of his briefings in Germany. He reasoned that aircraft on routine patrol from either Freetown or Ascension were sure to spot the debris, triggering an extensive hunt for *U 852*, which, even if run at full surfaced speed, would only reach a distance of 200 miles from the scene. Within minutes (according to the accepted version of events) Eck had decided that he would have to destroy all traces of the Greek steamer and ordered machine guns brought to the bridge as Lenz and Colditz argued with their captain about the wisdom of his decision. Eck dismissed their protests, stating that the destruction of the floating debris was an 'operational necessity' to protect *U 852* from being found.

What ensued remains the only documented account of a U-boat firing on survivors in the water during the Second World War. Eck ordered the two machine guns mounted on the '*Wintergarten*'s stern railings, one to starboard the other to port. Lenz went below while Eck ordered the guns manned and ready to fire. It is fairly certain that he never ordered the survivors specifically to be killed, although the natural assumption would be that the destruction of the liferafts would achieve the death of their occupants. Eck reasoned that the liferafts, in particular, were mounted on hollow floats and would immediately sink if pierced. He was wrong. Eck ordered the starboard machine gun manned by the Medical Officer, Weisspfennig, who opened fire as the dark, drifting shapes of the rafts hove once more into view. After only a few rounds his weapon jammed. Hoffmann cleared the breech and took over the trigger. Bullets arced into the darkness and pandemonium erupted in the rafts as men were hit, both those on the debris and those in the water, Liossis later remembering Kostantinidis crying out in pain and doubling over into the raft's bottom, where he died. Hoffmann continued to fire sporadically at the rafts. They refused to sink, and Eck then ordered the U-boat closer to investigate why. It transpired that, rather than being mounted on hollow floats, they were filled with buoyant material. Hoffmann soon changed to the twin 2cm flak weapons in an attempt to destroy the wreckage by blasting it to pieces. Still achieving nothing, however, Eck ordered hand grenades brought up from below and Hoffmann proceeded to throw them at rafts, killing more of the helpless merchant seamen and wounding Liossis in the back with shrapnel.

Below decks only Lenz was aware of the significance of the shooting, although as *U 852* continued her macabre mission the lookouts were changed, the two pale seamen who came below from the bridge soon telling of Eck's deeds. Colditz, who had taken no part in the killing, came below as well, replaced as watch officer by Hoffmann, who was still engaged in firing at the rafts. One of the newly enlisted lookouts, *Matrosenobergefreiter* Wolfgang Schwender, was ordered by Eck to man the port-side machine gun and he too began to fire at the clustered debris. At this point one of the most bizarre twists to the story appears. Schwender also suffered a blockage in his machine gun, and as he cleared it Lenz came back to the bridge from below and shoved the seaman away from his gun, taking over the task of firing himself. His later rationale for this strange act was that Schwender was not a 'satisfactory seaman'. He felt that the Greek officer he had questioned may have been on the raft that Schwender fired at and he did not want him 'hit and killed by bullets fired by a soldier who, in my view, was bad'. If he were to die, it would be at the hands of an honourable man.

By 0100hrs *U 852* had been at the scene for nearly five hours, also attempting to destroy wreckage by ramming. The immediate goal had failed utterly and debris still floated on the lazy swell, surrounded by bodies of men cut down and virtually torn to pieces by bullets, cannon shells and shrapnel. Finally, and with dawn only hours away, Eck abandoned his attempt and ordered guns stowed, and *U 852* sailed off at full surfaced speed. Behind them four men still lived, although only three—Liossis, Said and seaman Dimitrios Argiros—survived to be rescued after 35 days by the Portuguese steamer SS *Alexandre Silva*.

Despite his rationale that he was firing at the rafts and not the men, Eck had committed a war crime, and several officers and seamen were guilty by association in the terrible attack on the *Peleus*'s survivors. Morale on board *U 852* plummeted as word of the massacre rapidly spread, and Eck was obliged to address the crew to explain why he had done what he had done—although this failed to alleviate the mood of the crew. *U 852* escaped from the scene to continue her southward journey. Eck had transmitted a short message to BdU relating the sinking of the *Peleus*, but British HF/DF detected the Morse signals and followed the boat's general progress towards the Indian Ocean. On 1 April *U 852* torpedoed and sank the SS *Dahomian*, the survivors later being rescued by South African minesweepers after remaining unmolested. *U 852* then entered the Indian Ocean under intensifying pressure from enemy aircraft. The sinking of the *Dahomian* was the first in South African waters since August 1943 and a strong ASW group was assigned the hunt.

Eck escaped once more and, after unsuccessfully lingering near Cape Town, proceeded north towards Somalia. Regular radio reports were intercepted by British HF/DF, and finally, on 2 May 1944, RAF Wellingtons from No 621 Squadron, based in Aden, were despatched to find *U 852*. The boat was eventually located as she travelled, surfaced, shortly after dawn. Hoffmann had the bridge watch as the British bombers streaked from out of the sun and strafed and bombed *U 852*, and the Germans were taken completely by surprise. The boat frantically attempted to dive as six depth charges straddled her, causing severe damage as she plummeted downwards. Flooding threatened to engulf the boat, which soon suffered the deadly threat of chlorine gas from cracked battery cells as acid spilled into the bilges. *U 852* rocketed back to the surface, whereupon the Wellington bombers continued their attacks. As the flak crews raced for their weapons, British bullets slashed across the conning tower, killing two men, one of them IWO Colditz. *U 852* lay down by the stern and Eck knew that his boat was lost. More men succumbed to the strafing bombers' attacks but the German flak managed to keep them at bay sufficiently that Eck was able to head for the Somali coast. He could not save his boat, but he could at least try to save his crew by beaching the wrecked U-boat.

Hours later and still under attack, *U 852* ground on to the bottom next to Somalia's barren coast and the remaining Germans abandoned ship, under fire as they struggled, unarmed, through the water to the shore. A Royal Navy landing party, supported by a unit of the Somaliland Camel Corps, captured the 59 survivors the following day. Eck had unsuccessfully attempted to blow up the shattered boat but the hulk, listing to port against the coast, yielded invaluable information to British investigators. More damning for Eck was the fact that, although he had destroyed his Enigma and cipher material, the boat's KTB was found still aboard, revealing that *U 852* had been responsible for the massacre of *Peleus*'s survivors, who had since told their story to British naval authorities. By June 1944 Eck, Lenz, Hoffmann, Weisspfennig and Schwender were under arrest for murder, although their trial was postponed until Germany's defeat lest Hitler order a retaliatory trial of captured Allied servicemen. Thus on 16 October 1945 the five men were charged with having committing war crimes. Eck, Hoffmann and Weisspfennig were sentenced to death after a four-day trial, while Lenz and Schwender received prison sentences. On 30 November 1945 three more crewmen from *U 852* were added to the boat's casualty list as the capital sentence was carried out by firing squad.[6]

Despite the heinous nature of the crime committed by Eck in his exaggerated compliance with operational orders, debate continues to rage over the validity of the death sentences. Similar accounts of firing at survivors by the submarines USS *Wahoo* and HMS *Torbay*, and by British destroyers at Narvik, among others, remain unanswered to this day; moreover, the sentences handed out to Eck and his officers were almost a foregone conclusion at the time of the trial. The defence that Eck ordered the destruction of wreckage, not the deliberate shooting of survivors, fell short of explaining his actions. Strenuous attempts were made by the prosecuting counsel to make Eck claim that Dönitz had ordered the killing of survivors, either specifically or by implication in compliance with the 'Laconia Order'—a charge that could have allowed Eck to live but one that the young captain steadfastly (and properly) refused on all grounds. Eck's legacy is one of confusion over his appalling act and his bizarre interpretation of orders, as well as one of fiercely divided opinion over whether the trial was an example of *Siegerjustiz* (Victor's Justice).[7] Many who knew Eck before and during the war remember him as quite 'soft and sentimental'. Their point of view reveals an alternative chain of events to those quoted above, holding that Eck was under the influence of junior officers who possessed perhaps more ardour for the National Socialist doctrine and its demands for 'total war'. Regardless of Eck's motivation for his tragic misjudgement, he, as captain of a fighting vessel, was ultimately responsible for its conduct—a responsibility he did not shirk during his subsequent imprisonment and trial.

During Eck's gruesome and ultimately doomed voyage, ten more U-boats had departed from Europe bound for the Far East after action in the Indian Ocean, although, because of effective aerial patrolling that dramatically hampered U-boat penetration of the South Atlantic, six of the ten were destroyed, four of them failing to even reach the Cape of Good Hope. The first to fall foul of the enemy was *U 1059*, another Type VIIF that had been despatched from Germany to Penang. She sailed from Kiel on 4 February and lasted less than two months at sea. On 19 March *Oberleutnant* Günter Leupold had stopped for a swimming break west-south-west of the Cape Verde Islands, an extremely hazardous undertaking at that stage of the war. In an extremely unprepared state—Leupold, his IIWO and LI, as well as fifteen other men were splashing about in the water—his boat was sighted by aircraft from the escort carrier USS *Block Island*, which had been vectored into the area after 'Ultra' intercepts of a refuelling rendezvous with *Milchkuh U 488*.[8] A Wildcat immediately strafed the boat as German crewmen raced for their flak weapons, all but one of those in the water managing to scramble back on board before the first bullets arrived. An Avenger piloted by Lt N. T. Dowty dived to the attack and managed to drop two depth charges astride the U-boat before anti-aircraft fire smashed into his cockpit, killing Dowty and sending the Avenger into the sea. The depth-charge detonations caused a sympathetic explosion of some of the 39 torpedoes aboard *U 1059* and the boat lifted from the water, breaking in two and sliding beneath the waves. The sole survivor of the Avenger's crew, Ensign Fitzgerald, swam away from the wreckage of his aircraft and inflated a small dinghy, aboard which he clambered. He later assisted a badly wounded German sailor from the sea into another liferaft that had been dropped by an Avenger as more survivors climbed on to the rafts. Fitzgerald applied a tourniquet on his wounded companion's leg and treated other wounds suffered by the Germans, including a severe gash to Leupold's knee, keeping the German survivors initially under control by wielding both a knife and .38 pistol over them. Eventually spirits mellowed and the men clustered together in the two lifeboats to await rescue. Later that day the destroyer USS *Corey* rescued Fitzgerald and eight German survivors, including Leupold. Leupold's rash decision to allow a swimming break for his men had cost him his boat and most of his crew their lives. The days when German U-boat men could bathe

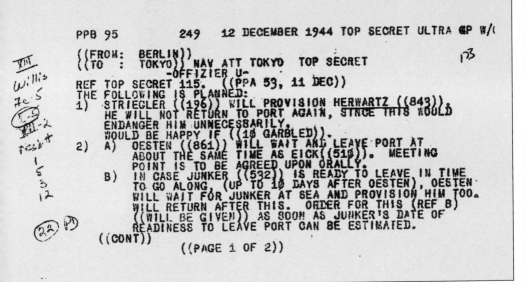

((FROM: BERLIN))
((TO : TOKYO)) NAV ATT TOKYO TOP SECRET
                    -OFFIZIER U-
REF TOP SECRET 115. ((PPA 53, 11 DEC))
THE FOLLOWING IS PLANNED:
1) STRIEGLER ((196)) WILL PROVISION HERWARTZ ((843)),
    HE WILL NOT RETURN TO PORT AGAIN, SINCE THIS WOULD
    ENDANGER HIM UNNECESSARILY.
    WOULD BE HAPPY IF ((10 GARBLED)).
2) A) OESTEN ((861)) WILL WAIT AND LEAVE PORT AT
        ABOUT THE SAME TIME AS EICK ((510)). MEETING
        POINT IS TO BE AGREED UPON ORALLY.
    B) IN CASE JUNKER ((532)) IS READY TO LEAVE IN TIME
        TO GO ALONG, (UP TO 10 DAYS AFTER OESTEN), OESTEN
        WILL WAIT FOR JUNKER AT SEA AND PROVISION HIM TOO.
        WILL RETURN AFTER THIS. ORDER FOR THIS (REF B)
        ((WILL BE GIVEN)) AS SOON AS JUNKER'S DATE OF
        READINESS TO LEAVE PORT CAN BE ESTIMATED.
((CONT))
          ((PAGE 1 OF 2))

Above: The Germans' Achilles' heel: 'Ultra' decryption of the Enigma code network. Messages such as this, intercepted and decoded in December 1944, provided extremely accurate intelligence estimates to be drawn by Allied naval planners. Messages were often so detailed that U-boats were sunk with successful ambushes laid directly as a result of 'Ultra'. (Jürgen Oesten)

Below: The wide sweep of the Type IXD2's deck can be seen from this photograph. In the foreground two yellow bands have been painted to allow identification by friendly Japanese aircraft. The forward torpedo-loading hatch is open and the winch is ready for use. (Jürgen Oesten)

Above left: The Type IX U-boats had such a wide deck that a small cradle was used for exterior torpedo transfers. Here a reload is withdrawn from its port-side storage container on to the gurney that ran along fixed rails. (Jürgen Oesten)

Above right: Once the torpedo had been moved from the stowage area to the loading hatch it could be tipped and lowered to the U-boat's interior torpedo room—not an operation to be undertaken if there was a possibility of an air attack. (Jürgen Oesten)

Left: Makeshift repairs were often carried out during the long patrols within the Indian Ocean. Here a crew member with lead-soled shoes is lowered over the side of a Type IXD2 to carry out a check on suspected damage to the hull. Generally other armed crewmen would keep lookout for sharks in these warm waters.

Right: Portrait of a U-boat man: *Obersteuermann* Berthold Wendelmuth photographed aboard *U 861* outbound from Europe. (Jürgen Oesten)

Below: Despite its size, the conning tower of a Type IXD2 could still appear crowded. Here two men sit upon the *Bachstelze* platform, while in the foreground crewmen are flanked by twin 2cm flak weapons. At left is the dipolar antenna head, with the well for the U-boat's attack periscope visible below. (Jürgen Oesten)

eft, upper: Arrival in Singapore. It was here that heavy work was undertaken on U-boats, including the ▸ading and unloading of material stored inside their keels. (Jürgen Oesten)

eft, lower: *Kapitänleutnant* Jürgen Oesten after his arrival at Singapore. He and his crew had already ▸ad an opportunity to spruce up both their own personal appearance and that of their boat at Penang ▸efore transferring to Singapore. (Jürgen Oesten)

▸bove and below: Mixed Japanese and German welcoming committees were always on hand to bring ▸rriving U-boats into port. (Jürgen Oesten)

Left: Among the guests to board *U 861* in harbour was this rather unusual one—a small monkey. (Jürgen Oesten)

Below: Crew chief *Bootsmaat* Max Schley and two Japanese naval personnel photographed during *U 861*'s overhaul. Many German engineers harboured anxieties about the presence of their Japanese counterparts aboard their boats, although there is no evidence of that in this photograph. (Jürgen Oesten)

Above: Enjoying *terra firma* once more, Jürgen Oesten (right) and Wilhelm Dommes (centre) take a stroll with the rest of *U 861* 's officers. (Jürgen Oesten)

Right, upper: Oesten photographed with *Taisa* Fujii, his Japanese liaison officer. (Jürgen Oesten)

Right, lower: Fresh food—often of different varieties from that available in Germany—was one of the most welcome aspects of landfall after long voyages from Europe. U-boat personnel received some of the best rations available to the *Wehrmacht*, and those serving on board the Far Eastern boats were no exception. (Jürgen Oesten)

Left, top: Oesten's relationship with his Japanese hosts was always cordial and often better than that. (Jürgen Oesten)
Left, centre: The German officers' billet on Gilstead Road in Singapore. (Jürgen Oesten)
Left, bottom: All the U-boat rest areas were opulent—the remains of the area's British and Dutch colonial past. (Jürgen Oesten)
Right, upper: This photograph is perhaps more telling of some of the frustrations experienced by Germans working alongside the Japanese military. While a mixed group of naval personnel have assembled (at right) to welcome an incoming U-boat, the two men at left are from the Japanese Army. The bollard on which one of them sits belongs to the Army: therefore he will not relinquish his seat—or even acknowledge the incoming Germans—lest naval personnel attempt to use what is the Army's territory. (Jürgen Oesten)
Right, lower: *UIT 24* inbound to Penang, 3 April 1944. This Italian submarine had been seized by the IJN in 1943 on Italy's surrender and later handed over for *Kriegsmarine* use.

Left: This close-up view of the conning tower of *UIT 24* shows that strange mix of German and Italian equipment with which the reconfigured transport boats were equipped. *UIT 24* was the first '*Merkator*' boat to attempt to sail from East to West, but her mission was scrubbed after the Indian Ocean tankers were sunk by Allied attack.

Below: Two Type XB U-boats — the largest built by the *Kriegsmarine*—were also assigned transport duties to the Far East. The size of the Type XB can be gauged by this photograph of one next to a Type VIIC in Germany during the boats' working-up trials.

Right, upper: In Penang and the other Eastern ports the German crews undertook most work on their boats. Local men were drafted for more menial labouring, and an armed guard from the crew was always on watch. (Jürgen Oesten)

Right, lower: Two German sailors examine the wares of a Malaysian market place. The national cockade was a part of the walking-out dress for U-boat men, prominently displayed on the left breast of their white shirts. (Jürgen Oesten)

Below: A Japanese submarine is provisioned in Singapore (right) while men from a German U-boat observe (left). The U-boat is a Type IXC of the 2nd U-Flotilla, its flotilla emblem visible on the conning tower front beneath the extended canvas awning.

Left, top: The heat of South-East Asia was a new experience to the majority of German crewmen and makeshift canvas awnings became commonplace to provide some shade in which to rest. (Jürgen Oesten)

Left, centre: Making the most of a brief break during their work, German submariners lie where they can to rest aboard their U-boat. (Jürgen Oesten)

Left, bottom: Local transport was used to ferry equipment and men about Penang dockyard. Here *Bootsmaat* Max Schley rides as passenger with a Malaysian driver. (Jürgen Oesten)

Right: For *U 861*'s return to Europe every inch of storage space was used for cargo, including the exterior torpedo canisters, seen being loaded here with blocks of raw rubber. (Jürgen Oesten)

Below: 'Freight coachmen are also necessary. Most important thing is: Always hold up the flag of ideals. Penang base wishes a happy homecoming in a victorious Germany': *U 861* prepares to depart for Europe on her home run, the Guest Book recording the moment for posterity. (Jürgen Oesten)

Top: Another German-Japanese garden party: in this photograph Dommes (facing away from camera in centre) is introducing *Kapitänleutnant* Heinrich 'Tute' Timm (left of Dommes) to his new hosts. (U-Boot Archiv)

Above: When traversing the waterways that flanked Malaysia, the majority of crew were ordered on deck with lifejackets. However, even the threat of enemy submarines could not prevent men enjoying the warmer water than that experienced in Europe. (Jürgen Oesten)

Right: *U 843* approaching another U-boat in the distance— possibly *U 181* —during their homeward voyages. This photograph was developed in 1958 after the film was found aboard the wreck of *U 843* when it was raised from the Kattegat. *(RNSM)*

Below: *Kapitänleutnant* Heinz-Wilhelm Eck's *U 852* lies wrecked and beached on the Somalian coast. It was the end of a cruise that had witnessed the U-Boat Service's only accurately documented war crime. *(RNSM)*

Left, upper: Happy to be approaching port: petty officers aboard *U 861* relax for the camera while approaching Penang in 1944. (Jürgen Oesten)

Left, lower: Pleased to have reached Norway: *Kapitän-leutnant* Jürgen Oesten (in white cap) talks with flotilla chief *Korvettenkapitän* Günther Kuhnke after *U 861*'s arrival at Trondheim, 19 April 1945. His was one of only four U-boats successfully to complete the wartime round-trip between Europe and the Far East. (Jürgen Oesten) with impunity within the 'Atlantic gap' beyond the range of Allied air power had ended months before.

Interestingly, particularly in the light of Eck's experience, Leupold, an avowed anti-Nazi, later made some astonishing claims to US interrogators, recorded by the American intelligence officers:

> Prior to departure from Kiel, Leupold had an interview with K. K. Oskar Moehle . . . In the course of issuing orders for the patrol, Moehle transmitted to Leupold specific oral orders from the Admiral commanding U-boats [Godt] that if any ships were sunk, all survivors were to be exterminated. When . . .[Leupold] expressed surprise and indignation at such an order, Moehle told him that it was a positive order from the commander-in-chief [Dönitz] and was a part of the total war that was now being waged.[9]

Dönitz had long resisted calls by Hitler to order the killing of survivors, and evidence such as Leupold's testimony to the Americans perhaps pointed to a harsh interpretation of instructions such as the 'Laconia Order', given through the words of Oskar Moehle, rather than strictly literal BdU orders. This sort of 'interpretation' would occur once more during the Allied invasion of Normandy with the apparent issuing by FdU West of the so-called 'Ramming Order'. Similar debate continues to this day about the validity of claims made by several U-boat veterans that they were ordered by BdU to ram their submarines into Allied landing ships as part of a 'total commitment' to the action.[10]

The next to fall was *Korvettenkapitän* Hannes Weingärtner's *U 851*, missing in unknown circumstances after making her final position report to BdU on 27 March. BdU listed the boat as missing from 8 June, although British speculation of the date of loss as some time during the last three days of March seem to be more likely. Weingärtner, a pre-war veteran of U-boat service and Flotilla Chief of the 24th U-Training Flotilla, had achieved nothing during his inaugural combat mission.

An earlier departure, *U 843*, which had slipped from Lorient on 10 February, managed to dodge Allied hunter-killer and patrol groups and reached Jakarta, and the three U-boats despatched from Europe after *U 851* also slipped through the stiffening cordon. *U 196* departed La Pallice on 11 March and *U 181* five days later, both boats reaching Penang during August, *U 181* on the 8th of the month and *U 196* two days later. The third of the successful trio, *U 537*, had sailed from Lorient on 25 March and reached Jakarta on 2 August. The successes enjoyed by these three boats, such as they were, can only be described as meagre, amounting to a confirmed total only five ships totalling 30,323 tons, with both machines and men worn to exhaustion by the arduous voyages.

However, although relatively unsuccessful, the trio at least survived a stiffening Allied defensive and offensive presence in the Atlantic. The four U-boats that followed were not so fated, all falling to enemy forces while en route to the East. The first to depart was *U 1224*, crewed by Japanese sailors and a legacy of the successful Japanese supply missions to France. The Type IXC-40 U-boat had been handed over to the Imperial Japanese Navy on 15 February, officially commissioned into her new branch of service thirteen days later and renumbered *RO-501*, and was known to the *Kriegsmarine* as *Marco Polo II*. The boat was crewed by 48 Japanese sailors who had been brought aboard the Type J3 *I-8* during September 1943 when the blockade-breaking submarine arrived in France. *I-8* had left Kure in company with *I-10* and the tender *Hie Maru* on 1 June 1943, bound for Lorient on a *Yanagi* mission. She was the second Japanese submarine after *I-30* to be given such a task and her cargo included two Type 95 'Long Lance' torpedoes, drawings of an automatic trim system, Type 95 submarine torpedo tubes and a new model Japanese naval reconnaissance plane. *Chusa* Sninji Uchino also carried *Shosa* Norita Sadatoshi and the spare crew aboard his massive submarine (Norita scheduled to assume command of *U 1224*) as well four translators and code clerks, a *Shosa* medical officer and a technical *Chusa* expert on torpedo boat engines. With approximately 160 men and cargo aboard the cramped *I-8*, the spare crew was accommodated mainly in the torpedo room, where only six torpedoes were carried within the tubes (including the two Type 95s, destined for German scrutiny).

The first leg of the arduous journey involved short passages first to Singapore and then Penang, where an additional cargo of quinine, tin and raw rubber was taken aboard, the E14Y1 floatplane, its two pilots and its maintenance crew of four being disembarked to make extra room. On 27 June 1943 *I-8* departed Penang, refuelling on 8 July from *Chusa* Tonozuka Kinzo's *I-10* before rounding the Cape of Good Hope, where the boat was battered for ten days by fierce storms that reduced the her top speed to five knots, damaged the upper deck and bridge and caused the aircraft hangar to sway so much that it shifted on its mounting. Crewmen twice had to make emergency repairs in the teeth of the fierce 'Roaring Forty' gales, tethered to the submarine by stout lifelines.

On 24 July *I-8* received her first radio signal from the *Kriegsmarine*, warning of Allied air power within the Atlantic and the growing threat from radar. On 20 August Uchino successfully rendezvoused with *Kapitänleutnant* Albrecht Achilles' *U 161* in heavy seas, taking aboard *Oberleutnant zur See* Jahn and two petty officer radiomen the following day to assist in bringing *I-8* safely into the French port. *I-8* had been codenamed '*U-Flieder*' (Lilac) by the Germans and a *Metox* 600A radar detector had been installed on her bridge. Upon completion of this task the Japanese crew presented *U 161* with a four-gallon tank of coffee. Achilles then headed away for Brazil where his boat was sunk during September, Jahn and the two petty officers the only crewmen to survive her last patrol.

Aircraft of the *Luftwaffe*'s KG 40 provided air cover and the *Torpedoboote T 22*, *T 24* and *T 25* also arrived to shepherd the Japanese boat into Brest harbour, their arrival filmed by German propaganda reporters. *Admiral* Theodor Krancke, *Oberbefehlshaber West*, who presented Uchino and his men with varying grades of the Iron Cross while a *Wehrmacht* band added its own pomp to the ceremony, greeted Uchino and his weary crew. *I-8* was berthed in Pen 'A' of Brest's huge U-boat bunker as the crew began the difficult task of unloading. Sadatoshi and his 48 men were transferred to Hamburg, where they began training with the 31st U-Training Flotilla in the use of their new boat.

I-8 remained in France until 5 October 1943, when she left Brest under escort by two minesweepers and carrying a mixed cargo homeward. Within the hull were stored six 13mm Rheinmetall-Borsig aircraft MG 131 machine guns with full ammunition, dive-bomber and level-bomber bombsights, one Daimler-Benz torpedo boat engine, radars (including the '*Rotterdam Gerät*'), sonar equipment, quadruple 20mm '*Flakvierling*' AA guns, G7e electric torpedoes, naval chronometers and penicillin. The passengers aboard Uchino's boat included *Shosho* Yokoi Tadao, the former Naval Attaché to Germany, and *Taisa* Hosoya Sukeyoshi, the former Naval Attaché to France, as well as three German naval officers, including the Japanese-speaking *Leutnant* Koch, one German Army major and four radar and hydrophone technicians, including a *Dr* Jakob and a *Dr* Müller.

The progress made by *I-8* was plotted by Allied HF/DF interception of her position reports to Germany, although air attacks failed to hinder her progress. The last attack within the Atlantic sent *I-8* plunging below, nearby bomb blasts causing some leakage which was soon traced to a loose valve and halted. The Japanese endured similar conditions to those experienced while outbound south of Cape Town before entering the Indian Ocean on 13 November, the same day that *I-34*, the next submarine en route to Europe, was torpedoed and sunk 30 miles south of Penang. Uchino received fresh orders to proceed to Singapore despite fuel running ominously low aboard *I-8*. After receiving no reply to radio transmissions aimed at the Penang base, *I-8* arrived at Singapore via the Sunda Strait on 5 December, anchoring near *Chusa* Kinashi Takakazu's *I-29* that had arrived recently from Kure and was being loaded for a *Yanagi* trip to France. The *Metox* radar detector gear was passed over to Takakazu. Finally, on 21 December 1943 *I-8* arrived at Kure, having completed a voyage of 30,000 miles and the only Japanese submarine successfully to conclude a round-trip voyage from Japan to Europe during the Second World War.[11]

During November 1943 *I-29* (codenamed '*U-Kiefer*' by the *Kriegsmarine* and '*Matsu*' by the Japanese) departed Penang with fourteen passengers from Japan, including *Chujo* Kojima Hideo, the new Japanese Naval Attaché for Berlin, *Chusa* Muchaku Senmei, the Naval Attaché to Spain, *Chusa* Ogi Kazuto, the Assistant Naval Attaché to Germany, engineers and scientists, as well as 80 tons of tungsten, 50 of tin, two of zinc and three of quinine, opium and coffee. On 8 January 1944, as *I-29* passed south of Madagascar, Allied 'Ultra' codebreakers deciphered a signal indicating that *I-29* would be at 39°S 42°E on 11 January, although attempts to find the Japanese boat failed. With Allied 'Ultra' decrypts tracking the boat's progress toward France, *I-29* successfully rendezvoused with the outbound *U-518* south-west of the Azores to receive three German technicians, who installed a FuMB 7 '*Naxos*' radar detector. She later refuelled from the *Milchkuh U 488*, after which the Japanese boat was spotted by an RAF patrol aircraft though managed to shake the pursuer loose. On 4 March, off Cape Finisterre, a surfaced *I-29* was found once again by the RAF, illuminated by the penetrating glare of a Leigh-Light, but once again she managed to shake free of the attacker. Six days later *I-29* successfully rendezvoused with five Junkers Ju 88C-6 escorts and the German destroyers *Z 23* and *ZH 1* and torpedo-boats *T 27* and *T 29*. Kinashi was instructed not to dive in the event of enemy attack as the convoy headed for Lorient. However, alerted once more by 'Ultra', four RAF Mosquitos of No 248 Squadron, escorting two Special Detachment 'Tsetse' Mosquitos armed with 57mm cannon, were sent to attack the submarine and her escorts. The aircraft found their targets off Cape Penas, still under escort from eight Junkers Ju 88C-6s from *Zerstörergeschwader* (ZG) 1, based at Cazaux. The four Mosquitos attempted to draw the German fighter-bombers away so that the 'Tsetses' could attack the ships below and succeeded in downing one Ju 88C-6 (that flown by the German flight leader), but the crucial target, *I-29*, escaped unscathed. After 1700hrs *I-29* and her escorts were attacked by more than ten Allied aircraft, including RAF Bristol Beaufighter flak-suppressors and Consolidated B-24 Liberator bombers but, again, all the bombs aimed at *I-29* missed, and on 15 April 1944 the boat arrived safely at Lorient.

The Japanese submarine's cargo of rubber, wolfram and two tons of gold bullion was unloaded as the huge boat lay within the sprawling Kéroman bunker complex. German technicians took the opportunity to inspect the submarine, which was far larger than anything in *Kriegsmarine* service. They were relatively unimpressed, later criticising Japanese submarines for excessive hull vibration as well as the extended and unnecessary use of underwater signalling by their allies, potentially betraying the boat's position to enemy units. Their boat safely ensconced within Kéroman, the Japanese crew were transferred to Lager Lemp with their 2nd U-Flotilla hosts, enjoying the local U-boat recreation centres, touring subjugated Paris (and taking in a visit to the Palais de Chaillot that houses the French Maritime Museum and overlooks the Eiffel Tower) and indulging in the hitherto unfamiliar game of football against the German flotilla's team. *Chusa* Kinashi travelled on to Berlin, where Adolf Hitler presented him with the Iron Cross 2nd Class for sinking the carrier USS *Wasp*. Four Japanese Type 96 2.5cm AA guns were removed from *I-29* and replaced by a German 3.7cm Krupp AA gun and one quad 2cm Mauser *Flakvierling*, and the submarine left Lorient on 16 April for her three-month transit voyage back to Penang, again carrying passengers and cargo. This time she had embarked 18 passengers (including four Germans) and taken on board an HWK 09A-1 rocket motor used in the Me 163 *Komet* interceptor and a Jumo 004B engine used in the Me 262 jet fighter, as well as blueprints for both aircraft. Kinashi's boat also carried drawings of the Isotta-Fraschini torpedo boat engine, a V 1 fuselage, TMC acoustic mines, bauxite, mercury-radium amalgam, technical plans for a glider bomb and radar equipment, together with twenty Enigma coding machines. On 11 June *I-29* and *I-52*, the next '*Yanagi*' submarine en route to Lorient, passed each other and Kinashi entered the Indian Ocean eighteen days later.

On 14 July *I-29* arrived safely at Singapore under escort by 'Betty' bombers, disembarking her passengers but leaving the majority of the German scientific cargo aboard. The following day Allied codebreakers intercepted a signal indicating that *I-29* had arrived at Singapore and revealing information for Tokyo from Berlin concerning *I-29*'s cargo. Five days later Kinashi ordered that a detailed itinerary be transmitted to Japan, which the US Navy's Fleet Radio Unit Pacific's (FRUPAC) communications-intelligence at Hawaii intercepted and immediately deciphered. FRUPAC alerted CINCPAC of *I-29*'s planned route and schedule from Singapore to Japan, and CINCPAC in turn immediately despatched three submarines to intercept her, the USS *Tilefish*, *Rock* and *Sawfish* racing for the Luzon Strait. One 22 July at 0800hrs *I-29* departed Singapore for Kure and was sighted by *Sawfish* four days later at the western entrance of the Balintang Channel. At about 1700hrs *Sawfish* detected *I-29* running on the surface at 17kts and Cdr Alan B. Banister fired four torpedoes. These were spotted by the Japanese lookouts and Kinashi made a frantic attempt to comb their tracks. It was, however, too late: three of the four impacted on target and *I-29* immediately sank. Three of the Japanese crewmen were blown overboard but only one survivor managed to swim ashore to a 'small Philippine island' and report the loss. *Chusa* Kinashi, who was at that time Japan's leading submarine 'ace', was among the 105 crewmen and passengers lost. The loss of the German aircraft aboard *I-29* dramatically slowed the Japanese development programmes for jet- and rocket-propelled aircraft programmes, although, using the blueprints that had been flown to Tokyo from Singapore, the Japanese were later able to develop the Nakajima *Kikka* (Orange Blossom) based on the Me 262 and the Mitsubishi J8MI *Shusui* (Sword Stroke) based on the Me 163. Both aircraft were, however, produced too late for active service.[12]

The passengers from *I-8* who had transferred to Hamburg for U-boat training took *U 1224* from Kiel on 29 March 1944, but 'Ultra' intelligence tracked *Shosa* Norita Sadatoshi's boat until she was located by the USS *Francis M. Robertson* of the hunter-killer group centred on the carrier *Bogue* north-west of the Cape Verde Islands. The American destroyer made a firm ASDIC fix on the submerged *U 1224* and a single 'Hedgehog' and two depth-charge attacks made the trace disappear. No debris or oil marked the end of the *Marco Polo* boat promised to Tokyo by the *Führer* as *U 1224* plummeted thousands of fathoms to oblivion.

The next boat to leave Europe had been the *Schnorchel*-equipped *U 859*, sailing from Kiel under the command of veteran skipper *Kapitänleutnant* Johann Jebsen. The Type IXD2 left Germany loaded with stores for Penang and the Japanese forces, including 1,959 flasks of mercury, 624 bars of lead (weighing 25½ tons), extra lubrication oil, radar sets, machine parts, spares, ammunition and general supplies. Jebsen's first port of call was Marviken in Norway, where the boat received a final topping-up of her fuel tanks before heading across the North Sea towards the *Rosegarten,* from where *U 859* would skirt northwards around the British Isles.

U 859's first success was not long in coming as the Panamanian straggler MV *Colin*, from convoy SC.157, was torpedoed and sunk southeast of Cape Farewell, one of only four merchant ships destroyed by U-boats in the North Atlantic between January and 1 June 1944. Jebsen managed to elude an aggressive hunt by Allied ASW forces following his attack and rounded the Cape of Good Hope during late June. On 5 July *U 859* was sighted running fully surfaced 270 miles east-south-east of Durban by a Catalina of St Lucia's No 262 Squadron, the flying boat braving sustained and accurate flak to strafe the boat and drop five depth charges around her before being forced to withdraw with severe damage. The attack had also managed to damage *U 859*, and *Matrosenobergefreiter* Hans Boldt was killed and three other crewmen were seriously wounded, including the boat's IIWO. The *Schnorchel* lifting gear was disabled in the attack, two diesels had been knocked off their foundations and a fuel bunker had been punctured. Once again Jebsen managed to slip away from gathering ASW forces, and after his crew had toiled at repairing their damage he sailed northwards into the Gulf of Aden.

Jebsen reported sinking an escorted tanker on 27 August (a claim so far uncorroborated by Allied records) as well as the American Liberty ship SS *John Barry* south of Mirbat the following day (confirmed) and the British SS *Troilus* on 1 September east of Socotra (also confirmed). The *John Barry* went to the seabed 8,500ft below, carrying Arabian silver riyals worth $80 million and silver bullion worth another $300 million inbound and destined for Russia, while the demise of the British freighter brought *U 859*'s operations to a close, Jebsen subsequently laying course for Penang and arriving off the island on 23 September. Unfortunately his was not the only submarine in that area. Once again 'Ultra' had detected the periodic position reports from *U 859*, the most crucial having been her commander's rendezvous instructions with Japanese escorts off Penang. Two nights previously the 'T' Class submarine HMS *Trenchant* had received orders to proceed to a new patrol area off Penang, to be there no later than the morning of 23 September. By this stage of the war British submarines based around the depot ships *Adamant* and *Maidstone* at Trincomalee, Ceylon, regularly patrolled the Malacca Strait, ranging almost as far as Singapore. Lt-Cdr A. R. Hezlet immediately ordered course set: as he recalled in his memoirs, the recent success of HMS *Taurus* torpedoing *I-34* in December 1943, HMS *Tally Ho!* sinking *UIT-23* and the sinking of Japanese *I-166* by HMS *Telemachus* during July, all within this area, 'gave us hope of meeting a U-boat.'[13]

It was after dark on 22 September that the outline of Penang began to cloud *Trenchant*'s radar screen, Hezlet diving at 0448hrs local time after cruising slowly into position in a heavy swell and beneath periodic sheets of tropical rain. The long swell made depth-keeping difficult for the British submarine, and as Hezlet lay in his bunk he realised that the watch-keeping officer was expending all his energy and attention on simply keeping the boat at periscope depth and not actually using the scope to look for potential targets:

> I got up and went to his assistance, telling him to concentrate on the trim while I looked through the periscope. As soon as we were shallow enough, I raised the periscope and at once sighted a large German U-boat approaching on the surface from the westwards at about 14kts. The range was 2,700yds, and we were running in roughly at ninety degrees to her track. It was obvious that we were going to be too close and that the torpedoes would not have time to pick up their depth or indeed to run off their safety range. I at once put the helm hard-a-port, increased to full speed on the motors and went down to fifty feet.[14]

Hezlet frantically attempted to open the range slightly to give his torpedoes the required run-time in which to arm themselves, *Trenchant* going a full 180 degrees before he ordered a stern salvo prepared. Within ten minutes of the first sighting of *U 859*, two torpedoes arced from *Trenchant*'s stern, one impacting between the forward gun and conning tower after a run of only 30 seconds. The effect was devastating. *U 859* was lifted bodily from the water, broke open and plummeted to the bottom.

Inside *Trenchant*, there was jubilation at the obvious destruction of the U-boat, the noise of detonation and the collapsing hull echoing through the water. Hezlet raised his scope once more to survey the scene:

> The first things I saw were yellow liferafts bobbing about astern. A more careful look showed that there were definitely a number of survivors. I therefore took a careful look round and decided, although we were only ten miles or so from Penang, to surface. The U-boat sinkings assessment committee in the Admiralty were hard taskmasters, and to have some prisoners would definitely clinch the matter and provide proof of sinking.[15]

Trenchant surfaced and began pulling Germans from the water. Ten men were hauled aboard the submarine's casing before lookouts sighted a ship emerging from a distant rain squall. The British Second Coxswain was still dragging one man aboard when Hezlet blew his alarm whistle; the German was released to fall back into the water, the Coxswain running for the conning tower hatch. It therefore startled Hezlet when the German reappeared at the conning tower hatch as the hull began to submerge. 'Wait for me please,' he said in perfect English before being hustled below, the British captain treading on the German's fingers as they raced down the inner ladder:

> The German prisoners were very different from the Japanese. They were grateful for being rescued and for them the war was over. We did not need to guard them like the Japanese, and they were divided amongst the various messes according to rank . . . [they] were allowed a certain amount of freedom.[16]

In total *Trenchant* rescued eleven Germans, the most senior the boat's LI, *Kapitänleutnant (Ing.)* Horst Klatt. All the other officers had perished, many having been killed by the initial torpedo impact that destroyed the small officer's mess. Klatt had, ironically, been saved by contracting diarrhoea: he was absent from the mess and in the forward heads at the moment of the attack and managed to escape from the wreck after it had gone down. Apart from *Bootsmaat* Paul Pötter, *Funkmaat* Karl

Gaudeck and *Funkgefreiter* Rudi Teschner, the rescued survivors were engine-room personnel, all of them donning their *Tauchretter* escape gear and rising to the surface from the U-boat's flooded interior after it had settled on the relatively shallow seabed.

Behind him, Hezlet left eight men in the water, soon rescued by an approaching Japanese vessel, which detected no trace of *Trenchant*'s presence after plucking the dazed Germans from the water. Below their keel Jebsen and 46 crewmen lay entombed within their iron coffin. The survivors had all successfully escaped from the sunken hull, a feat recorded on 25 September in the BdU War Diary:

> *U 859* sank on 23.9 shortly after 0632hrs . . . just before entering Penang, by enemy submarine. Torpedo hit amidships. Boat lay at 30 metres. A total of twenty [*sic*] men were rescued from bow and stern compartments. Twelve [*sic*] of these were picked up by the enemy. Eight were rescued by Japanese submarine. Search is continuing.

Ironically, the sinking of *U 859* need not have happened at all:

> The loss of *U 859* at that time could have been avoided. Both boats, *U 859* and *U 861*, had received instructions from Penang to meet a Japanese E-boat just South of Langkavi island (north of Penang) at 0800hrs on 22 September. On that morning there was a tropical rainstorm and not much visibility. We [*U 861*] found the Japanese boat in time and got a German ex-merchant navy officer as pilot with detailed charts of the coastal area. We waited for *U 859* for two hours until we got a message from *U 859* that he could not find the meeting point and would proceed on the peacetime track to Penang. We, on the other hand, went close inshore, in shallow water to Penang. *U 859* might still be alive if her navigation had been better.[17]

U 860, a sister-boat to Jebsen's ill-fated *U 859*, fared no better during her attempt to break through the Atlantic to the Indian Ocean. Departing Kiel one week after *U 859*, she was commanded by the veteran U-boat captain *Fregattenkapitän* Paul Büchel, who had begun the war as a captain of the Type VIIA *U 32* before being transferred ashore for staff duties. Brought back to combat status by his assignment to *U 860*, Büchel sailed for Penang carrying a cargo that included 104.4 tons of lead bars, two Flak 38 cannon and ammunition, navigational instruments, FuMB sets and spares, communications equipment and spare parts and tools for the U-boat station. The boat carried only her interior offensive weapon load, the exterior torpedo storage canisters given over to accommodate quantities of the various spare parts that were in demand within the Far East.

Büchel followed operational instructions and proceeded through the North and South Atlantic, submerged by day and surfaced by night to allow the batteries to recharge; *U 860* possessed no *Schnorchel*. By early June he considered that the most dangerous regions had been passed and allowed the boat to run at an economical surface cruising speed by both day and night. Aircraft had already caused casualties on 21 April near Iceland when *U 860* had been forced to make an emergency crash-dive in the face of incoming aircraft, leaving *Matrosengefreiter* Alfons Robalewsky and *Bootsmaat* Rudolf Versic outside as the conning tower disappeared underwater. After resurfacing, Büchel scoured the storm-wracked sea before transmitting news of the loss to BdU—a radio burst which, once again, was deciphered by Allied cryptologists and led to the despatch of a hunter-killer group based around the carrier USS *Solomons*.

On 15 June an Avenger of *Solomons*' VC-9 discovered the surfaced boat. The incoming aircraft was detected by *U 860*'s *Fliege* radar detector moments before it appeared to the naked eye. Ensign G. E. Edwards immediately commenced the first of four attacks, all of which missed the target until, during the last attempt, his aircraft was hit in the bomb bay by a twin 2cm flak cannon. The Avenger was engulfed in flames and plunged into the sea only a matter of 1,000m away. Büchel unsuccessfully searched for survivors but the entire aircraft had quickly sunk, leaving little trace on the ocean surface. Edwards' report of the encounter failed to communicate the sighting to the USS *Solomons*.

Submerging and departing the scene, Büchel waited until shortly before sunset before ordering his boat surfaced. Apparently he had been dissatisfied with the performance of his flak gunners during the battle with Edwards and was determined that they should have more anti-aircraft gunnery practice. The bridge watch had just arrived at their stations atop the conning tower when an aircraft was sighted off the starboard bow. Almost simultaneously the *Fliege* shrilled its own warning and all flak guns were manned and made ready for action. The commanding officer of VC-9, Lt-Cdr H. M. Avery, had found his target and radioed for support as he began to skirt around the grey hull below. He had taken off in response to Edwards' report, conducting a normal square search gambit over the reported contact to look both for his colleague and for the submarine.

For nearly twenty minutes *U 860* also circled, keeping the enemy aircraft on her stern where the flak was at its most effective and firing with her 3.7cm guns whenever the aggressor wandered into range. However, his tactic could not last for ever and before long four aircraft, two Wildcats and a second Avenger, were at the scene and *U 860* was unable to dive because of the valuable seconds during which the boat would lay defenseless after the flak crews had managed to go below. Büchel faced little option other than to fight.

The four aircraft launched the first attack together, Wildcats strafing the boat while Avengers dropped depth charges slightly wide of the target and fired solid-nosed rockets in the face of devastating flak. All four aircraft passed over the U-boat within ten seconds. The blast of the nearby charges and twelve rocket hits brought telephone connections between *U 860*'s forward torpedo room and the control tower to an end as the boat took on a severe list to starboard with moderate flooding inside. One of the Avengers received serious damage to a wing tank and was forced to break away and head back to its carrier.

A second attack by the aircraft scored hits near *U 860*'s Chief Petty Officer's quarters and also damaged the bilges beneath the control room when a rocket passed straight through the compartment, allowing water quickly to flood in. With ruptured battery cells within the bilge, chlorine gas seeped noxiously into the U-boat's interior, bringing many men to their knees and possibly killing several. The boat trailed a thick wake of oil and had been slowed to a 3kt crawl when the third attack from port, by two aircraft, finally ended Büchel's torment. Avery streaked low overhead, spraying the boat with bullets, while the second Avenger, piloted by Lt (j.g.) Chamberlain, released two depth charges over target, both of which landed immediately in front of the conning tower and probably exploded on contact. The resulting blast wave dazed everybody aboard *U 860*, many only recovering their senses as the U-boat sank beneath them and they found themselves in the water. However, the attack had been too accurate for Chamberlain as well. As the charges exploded, flames engulfed his aircraft (which was at an altitude of only 50ft), starting a fire in the bomb bay and cockpit. Chamberlain held control of his Avenger long enough to make a 180-degree turn before landing in the water 500m ahead of the U-boat, but the three-man crew went down with their floundering aircraft.

U 860 had been mortally wounded, going under with the majority of her crew trapped within the interior by the deluge of water through holes and the conning tower hatch. Twenty survivors, including Büchel and his IWO, were picked up six hours later by the escort destroyers of the USS *Solomons* and were transferred soon thereafter to the carrier herself. One of the Germans recovered from the sea was dead when picked up and was later given a full burial at sea. Interestingly, US Navy Intelligence noted the effect of increased armour plating for German flak crews that had been added to U-boat conning towers in its afteraction report:

> The gunners aboard the submarine were well protected by armor because, despite concentrated strafing attacks, they continued to fire until the submarine went down. (Note: This fact is borne out by the physical condition of the survivors. Only one survivor was badly wounded by the strafing attacks. All other survivors had superficial fragmentation wounds caused by the explosion of the depth charges. Prisoners stated that only one man was killed outright by the strafing).[18]

Days later, on 1 August, BdU recorded the probable demise of *U 860*:

> The last message was picked up on 10.6 from FU 42. Short message from *U 860* relayed by *U 198* on 4.7, with time of arrival 1925hrs, report on air attack. No position given. According to dead reckoning, boat is in the Cape Town area. The boat was probably lost in this action.
>
> According to [the British] 'Calais' propaganda transmitter, the commander and nineteen men were taken prisoner; 42 men were killed.[19]

U 860 was not the last of the April departures to be destroyed: *U 198*, which had relayed Büchel's message, had also fallen foul of enemy forces after departing La Pallice on 20 April. With Werner Hartmann having left for a Staff position, *Oberleutnant zur See* Burkhard Heusinger von Waldegg, previously the IWO aboard Gysae's *U 177*, had taken command. His journey to Cape Town was largely uninterrupted, despite having to shake loose the attentions of an American hunter-killer group in the South Atlantic that established momentary contact. Arriving off South Africa in mid-June, von Waldegg attacked and sank the South African steamer SS *Columbine* on 16 June and remained in the area until early July, but he achieved no further success until the middle of the month.

While cruising off Durban during the forenoon of 6 July, *U 198* was harassed by two Ventura 200 aircraft, flak defeating the aircraft's attacks on the boat although some damage was sustained during the sharp battle. As *U 198* took a fleeting opportunity to dive, nearby depth charges punctured a fuel bunker and also released into the sea some of the U-boat's yellow rescue dinghies from under the upper teak decking. With the illusion of a destroyed U-boat, the two aircraft departed, allowing von Waldegg to creep away to safety. Heading into the Indian Ocean, *U 198* continued a small run of success alternating with weapon failure and enemy attack, as reported on 6 August to BdU:

> Sunk on 15.7 in KP 3568 [SS] *Director*, sailing parallel to coast between Durban and Beira.
> [Attempted attacks] at dusk on 19.7 large freighter in KP 3288, three corvettes, speed 13kts in KP 3332. Only explosions heard 130 seconds after e-torpedo running time, as a corvette was in ramming position. Depth charges.
> On 5.8. T5 missed Liberty ship. Torpedo circled, premature explosion near boat. Slight damage.
> 6.8 Sank [MV] *Empire City* on course 5 degrees, carrying coal from Lourenco to Aden.[20]

The following day von Waldegg sank the British MV *Empire Day* 200 miles east of Dar-es-Salaam, taking the ship's Master aboard as a prisoner. However, his small rash of sinkings and attempted attacks had attracted the almost undivided attention of a British hunter-killer group, Force 66, formed around the carriers HMS *Begum* and *Shah* and homing on HF/DF contact with von Waldegg's report to BdU. An Avenger of *Shah*'s 851 NAS sighted *U 198* on 10 August, although the rapidly submerging boat escaped both the aircraft and a frigate hastily summoned to the scene. The next day *U 198* was again sighted by one of *Shah*'s Avengers, and this time she was rocked by narrowly missing depth charges before clawing her way to the sanctuary of depth. That same day, some hours later, a British Catalina detected the boat surfaced once more, 200 miles north-north-west of the Seychelles, and homed the Indian sloop HMIS *Godarvi* and the British frigates HMS *Findhorn* and *Parret* to the scene. The U-boat, which in the meantime had submerged, was detected by ASDIC after a search that lasted into the afternoon. A series of 'Hedgehog' and depth-charge attacks yielded underwater explosions and upwelling oil, and von Waldegg and his 65 crewmen, as well as the Master of *Empire Day*, never resurfaced. The fate of *U 198* remained a mystery to BdU: '7 October 1944. *U 198* must be regarded as lost . . . last report on 8.8 from LT. She should have entered port by now at the latest. Cause and date of loss unknown.'

In Berlin it was not only the loss of the outgoing U-boats to Penang that prompted concern over the extent to which Allied forces had gained the upper hand at sea. The last of the *Yanagi* boats was overdue by the beginning of August. On the final day of July there was considerable confusion in both Berlin and Lorient as reports from the Japanese Naval Attaché in Berlin had reported communication from a blockade-running submarine from the Far East the previous day. Dönitz recorded in his War Diary: 'Japanese U-boat 'Föhre' [*I-52*] reported 36 hours off rendezvous, entering Lorient.'

Hurried preparations were made for an escort to rendezvous with the huge Japanese vessel inbound from Singapore carrying fourteen passengers, two tons of gold, 54 tons of rubber, three tons of quinine and wolfram, molybdenum (used in the manufacture of steel alloys) and tin totalling a further 230 tons. Five minesweepers and a single torpedo-boat were made ready to proceed at 0430hrs to Point *Leben*. The 2nd U-Flotilla placed engineers on standby, the men transferred from Lager Lemp to the bunkers themselves and living in the concrete confines of Kéroman II. However, *I-52* missed her first rendezvous, and another rescheduled for 0430hrs on 2 August. There was no sign of the phantom boat and by 3 August, after she had yet again failed to meet up with the escort ships, BdU logged the following: 'There is great anxiety concerning the Japanese U-boat "Fohre", from whom no messages have been received.'

The Japanese boat had picked up a German navigation officer and a *Naxos* set and its operator from *U 530* on 23 June, the U-boat later returning safely to Norway. The meeting, however, had been pinpointed by DF by an American task Force centred on the USS *Bogue*, and Avenger aircraft then tracked the Japanese submarine using radar and sonobuoys before hitting it in a combined depth charge and 'Fido' attack on 24 July west of the Cape Verde Islands. The next day American destroyers picked up 115 bales of crude rubber, splintered wood and a Japanese sandal as evidence of their 'kill': *I-52* was long dead and resting in 17,000ft of cold water when the Japanese Naval Attaché claimed to have received her message. Finally, on 4 August BdU admitted the probable loss of the ship adding the painfully familiar 'no information as to cause of loss and dates is available'.

Another transport boat sailed from Penang on 15 July, *Oberleutnant zur See* Karl Albrecht's Type VIIF torpedo-carrier, filled with cargo, putting to sea after an aborted attempt during late June. Forced to return with a defective compressor, *U 1062* narrowly missed destruction after torpedo attacks by HMS *Storm* while outbound through the Malacca Strait. The same good fortune protected Albrecht as he departed on his second attempt when he was missed by a bow salvo from HMS *Templar* a day out from Penang. However, *U 1062* successfully eluded pursuit and disappeared into the expanses of the Indian Ocean.

NOTES

1. BdU KTB, 'Most Secret Order for Merkator Boats', 26 December 1943, National Archives Microfilm, PG30337, Roll No 3980.
2. *UIT 21* was blown up by German troops on 25 August 1944.
3. Newsletter of the Catalina Association, Cape Town Branch, June 2001. It was, perhaps, an unexpected victory for 'Gar' Nash: he was described in the same newsletter as apparently having piloted a machine possessed of numerous mechanical faults and thus 'one of the slowest combat aircraft of WW2, wags [saying] that crews needed a calendar rather than a stopwatch to rendezvous with a convoy.'
4. This unglamorous assignment resulted in UIT 25's later commander, *Oberleutnant der Reserve* Alfred Meier, designing a humorous emblem showing a 'coolie' wearing the distinctive flat brimmed Chinese hat with a lifering suspended from one end of his carrying pole.
5. Only *U 1061* survived the war, damaged by grounding in February 1945 and surrendered in Bergen at the war's end.
6. Schwender was released on 21 December 1951, Lenz on 27 August 1952.
7. An excellent account of the trial, written by Dwight R. Messimer, can be found in *Silent Hunters*, Savas Publishing, 1997.
8. The Admiralty radioed specific instructions to commanders that they avoid attacking U-tankers during refuelling for fear of compromising the Enigma secret. The US Navy refused to comply, further exacerbating an already fractious relationship between the anglophobe USN C-in-C Admiral King and the British.
9. Clay Blair, *Hitler's U-Boat War. Volume Two: The Hunted*, pp. 536–7.
10. See Paterson, *First U-Boat Flotilla*.
11. Uchino was promoted to Captain on 1 May 1944.
12. Kinashi was honoured by a rare two-rank promotion to Rear-Admiral, posthumously.
13. Arthur Hezlet, *HMS Trenchant*, p. 76.
14. *Ibid.*, p. 78.
15. *Ibid.*
16. *Ibid.*
17. Correspondence with Jürgen Oesten, 14 September 2003.
18. Analysis of anti-submarine action by aircraft: Unit:VC-9, Report No 33, Incident No 6433; 15 June 1944.
19. BdU KTB, 1 August 1944, National Archives Microfilm, PG30353, Roll No 4066.
20. BdU KTB, 6 August 1944, National Archives Microfilm, PG30353, Roll No 4066.

Eight

Combat in the East, Defeat in the West

D URING THE SPAN of months between 1 February and 30
April 1944 eleven boats had sailed individually for the Far East
but only four had completed their voyages. On 19 February
U 843 had departed Lorient, arriving at Jakarta on 11 June having sunk
a single ship during April while still in the Atlantic and suffered considerable damage from two attacks south of Ascension Island by American
aircraft. *Kapitänleutnant* Oskar Herwatz had also stopped and inspected
the papers of two merchant ships west of the Azores, satisfying himself
that the neutral Portuguese and Spanish ships were not contravening the
U-boat blockade and allowing them to continue unmolested. The arrival of *U 843* and a cargo that included steel plates welded to the hull
represented the safe delivery of the first shipment of cargo for the Japanese military—as well as spares for the Penang base—that had been
assigned to a German combat U-boat.

    U 196, no longer commanded by the overbearing Kentrat but by *Ober-
leutnant zur* See Werner Striegler , had also sunk a single ship during
her voyage. Surviving the attentions of destroyers escorting the USS
Solomons in the central Atlantic, Striegler had achieved his victory when
he torpedoed the British merchantman SS *Shazada* in the Arabian Sea,
although he claimed two sunk for 12,107 tons. His voyage, begun on 16
March from La Pallice, ended at Penang on 10 August, his intention to
head for base having been radioed to Penang eight days previously.

    Another veteran, *U 181*, under the new command of *Kapitän zur See*
Kurt Freiwald, achieved far greater things, accounting for four ships

sunk between May and July 1944 totalling 24,869 tons—17 per cent the total of merchant ship tonnage sunk by U-boats anywhere during those three months. His first attack had come over a week after successfully meeting Lüdden's returning *U 188* to receive current intelligence about operations within the Indian Ocean. On 1 May Freiwald attacked a south-bound freighter in the Atlantic narrows, sending the SS *Janeta* to the bottom but mistaking the 5,312-ton vessel for either the SS *Birming-ham* or the *Beanavon*, which he considered 'more likely according to silhouette'. On 19 June, deep within the Indian Ocean, he torpedoed the SS *Garoet* (wrongly recorded as *Caroot* within his KTB) north-east of Mauritius as the Dutch steamer taking sugar and coal to Durban. His third victory came less than a month later when he sank the SS *Tanda*, scoring hits on the heavily laden British freighter amidships using one magnetic and one impact fuse. Although he was unable to surface to confirm the ship's identity owing to aircraft radar alerts from his *Fliege* detector, Freiwald departed from what he correctly considered a 'cer-tain sinking' though underestimated her tonnage at 6,000 rather than the Lloyds-registered 7,174. Freiwald's U-boat became the object of a six-hour depth-charge hunt by the Indian sloop HMIS *Sutlej* and supporting aircraft after being spotted by the aerial reconnaissance on 16 July near the Laccadives. While he was in pursuit of enemy freighters the twin-engine aircraft dropped four depth charges from a great height as *U 181* dived away in alarm, reaching a depth of only 40m before detonation and having stern torpedo tube No 6 bent, leaving a single T5 *Zaunkönig* lodged within the tube and rendering the latter *hors de combat*. How-ever, *U 181* managed to wriggle free of the uncomfortably accurate bom-bardment and effect repairs before heading for the Indian peninsula, Freiwald considering the engine damage as being contained 'within rea-sonable limits'.

A final close call served to illustrate the increasing attention from enemy submarines near Penang as *U 181* was narrowly missed by tor-pedoes fired by HMS *Stratagem*, lying in wait in the Strait of Malacca. Once more 'Ultra' decrypts had pinpointed the location of the U-boat as she awaited escort into Georgetown harbour. *U 181* finally docked on 8 August, having fired eight electric torpedoes in anger and suffering only a single malfunction. Freiwald's extensive report, forwarded through Japanese transmitters to Europe, listed his achievements, observations and criticisms of the patrol that he had successfully finished, including several disconcerting opinions of increasing, though often inexperienced, aircraft patrols and unreliable radio communications:

Anti-aircraft armament:
  3.7cm gun in action (full automatic) until the end, after numerous repairs. 2cm gun showed signs of wear and tear eventually, and was therefore unreliable.

Bachstelze:
  Torn away and lost during first attempt owing to faulty repair. Pilot saved.

W/T:
  Every W/T transmission from the operational area was a tragedy. No W/T messages were heard on the first sending, if ever. Short signal book 41 needs an overhaul. The immediate reaction of the enemy (also on the transmission of short signals) was often observed. All FuMBs were in action until the end. *Wanze* was only switched on in especially dangerous areas as there was an inadequate supply of spare parts.

Weather conditions:
  In general unfavourable during SW monsoon owing to numerous rain showers, squalls of hurricane strength and variable visibility.

Boat type:
  Proved its practicability. In areas with heavy air patrols, the small compressed air supply, which allowed only four crash-dives, was a dangerous weakness. Ventilation and air cooling apparatus inadequate for the tropics.

Crew:
  Again proved efficient. Owing to long submerged passage and extensive operations in equatorial areas, this operation tested the limits of endurance.[1]

Six days before Freiwald's entry into Georgetown *Kapitänleutnant* Peter Schrewe's *U 537* had entered the port of Tanjung Priok, Jakarta's harbour. He had claimed a FAT hit on a tanker of 7,000 tons in LD 4656 on 8 July and a *Zaunkönig* hit on a destroyer, but these victories remained unconfirmed: the detonations from his attacks south of Ceylon were clearly heard but were perhaps wishful thinking after his crew had endured over fourteen weeks at sea. The resultant depth-charge retaliation from HMS *Racehorse* and *Raider* shook both boat and men, although Schrewe managed to elude his captors and make for Jakarta.

July also saw the return of *U 183* to Penang harbour after an aborted raiding foray into the Indian Ocean. Denied the ability to range as far as the Atlantic Ocean in a bid to return to Europe owing to the sinking of the Germany's two-ship supply network east of the Cape of Good Hope, Fritz Schneewind had seen his boat plagued with problems over recent months, beginning on 3 May when she sailed from port in an attempt to reopen combat from Penang within the Indian Ocean. After only a day at sea Schneewind was compelled to return as a result of mechanical problems. The run of misfortune continued on 13 May when *Obermaschinenmaat* Erich Adelsheimer was killed in an accident while working on a diving cell in preparation for the boat's next patrol. Four days after Adelsheimer's tragic death *U 183* put to sea once more, charged with an anti-shipping patrol towards Ceylon, Addu Atoll and Chagos. The results were unspectacular: *U 183* returned to dockside in Penang having accounted for a single 5,259-ton British merchant ship, the SS *Helen Moller*, sunk north-east of the Salomon Islands in the middle of the Indian Ocean. Officially transferred off the roster of Lorient's 2nd U-Flotilla to the list of boats accommodated within the newly formed 33rd U-Flotilla at the end of September, the boat would carry out no more patrols before then, transferring without incident to Singapore during August and later on to Kobe for the major task of battery replacement within the Japanese dockyard that would drag through until November.

Although it was not until January 1945 that *Korvettenkapitän* Eitel-Friedrich Kentrat would take command of a newly established official German mechanical station at Kobe, July 1944 also saw the opening of the Dutch naval base at Surabaya, Java, as a German port for maintenance when conditions permitted. *Kapitänleutnant* Konrad Hoppe had been freed of his position as temporary IWO aboard *U 168* after the latter's return to Jakarta in March 1944 laden with survivors from *Brake*. Since that time the boat had been undergoing extensive repairs and Hoppe had departed to take command of the new post as *U-Stützpunktleiter* Surabaya. As Jakarta had no complete repair facilities the nearest place for German use would have been Surabaya. However, by December 1944 there was a constant flow of Japanese battle-damaged ships that required the use of most of the facilities available. As a result it was very difficult for the German U-boats to be allocated space within Surabaya and thus the U-boats were ordered into the port only when the schedule permitted.

Still more U-boats continued to sail individually for the Far East from an increasingly beleaguered German-occupied Europe. *U 861* put to sea from Kiel on 20 April, followed the next month by the *Milchkuh U 490* and Type IXD2 *U 862*. By the end of August *U 863*, *U 180*, *U 195*, *U 219* and *U 871* had all sailed, each having stowed varying equipment and goods bound for Penang, Jakarta and Surabaya's U-boat stations. The Germany that they departed was being increasingly battered by Allied round-the-clock air raids, while in France the very existence of the German-held ports was directly under threat.

Since the Allied landings in Normandy in June 1944 preparations to defend the four Atlantic U-boat bases had been intensified, while the equipping of hopelessly outclassed and outmoded U-boat designs with the *Schnorchel* in a belated attempt to provide some sanctuary for diesel boats, perilously required to surface in order to recharge their batteries, was finally stepped into high gear by the *Kriegsmarine*. Dönitz's and his staff's realisation that this imperfect device provided the last possible hope of improving an already obsolete fleet of Type VII, IX and X U-boats had, however, come too late. During the *Landwirt* group's attempted interception of D-Day landing traffic U-boats were destroyed at a staggering and unsustainable rate. American troops raced for the Atlantic coast of France as the possibility of capturing the valuable ports and disrupting German submarine operations in the Atlantic seemed within the grasp of the Allies, and *Wehrmacht* troops reeled back in disarray from the juggernaut that threatened to roll over and crush the German lines in France. Brest came under siege first, followed soon afterwards by Lorient, while the almost unopposed landing of Allied troops on 15 August in southern France—Operation 'Dragoon'—posed a direct threat to Bordeaux, home of the 12th U-Flotilla that operated the majority of the long-range boats stationed in Penang. While other ports were put under varying degrees of siege warfare, Bordeaux itself was not able to hold out, and on the day the 'Dragoon' forces swarmed ashore and raced inland the final winding down of U-boat operations from the harbour at Bordeaux was announced: '12th U-Flotilla closed down wireless telegraphy station; personnel who cannot be evacuated to Germany (nucleus) will be incorporated into infantry.'

The base would last only weeks after this curt note within BdU's operational record. On 25 August two submarines, *U 534* and *U 857*, sailed from the harbour basin through the heavily mined Gironde river and into the dangers of Biscay—the last U-boats to depart the port. Behind them, still ensconced within the towering concrete bunkers, were *UIT 21*, *U 178* and *U 188*, the last two worn beyond use by their Far

Eastern cruises, immobile and with their batteries useless and *U 188*'s propeller shaft bent and inoperative. The return of *U 178* and *U 188* to Bordeaux marked two of only three successful round trips that had begun and ended in France. For her part *UIT 21* had never become operational during her tenure with the *Kriegsmarine* and was scuttled at Bordeaux.

Wilhelm Spahr's *U 178* had completed her crossing from Penang on 24 May, arriving with his cargo of rubber and tungsten before being consigned to the Bordeaux bunkers for weeks of expected repairs. However, with few maintenance man-hours and materials available the battered boat was still unseaworthy when the time came to evacuate Bordeaux's German installations. Spahr travelled back to Germany while the lines of communication remained open to take charge of the 23rd U-Training Flotilla. His Chief Engineer, *Kapitänleutnant (Ing.)* Karl-Heinze Wiebe, was awarded the Knight's Cross on 22 May for his exemplary service aboard *U 178* during the Indian Ocean patrols.

U 188's saga mirrored that of her flotilla-mate. After the sinking of the supply ship *Brake*, Lüdden met with the outbound *U 1062* to take on board mail and ciphers for use in the Atlantic. Following a turbulent rounding of the Cape of Good Hope during which *U 188* took a pounding in the 'Roaring Forties', the boat met up once more with another heading east, rendezvousing with *U 181* and taking on board lubricating oil and a commander-in-training who had accompanied Freiwald for the first half of the journey. A final meeting with *U 129* provided *Naxos* and *Borkum* equipment for the run through the Bay of Biscay.

During 1 May Lüdden was issued with emergency instructions to make contact with *U 66*, one of the oldest Type IXs still in service and a boat desperately short of supplies. Dönitz had ordered both *U 68* and *U 515* to meet with Seehausen's boat, but the radio messages had vanished into the ether, both submarines already long sunk. By the time that Lüdden received his orders *U 66* was in grim shape after nearly four months at sea. Fuel and rations were extremely low and the boat's qualified though inexperienced Medical Officer, *Sanitätsmaat* Wolf Loch, had discovered to his horror that, thanks to an error made while supplies were being packed, the large amount of vitamin pills that he had expected to carry on such an extended patrol had turned out to be one small, inadequate bottle's worth. By early May the crew were beginning to suffer a disease associated with the days of sail, exhibiting several of the classic symptoms of scurvy—yellowing skin which frequently bruised, loosening teeth, painful joints, reduced mental capacity, and lethargy. While the men waited for replenishment they were forced to spend more and more time on surface as the ageing batteries ran lower and lower, unable to hold a full charge.

On 6 May, as *U 188* made all speed for the ailing boat, Seehausen's final messages to BdU signalled the end of *U 66*:

0518hrs: Lüdden [*U 188*] not met. Supplying impossible since [we have been] D/Fed constantly since the 26th . . . Central Atlantic worse than Biscay . . .
0615hrs: Plane keeping in touch.
0622hrs: Being attacked by destroyer.[2]

In the action that ensued with the USS *Buckley*, detached from the hunter-killer group centred on the carrier *Block Island*, during which the two vessels became interlocked, with men fighting hand-to-hand aboard the American vessel's decks, *Kapitänleutnant* Gerhard Seehausen and 23 of his men were killed in action. *U 66* went to the seabed with them.[3] Lüdden received a message from BdU shortly afterwards: '6.5. 1215hrs. Order from Control: rendezvous cancelled.'

Lüdden was experiencing his own problems. His boat was short of lubricating oil after the high temperatures of the Indian Ocean had consumed vast quantities of the fluid and the radio transmitter had ceased to function, the boat unable to request resupply at sea. Forced to detour around *Block Island*, Lüdden proceeded slowly for home, spending much time submerged. With no means of communicating with BdU there were genuine fears for the boat's safety, but these were finally dispelled on 19 June when the boat entered the lock leading to the Bordeaux bunker, eleven days short of a year after departing Europe.

Lüdden's ordeal had not yet finished. Ordered to report in person to BdU in Berlin for the standard debriefing, he departed Bordeaux but his convoy was ambushed by French partisans as it made its way inland. With the approach of American troops, the activities of the French Resistance had begun to intensify, particularly ambushes of unsuspecting road convoys. Lüdden was captured after the disablement of his vehicle and his KTB—including a special section detailing the U-boat approaches to Penang, Singapore and Jakarta—was taken by the *Maquis*. Although

Lüdden himself escaped, the loss of these documents was a blow to Dönitz.[4]

In Bordeaux after the departure of the last seaworthy U-boats, dozens of ships, including erstwhile blockade-runners, *Sperrbrecher*, mine-sweepers, patrol ships and even a destroyer, were scuttled in and around the harbour and within the basins. The German installations, including the interiors of the U-boat bunkers with their three lame boats inside, were dynamited. The men left behind prepared to attempt to fight their way back to Germany, organised into the *Marinebrigade Weber*, the men of the 12th U-Flotilla and those few remaining Italians from *Betasom* a part of *Marineregiment* Badermann. The German columns departed from Bordeaux on 26 August, but under sporadic *Maquis* attack, and after meeting advancing American forces, *Marinebrigade Weber* surrendered on 15 September south of the Loire valley. Bordeaux had fallen, and with it the home of the 12th U-Flotilla and its cruiser U-boats.[5]

The boats of the Far East were transferred, on paper at least, to the strength of the 33rd U-Flotilla, formed in Flensburg during September 1944. However, as they were thousands of miles away the benefits of this redesignation was largely irrelevant to the *Monsun* boats still within the Indian Ocean. Dommes acted as a *de facto* flotilla chief for the purposes of co-ordinating his logistical requirements with the Japanese.

With chaos engulfing the *Kriegsmarine* command in western France, those boats sailing for the East continued their difficult voyages, their captains and crew focused on survival against the odds. On 8 August BdU recorded the apparent loss of one of them:

> *U 490* must be presumed lost. The boat put out of Kiel on 4.5 for Penang and was to supply homeward-bound Type IXC boats in the Indian Ocean en route, subsequently to return with cargo of military importance. The last message was a short weather report from CD 23 on 11.6. Since then, no reply to repeated request for position report. No details of date of loss or reason. The last XIV boat is therefore gone.

Oberleutnant zur See Wilhelm Gerlach's *U 490* had been systematically tracked by 'Ultra' since departing Germany on her maiden voyage, the final Type XIV boat to put to sea. Gerlach's boat had been commissioned on 27 March 1943 and was the last of the ten *Milchkühe* to enter *Kriegsmarine* service. However, she was dogged by mishap as she prepared to take her place amongst the submarine refuelling fleet. Following commissioning, and during a break amid trials with the AGRU

Front at Hela, a battery explosion resulting from a build-up of combustible gases after exhaust lines had been left closed as cells were being changed caused severe damage to the battery itself and its below-decks compartment. Returned to Kiel, the trials broken off, *U 490* was docked for a further month as repair work was undertaken. The return to the AGRU Front was completed successfully during June 1943, after which the boat completed underwater sound tests off Rönne before heading for Gotenhafen in July for tactical exercises as a part of the 4th U-Training Flotilla. However, once again misfortune struck as, during the course of a practice dive on 23 July, the main air induction valve was left open and *U 490*'s diesel compartment suffered a deluge of seawater flooding, completely filling the adjacent electric motor room and causing the U-boat to plummet out of control to the seabed. With an extra 60 tons of water aboard, she was barely refloated by her crew, and she returned to Gotenhafen with very little freeboard and at a slow speed. Gerlach narrowly avoided being attacked after another training boat mistook her altered silhouette for a Russian submarine, but *U 490* made port for emergency repairs before moving once more to Kiel's shipyards. Six months of drydock followed as the electric motors were replaced and flak weapons installed on an enlarged conning tower to which armoured shelters were added, a three-man shelter to starboard and a one-man shelter to port. Heavy aerial bombing of the docks and city hampered the maintenance work and *U 490* did not sail until January 1944.

Finally completing her exercises, *U 490* had a *Schnorchel* added to the port side of the conning tower during March. The final run-up to departure was occupied with refitting and loading and Gerlach put to sea on 4 May under *Sperrbrecher* escort and accompanied by a Type VIIC. After a final topping-off of fuel at Kristiansand the *Milchkuh* began her passage into the Atlantic.

U 490 was the last of her type still in action. The penultimate tanker, *U 488*, had been sunk with all hands on 26 April and Gerlach was probably aware of the narrow chance he had of running the Allied gauntlet: he was remembered by his crew as seemingly extremely nervous as the boat sailed west, maintaining a strict radio silence and running submerged for as much of the passage as possible. It was one of his few transmissions that would indeed seal his boat's fate.

Despatched to hunt for the tanker known to have sailed thanks to 'Ultra', Task Force 225, centred around the carrier USS *Croatan*, finally 'DFed' a brief high-frequency transmission from Gerlach as he made his short weather report 40 miles west of the carrier and her hunter-killer group within the central Atlantic. Three ships of the group obtained accurate ground wave bearings and shaped course to intercept while aircraft were recalled from the hunt owing to bad weather. As *Croatan* turned into the wind to conduct landing operations the destroyer USS *Frost* made sonar contact at a range of 650yds, the USS *Huse* being assigned to assist as the carrier made an emergency turn away from the enemy. Streaming 'Foxer' gear behind them to ward off retaliation with *Zaunkönig* torpedoes, the destroyers began their attack on *U 490*.

Gerlach and his crew were surprised by nearby explosions at 1100hrs as *Frost* opened her assault using the ahead-throwing 'Hedgehog' while *U 490* cruised at 80m, the German hydrophones having failed to detect the incoming destroyers. Gerlach immediately dived, taking *U 490* to 240m and rigged for silent running. *Huse* added weight to the attack by dropping depth charges, which detonated close by the target, and then the two destroyers began to pound the submarine systematically. The boat's LI, *Oberleutnant (Ing.)* Ewald Rotter-Woletz, took the boat deeper still, to 300m, beneath the continuing barrage as the sound of ASDIC and the 'circular saw' of the Foxers echoed through the iron hull.

Seventeen hours of depth-charging shook the boat and caused morale on board to plummet dramatically. Although below the effective reach of the exploding charges (which were set for a maximum of around 200m), *U 490* still suffered from the blasts, not least of all the twelve guinea pigs—known aboard as '*Schnorchel* pigs'—that had been accommodated for experimental purposes by the surgeon, *Marinestabsarzt* Herbert Stubbendorff. The terrified animals' squeals tore at raw nerves and, afraid of the effect they were having on his crew and the possibility of the noise travelling through the water to the attackers above, Gerlach ordered them killed by Stubbendorff.

Although the boat suffered only minor damage, her interior became clouded and foul and potash cartridges were handed out to the exhausted and demoralised crew. Batteries ran lower and lower until Gerlach was faced with little choice but to take his sluggish boat to the surface and attempt to escape with diesel power. Above him the Task Force's commander had anticipated this move and had placed the USS *Snowden* five miles to the south of the U-boat's estimated position as *Frost* and *Inch* continued the inexorable creeping attacks on *U 490*. Finally, at 0027hrs local time radar contact was made with a large surfaced object between *Frost* and *Snowden* as *U 490* burst through the surface and ignited her diesels. Gerlach and his lookouts raced for the conning tower where they were soon blinded by searchlights and starshell that held their boat beneath an uncompromising glare. With no chance to escape, Gerlach ordered the boat to be scuttled and his crew to abandon ship. Gunfire of all calibres began to crash on and around *U 490* as Gerlach ordered light semaphore flashed to his attackers: 'SOS: please take our crew.' Within 30 minutes *U 490* had upended and slid, stern-first, beneath the waves; a large underwater explosion was heard as her entire complement of 61 was rescued by the Americans.

With the destruction of *U 490* the last opportunity of having a refuelling vessel within the Indian Ocean to facilitate the return of the Type IXCs had gone. Dönitz's intention—that Gerlach transfer diesel to homebound boats before making for Penang himself—had been frustrated by the Allies' ability to track U-boat movements through combined cryptographic breakthroughs and highly efficient HF/DF location of the intercepted signals required by BdU's tight hold of the operational reigns within the Atlantic.

Gerlach's was not the only Malaysia-bound boat to fail in an attempt to break through the Allied cordon: of those nine boats that had sailed between April and the end of August 1944 *U 490* had fallen first, but she was followed by *U 198* and *U 180* during August, *U 871* on 26 September and *U 863* three days later.

The Type IXD1s *U 180* and *U 195* had both had their experimental high-speed engines removed after their first voyages, during which Bose had been transferred by *U 180* to *I-29* and *U 195* had raided off Cape Town. They had been ensconced within Bordeaux's U-boat bunkers from October 1943 to April 1944 and the decision had been taken to convert them to transport boats for a return voyage to the Indian Ocean, this time destined for Penang. The two boats had *Schnorchel* fitted, their propulsion units had been replaced by the same diesels as those used by the Type VIIC and the torpedo tubes had been removed, allowing 252 tons of goods to be taken to Penang and a similar quantity to be brought home. Recommissioned during April, *U 180* was commanded by a new captain, *Oberleutnant zur See* Rolf Reisen, and she left Bordeaux on 22 August.

Reisen sailed alongside sister-boat *U 195* and Type XB *U 219*, the former now captained by *Oberleutnant zur See* Friedrich Steinfeldt, formerly the commander of the inoperative *UIT 21*. Inside *U 180*'s keel and pressure hull there was an impressive and diverse cargo for Penang, including 6,669 aluminium bars, spare torpedoes, 1,843 bottles of mercury, six tons of steel, 6.8 tons of raw, uncut, optical glass, Enigma machines and ciphers for 1945, Junkers compressors, spare parts, tools and engine components, as well as radio and medical equipment. Steinfeldt's *U 195* carried an even more diverse collection of *matériel* and men: as well as transporting *Chusa* Iwatani Eiichi and blueprints for projected jet aircraft projects, she held rocket parts, spare torpedoes, ammunition, 54.4 tons of mercury, 78.5 tons of raw glass, spare diesel engine components, a spare propeller, medical supplies, radar construction plans, radio and navigation gear, 9,100 aluminium bars, 14.7 tons of steel and 64.37 tons of lead. Both boats were loaded to capacity as they traversed the turbid waters of the Gironde river to the Bay of Biscay.

Hopes of resupplying the poorly equipped garrison in Malaysia were partially frustrated once more as, only days from port, *U 180* disappeared, lost probably to Allied aerial mines west of Lacanau-Océan. The 56-man crew and their valuable cargo disappeared into the maelstrom of Biscay, though the boat was not officially listed by BdU as missing presumed lost until 3 October.

The losses of both *U 871* and *U 863* were more readily explained, neither succeeding in escaping the Atlantic. *Kapitänleutnant* Erwin Ganzer's *U 871* was sighted by a B-17 Flying Fortress of RAF Coastal Command's No 220 Squadron engaged as escort cover for convoy CU.40 north-west of the Azores. At 1300hrs on 26 September Flt Lt A. F. Wallace was circling the merchant ship SS *Irish Rose*, which appeared to have suffered mechanical failure, when a flash report from a second No 220 Squadron Fortress reported a surfaced U-boat nearby. Arriving over the scene as the other Fortress circled the spot where the boat had dived, Wallace's Second Pilot sighted a periscope, or possibly a *Schnorchel* wake, which was duly attacked with three depth charges only moments before the conning tower began to break the surface. As the charges detonated astride the tower *U 871* dipped under again, a huge oil patch forming as bodies and debris floated to the surface of the sea. Ganzer and his 68 crew members were dead.

Kapitänleutnant Dietrich von der Esch's *U 863* was similarly destroyed by aircraft, having been spotted and attacked by a US Navy Liberator of VP-107 based in Natal, Brazil. Five depth charges straddled the boat and brought her speed immediately down, with oil leaking behind the crippled craft. A second attack was greeted by flak as the depth charges initially failed to release from within the Liberator's bomb bay. By this time a second Liberator had arrived on the scene, and after a duel that involved further bomb hang-ups, strafing from the aircraft and fierce flak from, and manoeuvring by, *U 863*, the boat was straddled by three depth charges, after which the crew began to abandon ship. *U 863* slid rapidly beneath the waves, helped along by another depth charge attack on the oil slick and her scattered German survivors. Once the boat had gone, liferafts were dropped to the twenty or so men still seen in the water, although none of the 68 crewmen was ever rescued.

Of the four boats that survived the attempted journey to Malaysia, *Korvettenkapitän* Heinrich Timm's *U 862* was the first to dock in Georgetown, arriving there 9 September. Timm, a veteran of Arctic U-boat operations, had achieved rare success during his cruise, sinking five merchant ships within the Atlantic and Indian Oceans. He sported the nickname '*Tüte*' in recognition of the conical paper container used for boiled sweets and its similarity to the shape of the gramophone speaker that Timm used to listen to classical music—at high volumes, much to the dismay of many around him. Timm had carefully taken his boat through the treacherous Atlantic, weighing warily the chances for offensive action against what he knew were extremely effective Allied HF/DF capabilities.

The cruise had begun inauspiciously after *U 862* had departed Kiel under escort and in company with several U-boats bound for the Atlantic on 20 May. The Type IXD2 was packed with provisions, ammunition and a cargo that included technical drawings, models and blueprints of German weaponry and equipment bound for Japanese evaluation, and a keel packed with flasks of mercury, lead, steel, uncut optical glass and aluminium. Timm was frustrated in his first attempt at breaking through the narrow passage between Iceland and the Faeroes and put into Bergen. A second attempt was also foiled after lookouts discovered a shimmering trail of oil in their boat's wake, emanating from a leaky fuel tank. Timm put into Narvik for repair and sailed once again on 3 June, this time skirting the ice-pack with which he was so familiar and, in thick fog and sporadic storms, making the break through the Denmark Strait into the Atlantic proper and using his *Bachstelze*, with the ship's doctor Jobst Schäfer as pilot, to navigate from above the fog banks into clear sea.

It was while heading cautiously into the South Atlantic on 5 July that Timm received news of his promotion to *Korvettenkapitän*, authorising a rare issue of weakened schnapps for the crew and cooled champagne for the officers. Twenty days later he made the first sinking aboard his new boat west-south-west of St Helena, torpedoing the 6,885-ton American merchantman SS *Robin Goodfellow*, which was en route to New York from Cape Town loaded with iron ore and general cargo. The attack had required the expenditure of five torpedoes, an initial attempt with two *Zaunkönig* T5s having missed the target and one of the errant weapons circling (which *U 862* narrowly avoided as Timm dived in alarm).

Timm was initially ordered to hunt off Cape Town in company with *U 181*, but positive reports of merchant traffic within the Mozambique Channel from *U 198* before her demise had led BdU to redirect both boats towards the Gulf of Aden. The three boats were, however, tracked by 'Ultra', which soon led to the destruction of von Waldegg's *U 198*. Timm experienced a small run of success, torpedoing the SS *Radbury* at the southern entrance to the Mozambique Channel and three other British steamers at the northern end—the SS *Empire Lancer*, the ammunition ship SS *Nairung* and the SS *Wayfarer*, representing half of the Allied merchant ships sunk in the Indian Ocean during the month of August. Timm attempted to report his success to BdU, allowing him to 'DFed' twice on 19 August, as indicated within the content of an Admiralty report on the Indian Ocean situation for the period August–October 1944:

> Five German U-boats operated in the Indian Ocean during August, one of which [*U 198*] was sunk by aircraft and escort vessels of Force 66 . . . The U-boats operated with extreme caution, and their achievements were almost negligible when compared with the amount of shipping in the Indian Ocean. As sinkings occurred between 1554N and 3058S and the U-boats in this part of the ocean

only broke W/T silence of five occasions, the difficulty in locating them is obvious.[6]

Timm's boat was among the few successful sightings on 20 August when a Catalina of No 265 Squadron, based on Madagascar, found *U862*, running surfaced, shortly after dawn. Radioing his position, Flt Lt J. S. Lough dived into the attack as Timm, realising that he had no time to submerge, ordered his flak weapons to be manned and readied. When the approaching aircraft was only 500m from his boat Timm ordered all weapons to open fire, but the Catalina kept a straight and steady course on its bomb run. The 3.7cm cannon scored several hits, causing debris to fall from the aircraft, before it jammed, the problem brought about by the effects of long periods of submersion despite large quantities of grease having been slapped on to the moving parts. However, the two double-barrelled 2cm cannon poured shells into the Catalina, which continued its shallow dive, flames engulfing the cockpit and Timm frantically ordering *U 862* hard to starboard lest the aircraft collide with him. Heeling over to one side as the diesels raced to maximum revolutions, *U 862* pulled herself out of the way as the Catalina skimmed overhead to crash and explode in the sea, showering the victorious Germans with water. Of Lough and his twelve crewmen there was no sign, although a single floating dinghy pulled aboard *U 862* yielded Lough's logbook, his navigation charts and some items of RAF clothing.

Sensibly, with aircraft scouring the region for the downed Catalina and its U-boat target, Timm decided to vacate the area at high speed—but to no avail. Constantly diving after his *Wanze* radar detector had chirped its audible warnings, he released three Aphrodite decoy balloons that trailed thin strips of radar-reflecting aluminium in an effort to mislead enemy hunters and elected to bring operations to a halt and head for Penang. His judgement proved correct as, unbeknown to him, the Royal Navy immediately ordered Force 65, built around the carrier HMS *Battler*, into the Mozambique Channel to hunt for him.

The boat arrived at the Strait of Malacca in early September, Timm mindful of information regarding the torpedoing of U-boats within the narrow waterway and the ineffectiveness of Japanese escorts and ASW forces. One of Penang's Arado aircraft overflew *U 862* as she awaited the arrival of a small Japanese torpedo-boat for the run into harbour. Radio warnings from Dommes in Penang telling of the need to 'reckon everywhere with enemy submarines' this time proved unnecessary, although it was only a delay by the British in decoding Timm's message detailing his arrival time that had failed to allow the diversion of any of four British submarines within the region for an ambush.

As the boat entered Penang an assembled reception committee that included Wilhelm Dommes' staff and Japanese *Shosho* Uozumi Jisaku (former commander of the *Haguro* and current commander of the 8th Submarine Division) was drawn up on Swettenham Pier. Dommes himself had met *U 862* at the harbour entrance after sailing out in a small pinnace to offer his own congratulations as well as immediate advice on how best to handle Japanese customs and courtesy.

While the boat tied up, the incongruous sight of an Indian military band blasting out the 'Lilli Marlene' and various other *Wehrmacht* favourites, flanked by the Japanese officers in immaculate dress whites, greeted Timm's crew. Speeches—incomprehensible to the assembled Germans since they were delivered in Japanese—followed, after which the men were given the kind of reception banquet that had become a distant memory in Europe.

As *U 862* lay at Swettenham Pier, Dommes took the opportunity to have her *Bachstelze* removed from the stowage canisters at the stern end of the '*Wintergarten*'. Although Timm had used the device both in the Denmark Strait and in the Indian Ocean, it had provided little by way of benefit and Dommes had greater need of the flimsy gyrocopter. One of the three Arado 196 aircraft that were operated by German pilots in Penang had burnt out, and by bartering Timm's *Bachstelze* (as well as one taken from *U 196* that had arrived after a barren patrol on 10 August) with the Japanese he was able to obtain a Japanese Reisui floatplane to augment his small aerial reconnaissance team.

The men from *U 862* spent three days in palatial accommodation within Penang's German station before their boat was moved to Singapore, where her keel cargo could be removed. Timm was suffering from a short though severe fever as his boat sailed through the Malacca Strait, fully alert to the threat of enemy submarines and with the majority of the crew on deck and wearing lifejackets. An Arado circled overhead as *U 862* set sail during the evening of 12 September, a second aircraft, with Dommes aboard, joining the boat early the next day before flying ahead to Singapore. It was a relieved Timm that docked his boat in Singapore. Cars and buses took him and his crew to Pasir Panjang on the island's eastern side, where Timm received news of his award from Dönitz of the Knight's Cross, effective from 19 September—the fourth for an Indian Ocean U-boat man. Fourteen Iron Crosses First Class and 36 Second Class were distributed amongst the crew as they celebrated their arrival that evening. Within days their boat was in drydock, her keel opened and emptied and the cargo replaced by goods bound ultimately for Europe.

Within days of his arrival Timm had already communicated an idea for an ambitious new assault to BdU in Berlin. Godt's diary entry for 14 September recorded the request as well as the status of two boats:

> U 862 requested permission for subsidiary operation off SW Australia, pointing out time which had been saved at sea, good condition of the crew, boat and batteries. In spite of low battery capacity, U 168 has made same request before basic overhaul in Japan. BdU concurs with suggestion (Commander of U 862 has sailed this route before as Merchant Navy officer).
>
> U 537 and U 843 ready to put to sea on about 10.10 for return passage home. Refuel arranged for somewhere in SW part of Indian Ocean by UIT 24 and a Type IXD boat.[7]

In fact U 843 would be held at Singapore for longer than at first anticipated as UIT 24 had been refitted at Kobe before embarking on the routine and perilous cargo runs between Japan and Singapore in accordance with the agreement with the Imperial Japanese Navy—narrowly escaping destruction by American submarines at least twice as they waited astride the well-travelled route. Plans for a return to Europe were scrapped in September shortly after Godt's confident diary entry owing to a lack of refuelling options within the Indian Ocean. His interest sparked by Timm's and Pich's joint suggestion, Dönitz added U 537 to the projected Australian operation, which was scheduled to begin in October.

Meanwhile a sister-boat to U 862 had also successfully docked at Penang, Kapitänleutnant Jürgen Oesten bringing U 861 into harbour on 22 September after an arduous voyage that had seen four ships destroyed and another badly damaged. Oesten was another veteran submariner, active within the U-Boat Service since pre-war days. Taking command of U 861 as the Type IXD2 lay within Bremen's A. G. Weser yards for final completion in August 1943, Oesten commissioned the boat into the Kriegsmarine the following month.

U 861 sailed on her inaugural patrol on 20 April 1944, destined first for operations off the coast of Brazil before moving onward into the Indian Ocean. Like Timm's and the other eastbound boats she carried a cargo consignment for Malaysia, including two 2cm Flak 38 weapons and ammunition, navigational instruments, spare Junkers compressor parts, motor, machine and workshop parts, 109.8 tons of lead for the Imperial Japanese Navy and 120 tons of mercury within her keel. Also on board was a war correspondent, *Leutnant (PK)* Hermann Kiefer, who embarked as the boat prepared to sail.

Oesten's outbound journey into the Atlantic was relatively problem-free, and *U 861* crossed the Equator on 23 June with all due ceremony. During early June *U 861* prowled the coast of Brazil, which country had recently entered the war against Germany. Although Oesten missed an opportunity to attack the American troopship SS *William A. Mann,* which had departed Rio de Janeiro on 2 July carrying Brazilian troops to Italy, he did sight the Brazilian auxiliary troopship *Vital Oliveira* carrying 150 people, also headed for Italy and under escort by the small patrol boat *Javari.*

While Oesten observed the ships through his periscope the escort left the troop transport's side and he followed the escort boat, firing a T5 torpedo but missing because of the target's small size. However, the *Vital Oliveira* was not so fortunate and the 1,737-ton vessel was attacked and sunk on 20 July. The sinking resulted in a heavy loss of life, and the lieutenant who commanded the patrol ship was later court-martialled for deserting his charge and allowing the U-boat attack to take place without retaliation.

Oesten recorded weak day and night air patrols off Brazil by both aircraft and blimps as he sank a second victim, the American Liberty ship SS *William Gaston* from convoy JT.39, south-south-west of Rio, again escaping detection. Shortly after this Oesten was ordered by BdU to proceed east towards Cape Town, where he was at first instructed to operate in loose company with *U 862*, an order rescinded after intelligence concerning the Mozambique Channel was received. During the early morning of 20 August (1215hrs on 21 August U-boat time) *U 861*, cruising northwards in search of targets, sank the SS *Berwickshire* east of Durban. That evening Oesten again made an attack, hitting twice and damaging the 8,139-ton British tanker MV *Deronia* from convoy DN.68

and recording her as 'probably sunk', although in fact the tanker managed to limp into Durban under her own power.

Buoyed by his success, Oesten decided on an impromptu celebration north of Madagascar after skirting the eastern shores of the island and finding nothing:

> On the way out [to Penang] on 2 September 1944, the boat had been in commission for exactly one year and I thought I should give the crew a treat. So we headed for a small atoll, Aldabra island, where we went into the lagoon, anchored and made ready to send a boat ashore and things like that. But then a Catalina flying boat came and, as I later learned, they were just on a transfer flight and weren't watching properly. We had all our guns trained on her, one 3.7cm, two double 2cm cannon, even the 10.5cm, but she didn't see us so we though, oh well, let it go, because we just went in there for fun, no military reason. But unfortunately the rubber lifeboat had to be recalled and never made landfall because within the lagoon the current was so strong, and the boat had no motor that I could see they were having problems.[8]

A final combat victory fell to Oesten three days later when he torpedoed the Greek steamer SS *Ioannis Fafalios* east of Mombasa. Before sinking the Greek vessel Oesten had used his *Bachstelze*, and one of the three seamen aboard trained in its use, to locate another merchant ship, but in the time taken to retrieve the gyrocopter their quarry had disappeared into the expanse of the Indian Ocean.

The crew of *U 861* remained in good health and good spirits throughout the voyage but Oesten understood the demands that were to be placed upon his predominantly young crew. Although he had managed to keep together a hard core of experienced seamen from his earlier crews, there were little things that, he recognised, would help the morale of his men as they spent week after week at sea. One such—small but valuable— was Oesten's alteration to the lookout duty times. The afternoon watch was split in half, i.e. between 1600 and 1820hrs and between 1820 and 2000hrs, so that his 'boys got their dinner at a reasonable time, also having the effect that their times on duty were constantly changing'. One of their most dangerous foes—boredom and its corollary, complacency—was kept at bay by means of activities organised for the crew and the production of an onboard weekly newspaper, *Der Monsun Bote* (written mainly by Kiefer during the voyage), which dispensed whatever world news was available, general information, crew matters, games, contests and poetry. Issue 17 came off Kiefer's typewriter on 17 September, the front page decorated with five sinking pennants that also flew from the raised periscope six days later when *U 861* entered Penang. Here the boat would remain in port for over a month, her crew resting on Penang Hill before they moved on to Singapore.

NOTES

1. BdU KTB, 14 August 1944, National Archives Microfilm, PG30353, Roll No 4066.
2. BdU KTB, 6 May 1944, National Archives Microfilm, PG30346, Roll No 4065.
3. See Paterson, *Second U-Boat Flotilla*, pp. 236–8.
4. Lüdden is often listed as having been killed in this ambush but this is incorrect. He was later transferred to the command of BdU Staff, responsible for artillery and navigational matters, but was mortally injured during an accidental fire aboard the training ship *Daressalam* on 13 January 1945.
5. Although Bordeaux was taken by American troops, the Festung Girondemündung that spanned the entrance to the Gironde river held firm until the end of the war, like similar 'fortresses' at La Pallice, St-Nazaire and Lorient.
6. Admiralty Anti-Submarine Warfare Report, October 1944.
7. BdU KTB, 14 September 1944, National Archives Microfilm, PG303354 Roll No 4066
8. Interview with Jürgen Oesten, Hamburg, 8 March 2003.

Nine

Australia and New Zealand

D ÖNITZ'S backing of a U-boat assault into the Pacific Ocean against Australia promised the possibility of opening new and potentially abundant hunting grounds for U-boats that were increasingly under pressure within the Indian Ocean, both through a lack of targets and because of improving and more aggressive enemy ASW activities. Helmut Pich's *U 168* had been laid up for extensive repairs at Jakarta since March 1944, and by the time BdU's agreement arrived for the new assault both he and his crew were more than ready for action. However, the message that approved the new deployment, despatched from Berlin on 14 September 1944, had been successfully decrypted by 'Ultra', and although the Allied naval command was unable to specify where the enemy might strike it was aware which boats were allocated for the new attack and of the likelihood that it would centre on south-west Australia.

U 168 was compelled to make a short voyage to Surabaya, where the boat could undergo battery trials within range of the shipyard before heading for Australia. As a matter of routine, details of the boat's transfer, including the scheduled departure and arrival times, intended speed and estimated position at the midpoint of the voyage, were given to the Japanese by radio signal, and this was in turn intercepted and immediately decoded by Allied intelligence who, as well as breaking the Enigma code, had long been reading Japanese ciphers. Indeed by April 1942 up to 30 per cent of Japanese naval coded radio traffic (JN 25) was being decoded, although periodic changes of the five-digit code continued to cause temporary 'blackouts' amongst the American cryptographers. However, the sinking of the submarine *I-1* in January 1943 by Royal New Zealand Navy trawlers near Guadalcanal and a subsequent examination of the wreck by divers yielded not only fresh cipher material but also the long-missing piece—a Japanese chart with the overlay for decoding grid references, hitherto unbroken and from that moment onwards open to Allied analysts.

Pich sailed from Jakarta before dawn on 5 October with a hostile reception already racing to intercept him. The Dutch submarine *Zwaardfisch*, attached to the 8th Submarine Flotilla, was active within the region and, guided by the precise intelligence reports, Lt-Cdr H. Goosens was submerged precisely on station at dawn the following day as *U 168* appeared, running surfaced and only 'five minutes late', according to Goosens. Pich was not steering a zig-zag course, perhaps lulled into false security by the lush surroundings and seemingly unhurried pace of life within Java. At a range of 900yds and only six minutes after sighting *U 168*, Goosens fired a full bow salvo of six torpedoes, which was spotted by an alert German as the 'fish' neared the target but too late to allow evasion. The result was devastating. One torpedo impacted at the level of the Petty Officer's Mess and detonated, a second pierced the pressure hull in the control room and failed to explode, while a third also hit and did not explode. However, one had been enough. Many men, both above decks and below, were killed by the blast as *U 168* upended and rapidly plunged to the bottom to a depth of 45m. While some of the crew were swept overboard by the explosion, others, including Pich and his LI and Medical Officer, were trapped within the control room. There they waited in darkness as the water level rose, allowing pressure to equalise and the hatch to be opened, the resultant air bubble blowing all of them to the surface.

Zwaardfisch surfaced and began to nose gently amongst the survivors, confident that no Japanese surface or air escort was nearby. Twenty-seven survivors were hauled aboard the Dutch submarine. Pich, his LI, his IWO, his Medical Officer and a seriously wounded leading seaman were kept aboard for return to Australia, the remaining men being handed over to a nearby Indonesian fishing vessel and later landed in Japanese territory. *Zwaardfisch* then departed the scene, sinking four more ships before returning to Fremantle, Australia, on 26 October.

The loss of *U 168*, yet another U-boat so close to the Eastern bases, was a shattering blow to BdU, not least because of the hindrance to *Unternehmen 'Australien'*, which offered the only fresh offensive possibilities for Far Eastern boats. Berlin was informed of *U 168*'s destruction the following day, although the cause of the disaster was initially thought by Tokyo to have been enemy aircraft. Pich was at first reported killed in the sinking, further information only coming to light on 10 October. Dönitz was furious at the lack of Japanese escort capability, not least of all the unwillingness of the Japanese to begin ASW operations before 1100hrs! However, the fault was not entirely theirs. Although Pich was considered cool under pressure and an effective U-boat commander, he had succumbed to the sort of *laissez-faire* attitude against which Dommes continually warned his men: 'It was my greatest problem to convince the captains of our boats of the size of the danger of hostile subs. When they reached the south, they simply believed they had entered a paradise after all the stresses behind them.'[1]

Strict instructions flowed from BdU to Penang on 13 October, designed to instil in the eastern boats an understanding of the dangers posed within then Malacca Strait:

To Penang and all Far East boats:

Everything possible is to be done to reduce the danger to U-boats on passage to and between the bases. This means:

1. Before every sailing, find out from Japanese exact details of enemy submarine positions, procedure and methods of attack, as far as known. Inform approaching boats by radio, especially new boats.

2. Avoid coastal routes and much frequented areas, haul out to sea, and enter port by shortest route. No fixed escort rendezvous.

3. Areas particularly dangerous to U-boats should be passed submerged. Arrange this with Japanese.

4. If boats have to proceed surfaced, high speed, zig-zags, vary speed degrees frequently. Radar interception gear switched on, in bad visibility also radar.

5. Investigate whether passage with Japanese escort is not more dangerous than passage without escort. Take action accordingly.

6. Insist on measures which appear necessary being carried out by the Japanese.[2]

This set of instructions was followed on 21 October by further measures: 'On account of submarine danger, when proceeding into any East Asian port, close down, crew on upper deck with lifejackets, officers to wear no insignia as officers have been taken prisoner by enemy submarines.'

However, extracting intelligence information from the Japanese was a forlorn hope. Despite repeated attempts by various captains to elicit whatever data they could from their Japanese counterparts, they gained little. While the Europeans considered this to be an example of Japanese inscrutability, it is very probable that they had little information to impart in any case. Japanese submarine operations had steadily diminished in the Indian Ocean and western Pacific, limited to bolstering the flagging defence of garrisons on Guadalcanal and other Pacific islands in the face of American invasion.

Reluctant to diminish the promise of a proposed attack on Australia, Dönitz ordered *U 196* to take over Pich's role for the forthcoming offensive on 4 November, *Oberleutnant zur See* Striegler's boat having moved to Singapore during October for the removal and replacement of the keel cargo and then on to Jakarta to be fitted out once more for operations. Striegler's new instructions were complicated, involving a run west into the Indian Ocean in order to supply fuel to *U 510* (which was scheduled to return to Europe) before heading for a month of Australian operations and from there to Kobe for a long overdue battery replacement.

Kapitänleutnant Peter Schrewe's *U 537*, the spearhead of the assault on Australia, left Surabaya at 1700hrs (Tokyo time) on 9 November. Helpfully, for the enemy at least, the Japanese naval picket at Surabaya radioed detailed instructions concerning the boat's departure times, course, diving tests and route, including estimated times for passing landmarks such as Tanjung Iboes on Bali. Issued five days before *U 537*'s departure, the message was intercepted by the joint American/Australian Fleet Radio Unit Melbourne (FRUMEL) and immediately decoded. In Darwin three large fleet submarines, the USS *Flounder*, *Guavina* and *Bashaw*, sailed just one day after arriving in port to replenish, putting out on 6 November as a 'co-ordinated search and attack group'. Racing to their planned interception area while avoiding contact with the many native sailboats and sampans spotted en route, they were at their allocated stations by early morning on 10 November. *Flounder*, commanded by the group's senior officer, Cdr James E. Stevens, occupied a prime position between the Kangean Islands and the Bali mainland.

Stevens, one of the few officers aware of the source of the intelligence that had allowed such precise positioning, ignored a small Japanese escort vessel that passed by the submerged *Flounder*, demonstrating the scorn with which Allied submariners generally treated Japanese ASW craft. Almost two hours later *Flounder*'s deck officer sighted what he took to be a small sailboat bearing 347 degrees and at an estimated range of 9,000yds. Within six minutes the object had hardened into the conning tower of a German U-boat.

U 537 travelled on the surface at 12kts, making regular zigzags as required by BdU instructions. Schrewe's boat had been held within the shipyards of Surabaya for longer than he had originally anticipated, and the outbound trip from Europe that had ended in August had been only his second war patrol aboard the Type IXC/40.[3] His last venture had yielded no confirmed successes, although both he and BdU believed that he had sunk a destroyer with the miraculous T5 *Zaunkönig*. His new designated area of operations was south-west of Fremantle.

Aboard *Flounder* the supposedly evasive course steered by Schrewe was too regular to be effective, a 'zig' towards the submerged American allowing Stevens to fire electric torpedoes from his four stern tubes, which he did 32 minutes after the initial sighting. At a range of only 1,000yds he could not miss:

0827 Observed hit about 40 feet inside the bow. There was a tremendous explosion and the whole target was obscured by smoke and flame . . . felt another hit.

0833 Another explosion.

0836 Another explosion. These were violent and seemed close and were thought to be aerial depth bombs, so we went to 150 feet and cleared the area. Subsequent consideration and information from the sound operators indicates that these were probably explosions inside the sinking sub because the sound operator reports that they were accompanied by breaking up noises and hissing.[4]

Schrewe and his 57 crew members had been taken completely by surprise by the wakeless electric torpedoes and there were no survivors. Japanese patrol craft remained oblivious to *U 537*'s fate. Mindful of the dangers posed by Allied HF/DF, neither Dommes nor BdU had expected to hear any further communication from *U 537* as she went forward to savage the Australian merchant lanes and her destruction went unreported until January 1945, when she was listed as overdue, missing presumed lost to unknown causes.

With two of the four U-boats known by the Allies to be destined for Australia accounted for, the chances of survival for Heinrich Timm's *U 862* appeared slim at best. However, Timm slipped from Jakarta at midday on 18 November, having transferred from Singapore to prepare for his voyage, and raced unchecked through the Sunda Strait and then south into the Indian Ocean. No betraying Japanese broadcasts had been made, and *U 862* sailed into rough seas heading almost due south, keeping well offshore and away from the routine air patrols that Timm suspected would cover the approaches to western Australia. Little intelligence material had been gathered before departure, and the Imperial Japanese Navy had not operated within the Australian region for months.

Timm, reliant on his knowledge of the area as a merchant mariner, opted to shy away from Schrewe's hunting ground off Fremantle and headed instead for the south-east of Australia and the shipping lanes around Tasmania. Facing heavy rolling seas and with his lookouts lashed by severe rainstorms, Timm sailed ever south, crash-diving at the sight of enemy aircraft between squalls and remaining undetected as he cruised for his patrol area.

The last of the 'Australian boats', *U 196*, with her complicated schedule of refuelling, war patrol and transfer to Japan, departed Jakarta on the final day of November. *Oberleutnant zur See* Johannes-Werner Striegler was due to take his boat from port through the Sunda Strait and make for a rendezvous with *Kapitänleutnant* Alfred Eick's *U 510*, which had sailed from Jakarta on 26 November. Eick carried the usual cargo from Java, including 19 tons of crude rubber stowed within the boat's free-flooding superstructure. However, serious leaks had developed within *U 510*'s exhausts and Eick was forced to abort his mission, returning to Java for repairs. A recall order was issued for *U 196* on the day of her departure, repeated six times but receiving no response. The presumed position of *U 196* continued to be charted, BdU's War Diary entry of 12 December illustrating the bewilderment and blind hope as to Striegler's whereabouts and trusting to a faulty communications problem as the cause of the persistent silence:

> According to report from naval attaché in Tokyo, *U 196* left Jakarta on 30 November. Supply of *U 510* by *U 196* foreseen earlier must have fallen through, since *U 510* entered port because of damage to her machinery.
> *U 843* left Jakarta on 10 December for Germany and will be supplied by *U 196*. Since the position of *U 196* is not exactly known, she will be requested

to send her position. After supply activities are completed, *U 196* will make a short patrol and then return to Japan to get new batteries.[5]

Finally, on 22 December BdU admitted the inevitable, informing Dommes that they considered *U 196* sunk by enemy submarines shortly after leaving Jakarta—probably ambushed in the Sunda Strait. In actuality the Allies, who had followed the signal exchange with interest, were equally perplexed as to Striegler's fate. Allied submarines within the area had made no claims and the Sunda Strait was not mined until weeks later by a Dutch submarine. *U 196* and her crew of 66 had simply disappeared.

By December 1944, unbeknown to Timm, *U 862* was the sole survivor of the Australian U-boat attack force. Aboard his boat Timm was slightly mystified as to the apparent regularity of stepped-up Australian air patrols, unaware, of course, that 'Ultra' had betrayed the operation's purpose. In his own War Diary he recorded his thoughts, deducing that perhaps Schrewe had opened his attack and thereby stirred a response from the RAAF. Timm cruised east across the Great Australian Bight, keeping well below the Australian subcontinent and weathering the severe conditions common within the southern ocean. Finally, on 6 December *U 862* came within sight of Kangeroo Island, south-west of Adelaide, Timm and his crew frustrated by a dearth of merchant shipping in what they had expected would be busy trade lanes. Lighthouses appeared on the horizon as *U 862* continued east toward Tasmania. On 9 December the patience of the Germans was rewarded when hydrophones reported piston-engine noises ahead.

Timm ordered his crew to action stations and immediately resolved to attack the unknown merchant ship. The vessel was sighted in heavy seas and was already on the U-boat's beam as acoustic conditions had allowed only a late detection. However, unwilling to let the target go and unable to manoeuvre in time for a submerged attack, Timm ordered his gun crews to their stations, despite vocal protestations from his IWO Reiffenstuhl, who considered the conditions to be completely unsuitable for such an attack. U-boats were notoriously unstable gun platforms in fine weather, let alone amidst the pitch and roll of the storm-wracked southern ocean. Nevertheless Timm persevered, and the first shot from his 10.5cm arced toward Greek freighter MV *Ilossis*, whose crew had sighted *U 862* but were convinced, by their location, that the newcomer was friendly. The first wide shot from *U 862* persuaded them otherwise, and the merchantman's four gunners raced for their own 4in stern gun in order to return fire. The *Ilossis* ran for the Australian coast as shells began to fall uncomfortably close to *U 862*, spray blanketing the U-boat and prompting Timm to rescind his decision and submerge in order to make an ignominious retreat. The Greek ship disappeared into a thick rain squall, neither side having scored a hit, and *U 862* dipped under the waves and headed away from the coast as plain-language distress calls flowed from the *Ilossis*. Aboard *U 862* Reiffenstuhl vented his feelings within his private diary:

> I am annoyed . . . because of this senseless enterprise. Now we have alarmed the whole coast to our presence; certainly over the next few days no more steamships will be sailing past . . . Because of this nonsense we have destroyed all our chances here. Nothing has been proved.[6]

Despite forces within Australia's Southern Defence Area having been whittled down dramatically during the previous months, two rocket-equipped Beaufighters arrived over the *Ilossis* within two and a half hours as the hunt for *U 862* began. Three corvettes joined the search, although Timm managed to slip away, aware of the corvettes' presence but powering through blinding rain both surfaced and submerged to put distance between himself and the Australians.

By 14 December the weather had moderated. Tasmania's southern mountain range appeared on the horizon, lighthouses casting their comforting glow over the scene and providing precise navigational fixes for *U 862*, which had positioned herself among the shipping lanes from Melbourne to New Zealand. A tanker that was sighted and chased escaped, oblivious to the German's presence. During the days that followed there were several sound contacts, but the targets remained elusive because of their speed and the obliterating rain squalls. It was not until a calm Christmas Eve, as the crew prepared for a small feast beneath a Christmas tree made of broom handles, wire and strips of canvas, that another target hove into view. The American Liberty ship SS *Robert J. Walker* was hit by an initial attack with two torpedoes 160 miles south-west of Sydney. The stubborn ship refused to sink as Timm observed it through his periscope. The ship's Master, Captain Murdoch D. MacRae, at first believed that his propeller had hit a mine, despite the fact that depth of water there precluded the use of minefields such as had been laid by German raiders in bygone years. With his propulsion destroyed, MacRae radioed for help. The small amount of flooding caused by the attack was soon brought under control and his crew remained calm, awaiting further developments.

Frustrated by his inability to sink the disabled ship, Timm fired a third torpedo, missing completely and causing him to pause and circle the scene as he decided on a course of action. He was unwilling to use too many of his valuable 'eels'. *U 862*'s weapon load-out was less that the standard load-out of a Type IXD2, thanks to a lack of stored torpedoes at Penang and an unwillingness to have external stowage of such weaponry for fear of the need to spend long periods of time on the surface in order to retrieve them. Timm hesitated for two hours, slowly circling at *Schnorchel* depth out of sight of the Liberty ship as he recharged batteries. Eventually he returned at periscope depth to finish off the *Robert J. Walker* off and a fourth torpedo was fired at the target, which was now partially obscured by a haze that hung low over the water caused by dust blown offshore by the freshening breeze. Aboard the Liberty ship the torpedo was quickly spotted and every available weapon opened fire on the approaching danger, hits from a 2cm flak weapon detonating it 100yds short of the ship's starboard flank. Mistaking the detonation for a hit, Timm was amazed that the American still refused to sink. Crewmen aboard the merchantman had discharged smoke floats into the water to attempt to throw Timm off his aim, and, believing they had been dropped by an aircraft, the U-boat commander was even more cautious in his next approach. Yet another of his precious 'eels' arced away from *U 862* and this time the deeper-running torpedo, unaffected by the fierce defensive fire, exploded against the empty No 4 hold, sending the stubborn vessel stern-first below the waves. It was an historic occasion: the SS *Robert J. Walker* was the only ship sunk by U-boat within the Pacific Ocean.

U 862 retreated to seaward still submerged, the Christmas party postponed as Timm attempted to make the most of the little oxygen aboard his boat. Unwilling to ventilate by either surfacing or using the *Schnorchel* owing to the certainty of enemy aircraft, *U 862* was in a weakened state as she headed to the south-east. The hornet's nest of Australian activity that followed, however, missed her entirely. As RAAF aircraft bombed phantom targets Timm hauled out into the Tasman Sea and headed east towards New Zealand. A ship sighted on 27 December escaped from an attempted attack after a single electric torpedo detonated prematurely only 300 metres from the U-boat. Timm imagined that their presence must have been detected by the zig-zagging ship and reported hearing distant aircraft bombs later that day, but in fact the target remained blissfully unaware of how close it had come to disaster.

Once more fierce gales ravaged the boat as Timm laid course for New Zealand's North Cape, rounding Cape Regina, the northernmost tip of the mainland, on 7 January. Settled into the lee of the North Island, *U 862* followed the shipping lane southward in calm seas, pausing near Auckland harbour to search for prey. Occasional targets of opportunity passed unmolested before *U 862* as Timm showed an extreme caution in engaging the enemy, unable to manoeuvre into a submerged firing position more than once as the unwitting steamers continuing on their way. Contrarily, Timm also took *U 862* into the shallows of Gisborne harbour at night on 15 January, watching people walking the streets and cars driving along; there was no sign of a blackout in this remote corner of the Allied world. However, finding no targets, Timm retreated from the harbour, ignoring a small coastal steamer and heading for Hawkes Bay and Napier, where he again approached the shore, stopped less than half a mile from land and allowed the crew to come on deck to observe the peaceful scene.

A small steamship exited Napier's harbour and *U 862* took up the chase, the merchant's navigation lights making pursuit easy. Diving to attack, Timm was foiled by another premature torpedo detonation that, once again, went miraculously unnoticed. As Timm sailed onward he received an urgent despatch on 17 January from BdU, directed at him and three other captains already dead: 'Von der Esch, Ganzer, Schrewe, Timm: return to Jakarta immediately.'

U 862's New Zealand adventure was over, and Timm brought his boat away from the undisturbed tranquillity to traverse the seas well south of Australia and make for Jakarta. This time nature unleashed its full fury on the German interloper as he sped west, enormous mountains of water cascading over the U-boat's hull as the heavily strapped lookouts struggled for survival. Timm, however, was exhilarated by the voyage, the seaman in him alive to nature's fury. Once well clear of western Australia *U 862* headed south to more clement conditions, and it was on

6 February 1945, outside his expected hunting grounds, that her commander chanced upon his final victim. The Liberty ship SS *Peter Sylvester*, carrying 317 army pack mules, 2,700 tons of mainly hay cargo and 106 US Army passengers, was hit by three torpedoes and immediately sank, the survivors dousing their emergency lights as *U 862* surfaced and approached, fearful of possible Japanese machine-gun fire. To the unfortunate Liberty ship went the unwanted accolade of being the last Allied ship sunk by enemy action within the Indian Ocean, and the only vessel destroyed by U-boat attack within that region during 1945.

Leaving another storm of Australian searching behind him, Timm headed for the Sunda Strait and a return to an uncertain future at the Far Eastern U-boat bases.

NOTES

1. Wilhelm Dommes' letter to Gus Britton, Royal Navy Submarine Museum, dated 29 November 1980.
2. BdU KTB, 13 October 1944, National Archives Microfilm, PG303356 Roll No 4066.
3. *U 537* had made one journey to the frigid waters off Canada, where crewmen established an unmanned weather station on Newfoundland—which remained undiscovered until 1981. The boat made no sinkings.
4. USS *Flounder*, Report of Fourth War Patrol.
5. BdU KTB, 12 December 1944, National Archives Microfilm, PG303360 Roll No 4066.
6. David Stevens, *U-Boat Far From Home*, p. 149.

Ten

The Rising Sun Finally Sets

WHILE TIMM had been at sea mounting his solo attack against Australasia, elsewhere the fortunes of the other Far East submarines had improved little. The two remaining U-boats that survived the Allied blockade had reached Jakarta within days of each other. The large Type XB *U 219* entered harbour after a marathon voyage that had endured one false start. She was commanded by *Korvettenkapitän* Walter Burghagen, born in September 1891, of the same graduating Crew of 1911 as Karl Dönitz and the oldest active submariner within the U-Boat Service. Burghagen had served as IWO aboard *U 44*, *U 49* and *U 50* during the First World War and was taken prisoner in 1916 after the last of his boats was sunk. Many of the younger men amongst his crew considered him too old for operations, although eventually his experience would keep them alive to witness the end of another world war.

The cavernous mine chutes of this, the largest U-boat constructed for the *Kriegsmarine* were filled with 24 pressurised containers holding a variety of supplies for Malaysia—an entire radio transmitting station destined for Kobe, spare parts for diesel repairs and the torpedo balancing station at Penang, hospital supplies, equipment for the German radio station at Singapore, spares for the Arado 196 aircraft and crated aluminium bars—while uncut optical glass and mercury in steel flasks were secured in the boat's keel.

Loaded with provisions for three to four months, the boat had departed Bordeaux for La Pallice at the end of April 1944 in order to take the opportunity to conduct diving and trim tests with the full load: a Type XB had never carried so much material before and its performance under those conditions was unknown. The trials were a near-disaster, as IWO Hans-Joachim Krug remembered:

> Nobody could say with confidence in their calculations whether the boat with all this freight would dive and so on, and with only six to eight metres' depth in the harbour basin before the bunkers, fresh water at that, it was impossible to make reliable trim tests. So it was decided by the flotilla that a shipyard engineer and the Flotilla's Chief Engineer would come with us for trim and deep-diving tests at the 200-metre line, the easiest thing to do afterward taking them on to La Pallice and leaving them there as we departed.
>
> It was lucky for us that the Flotilla Engineer was aboard. Because of the acute danger of air attack, we had planned to travel the whole day submerged. However, in order to find the navigation points for La Pallice, we wanted to trim the boat before dawn and surface in order to take a star fix in the twilight. We didn't have other possibilities like radio beacons etc. But it didn't work out like that.
>
> Immediately, with the first diving attempt . . . the boat sank like a stone. Only the experienced Flotilla Engineer succeeded in getting us back to the surface after five exhausting hours of underwater manoeuvres (All ahead full! Full reverse! With men running to bow and stern), rocking the boat and moving an air bubble within the diving cells back and forth.
>
> It was proven that, with this equipment and freight, the boat was too heavy and non-operational. Unfortunately, we also found [upon reaching periscope depth] that we didn't have any reliable location fix. The hope of taking a star sight in the twilight also went wrong, since a Sunderland appeared over us at exactly the time we wanted to surface. And of course, when one is in such a situation in the middle of the Atlantic, it was vital for the navigation of a mine-free entrance into a Biscay base.
>
> Nevertheless — by using our nose and plenty of good luck — we found the escort rendezvous for La Pallice and entered the bunker during early morning.[1]

U 219 eased through the lock and into the La Pallice U-boat shelter, where the boat was forced to reload her freight and provisions. Burghagen next returned to Bordeaux, where workers were racing to equip as many boats as possible with a *Schnorchel*. *U 219* received her *Schnorchel* installation, losing all vestiges of the equipment, including the heavy winch gear, she had used while acting as an auxiliary tanker on a previous war patrol. The boat also had her deck gun and its ammunition taken off; the weapon was of little use at that stage of the war anyway.

U 219 sailed once more from Bordeaux on 22 August after an Allied air attack on the Le Verdon roadstead at the mouth of the Gironde river. Accompanying *U 180* and *U 195* under escort into Biscay, she picked up signals of incoming Sunderland and Mosquito aircraft. Sporadic flak arced upwards but inflicted no damage on the British intruders, who in turn failed to hamper the outbound convoy. Once free of the coastline all three boats dived and proceeded submerged towards the Atlantic, *U 219* employing her new *Schnorchel* as Burghagen planned his journey to Malaysia. The complicated *Schnorchel* raising gear would malfunction in mid-September, rendering it useless until the sweating engineers aboard managed to effect makeshift repairs.

On 28 September Burghagen received fresh instructions to refuel from the inbound *U 1062*, which had left Penang on 15 July with 105 tons of cargo for Germany. *Oberleutnant zur See* Karl Albrecht's boat had been at sea for over two months when the refuelling rendezvous was arranged 600 miles west-south-west of the Cape Verde Islands but two days after BdU's message had been transmitted—and intercepted—*U 1062* was found by the Americans. Three destroyers from the screen around the carrier USS *Mission Bay* were sent to investigate the location of the proposed rendezvous, the USS *Fessenden* finding firm sonar contact which was attacked with 'Hedgehog' and depth charges. Four underwater explosions were heard, marking the end of *U 1062* and the 55 men aboard.

As *U 219* had cruised into the area of the meeting at dusk two days previously lookouts detected a strong smell of diesel from the oily water; distant explosions had already been heard through the hull during the boat's afternoon approach, their source unknown. Burghagen had brought his crew to battle stations as they awaited the refueller, flak guns manned and ready. At 1940hrs an aircraft was spotted, wrongly identified as a Skua; it was in fact a VC-9 Avenger, launched from the USS *Tripoli*. At first it appeared that the American had not noticed the U-boat below since it overflew the submarine with no offensive gesture, but then it wheeled around in the sky to roar towards *U 219*'s starboard beam. Silhouetted against the still-light western horizon, the Avenger, taking of concentrated 3.7cm and 2cm anti-aircraft fire, streaked overhead and dropped a single bomb that exploded to the U-boat's port side, soaking the German gunners as the aircraft ditched into the water in flames, its entire crew lost with their aircraft. Burghagen took the opportunity to order diesels full ahead in preparation for a crash-dive in case of further air attack. However, in the noise and confusion the helmsman within the conning tower misheard and ordered all diesels stopped, prompting frantic calls to get them restarted and the boat below the surface.

Strong explosions echoed through the water in the boat's wake as a Wildcat from *Tripoli* arrived on the scene and belatedly attacked. Once the boat had submerged, however, calm was restored and *U 219* headed south, away from the region. Distant depth charges continued to be heard through the dense water, their pitch raising and falling all through the following two days. At some point the sounds would have signalled the end of *U 1062*, although the men aboard *U 219* were distracted by the need for self-preservation as they again came under air attack, the transmitter choosing that moment to go down and their assailant later augmented by depth charges from unknown attackers after the boat had dived once more. Under nearly continuous bombardment *U 219* crept steadily south, Burghagen believing the enemy to have his position fixed but with no clear echo to fire at.

By 2 October the escort ships had faded into the distance, and *U 219* surfaced long enough for the radio personnel to clamber on deck and discover that water had seeped along the main antennae, shorting the wireless circuits. Warnings from the GSR gear alerted them to incoming radar-equipped aircraft and the communications men narrowly made it back to the bridge in time as *U 219* crash-dived once more. Soon the familiar high-pitched sound of a destroyer's propellers was overhead again and depth charges rained down.

U 219 was able to drift on top of a salinity layer that lay at between 75 and 85m, engines stopped to conserve battery power. Within the control room the boat's officers closely monitored the salinometer, an instrument comprising a 30cm graduated glass tube that tapered toward the top. Weighted with lead shot and floated in a metal cylinder connected with the outside seawater, the instrument was able to measure water temperature and density as well as salt content. The boat drifted west-south-west, differing salinity layers bending the probing Allied ASDIC and rendering *U 219* virtually invisible. With almost every light extinguished and all but the most essential personnel in their bunks, *U 219* lay for an incredible 68 hours, drifting nearly 120 miles in the Atlantic current. The carbon dioxide level crept steadily upwards until it reached ten times the normal level permissible. As the air quality deteriorated to the point of being almost unbreathable the lower deck was evacuated, followed by the lower bunks. Men even went as far as to put their heads in lockers, attempting to squeeze every molecule of life-giving oxygen from the dense fug around them. All the potash cartridges and three-quarters of stored oxygen from the pressure bottles had been used by the time Burghagen decided that the boat must surface, the enemy seemingly lagging far behind his U-boat. Stuporous, the crewmen took their stations and *U 219* climbed from the abyss to surface, unexpectedly breaking through the Atlantic into a blinding dust cloud blown from the nearby African coast. Fate had dealt *U 219* a lucky card: the choking sand miraculously masked her radar signature. As almost all of the crew came in turns to the bridge, a foul stench streaming from the boat's putrid interior, Burghagen fired diesels and *U 219* ran for four hours, away from the American warships, to charge her drained batteries.

All arrangements to meet *U 1062* now cancelled, *U 219* made good her escape, Burghagen diving once more as soon as his boat had been thoroughly ventilated and recharged. She sailed steadily south, surfacing only to recharge batteries at night and crawling submerged for the reminder of the day until the beginning of November, when the threat of aerial discovery was felt to have passed: '1/11/1944. Commandant intends to travel surfaced. After 68 days of night and CO_2, the sun is seen again.'

U 219 entered the 'Roaring Forties' during early November after meeting with Freiwald's *U 181* to pass over '*Naxos*' and '*Borkum*' equipment. Burghagen opted to give Africa a wide berth, heading east again once his boat had reached 46° south, just north of the fringe of drift ice from the polar region. Although divorced geographically from the fighting in Europe, the crew's morale rose and dipped with each new fragment of information: '10.11.44. *Wehrmacht* reports bring daily new worries. There was also concern about the situation at their destination when BdU ordered *U 219*, and any other boats headed for Penang, to divert to Jakarta instead. Burghagen was periodically employing his unreliable *Schnorchel*, though in early December vibrations from the device shattered the insulator through which the radio transmission antennae ran, causing huge if intermittent problems with communications. With the boat travelling surfaced, the antennae and their associated equipment had a chance to dry out; radio contact was regained and news of *U 196*'s sinking near Jakarta was relayed to Burghagen.

Finally, on 6 December *U 219* approached the end of her cruise, the War Diary recording the first of the crew's beards shaved off as they looked forward to sampling the exotic taste of Java. Within five days the boat was at the entrance to the Sunda Strait, making the brief radio transmission required to enable the Japanese to arrange an escort rendezvous at the 'Dwars in de Weg' island and the crew warily eyeing the surrounding sea for the slightest hint that they were not alone:

> When we neared Jakarta . . . because a boat had been sunk recently we moved in zigzags. We waited for our escort into harbour, continuing to zigzag in case of ambush. Then the Japanese sent out a small fishing boat as escort and it was so slow that we were just inviting an attack. So very soon we left the escort behind and used our speed to get home safely.[2]

Burghagen and his weary crew finally disembarked in Priok harbour on 11 December 1944. Although none of them could know it at the time, theirs was the last but one U-boat to reach the Far East.

On 28 December *U 195* also tied up at Jakarta, having been escorted towards harbour by an Arado 196. However, Tanjong Priok appeared blackened by smoke as Oberleutnant der Reserve Friedrich Steinfeldt and his crew lined the deck for their reception. Less than twenty-four hours earlier the 1,135-ton Japanese ammunition ship *Taicho Maru* had exploded, wrecking the harbour's facilities and causing many casualties and light damage to *U 219* anchored nearby. The reception by the Japanese officers in their crisp white dress uniforms was nevertheless still formal and courteous, and their German counterparts were also assembled to bid welcome to the last new arrivals from Europe.

Steinfeldt, who had experienced a relatively uneventful voyage, had stepped into the void left by the destruction of *U 196* and refuelled the Europe-bound *U 843* on 20 December, only days after the latter's voyage for Norway had got under way. *U 195* had been forced to make Jakarta at low speed, eking out her fuel reserves, and was given the opportunity of making rendezvous with *U 181*, which was on an abortive run to Europe, in case fuel was needed. Like Burghagen's, Steinfeldt's boat had been originally destined for Penang before BdU's redirection order had come through—a fact unexplained to the men until they arrived in Java.

The increasing pressure on German and Japanese forces applied by the seemingly miraculous presence of enemy submarines so close to Penang rendered the port untenable by the middle of November. Discussions had been taking place between the German and Japanese authorities, and as early as 26 October 1944 the Japanese had concurred with the German reluctance to use Penang as a permanent U-boat station, although they were unwilling to relinquish the port completely:

> After going into the question thoroughly with the Japanese Navy, consulting stations in the Southern Area, I advise against giving up Penang. For the present, however, in view of the Nicobar Islands operations and the fact that the defences of Penang cannot be strengthened, boats should only put into Penang for the present in urgent cases, and they should approach and leave the other ports via the Sunda or Lombok Straits [at the northern and southern tips of Java]. Preparations are being made to transfer the main radio stations in the Southern Area from Penang to Jakarta.[3]

To reinforce the perilous situation facing Penang, British Liberator bombers from No 159 Squadron, based at Kharagpur, India, laid 60 mines in the approach channels to the port during the night of 27 October. With only ineffective Japanese minesweeping forces available, it had become apparent to the Germans that the time to withdraw from Penang had come. The *Kriegsmarine* pilots took their two Arados and the Reisui floatplane to a new station in Jakarta during November 1944. U-boats also withdrew to Jakarta and Surabaya, at which latter port they joined the small number of Japanese I-boats still located regionally. Penang became the object of further unwelcome attention on 5 November, when five Allied photo-reconnaissance missions overflew the city. The Japanese-controlled local newspaper *Penang Shimbun* reported them 'driven away', although this appears to have been little more than propagandist wishful thinking.

During December 1944 Dommes officially took up his new appointment as *Chef der U-Bootsstützpunkt Südraum* and relocated permanently from Penang to Singapore; Erhardt flew to Penang to oversee the winding down of operations there and returned to Singapore during February. As of 26 November the main combat base for U-boats in the Far East was officially declared to be Jakarta. By 1 January 1945 the *Kriegsmarine* had a presence at six Far Eastern bases. Penang's facilities had been scaled down and the port was no longer fully operational, although not yet under direct enemy pressure. Jakarta remained the primary site for equipping combat boats for sea. Surabaya was used for both loading and maintenance. The newly established base under Kentrat in Kobe, as well as that at Singapore, was exclusively for repair, the former generally for battery maintenance, while Yokohama continued to host a small loading depot.

It was during the move by Dommes to Singapore that he received notification from the Japanese Naval Staff that they expected an Allied combined fleet attack against both Penang and Singapore and could no longer guarantee the security of either. The broadcast ordering Timm to return to Java had been sent because the German authorities were concerned that the loss of the transmitter at Penang would cut off communications with U-boats at sea.

It was not only from the west that the Malaysian and Indonesian bases were under threat. On Friday 20 October the US Sixth Army began its landings in the Philippines, on the east coast of Leyte. Offshore the naval Battle of Leyte Gulf saw four Japanese carriers, three battleships, six heavy cruisers, four light cruisers, eleven destroyers, one submarine and nearly 500 aircraft lost in a fierce though decisive engagement. The Japanese resorted to *Kamikaze* missions for the first time as American troops stormed onward in the face of fierce opposition. By 25 December the last Japanese port on Leyte had been captured and General Douglas MacArthur declared the area secure for the Allies. The threat of near-encirclement loomed large in the mind of Dommes and his staff.

Between November 1944 and February 1945 a total of twelve aerial reconnaissance missions were flown over Georgetown as well as Prai and Butterworth on the adjacent Malaysian mainland. Intelligence officers compared the results with information provided by pre-war maps and photographs compiled by Oxford's Inter-Service Topographical Department and photographs taken during December 1941 and January 1942. In this way it was possible for the Allied military command to deduce which installations the Japanese and German occupation forces had constructed.

Twice during this period, first on 11 January then on 1 February 1945, the USAAF's India-based XX Bomber Command's 58th Bombardment Wing carried out air raids on Penang, designated a secondary target after Singapore's King George VI Graving Dock and Admiralty IX Floating Drydock, which had been subjected to heavy aerial bombardment since 5 November, when the Graving Dock was rendered non-operational for three months as a result of the heavy damage inflicted. On 11 January 25 B-29s attacked the two drydock facilities in Singapore while fifteen of the Wing's B-29s bombed Georgetown as well as targets of opportunity in Mergui and Burma. Two of the big bombers were downed over Malaysia by defending Japanese fighters. In Penang, in particular, the damage was relatively light, the B-29s having dropped their bomb loads from high altitude: the government office building, the clock tower near Fort Cornwallis, the post office and the Daimaru department store weathered the brunt of the attack. Residents began to leave Georgetown for fear of more and heavier attacks and were given permission to do so by the Japanese authorities if their dwellings had suffered damage.

The attack on 2 February was mounted by B-29s, 67 of which attacked Singapore's Admiralty IX Floating Drydock as well as vessels in the immediate area while 21 others unloaded their high-explosive and incendiary bombs on the West Wall area of the Singapore naval base. Elsewhere a further 21 B-29s once again attacked alternative targets in Burma, Martaban and Georgetown and two were brought down by the Japanese defenders. Georgetown's shower of explosives lasted for four hours. The damage was greater than that previously suffered and the next day the city was eerily quiet as many residents had already moved to safer areas, the authorities having lifted restrictions for four days on all residents departing the city. By 7 February throngs of people were choking the residential streets of Georgetown, anxious to flee. With the business area deserted looting broke out once again, reminiscent of that in the wake of the departing British nearly four years before; this time it was Japanese troops who battled to quell the disorder.

In Singapore worse was to follow when, on 24 February, 105 B-29s launched an all-incendiary attack on the Empire Docks, burning out nearly 40 per cent of the warehousing facilities used by both Japanese and German naval personnel. Plumes of thick black smoke rose from the buildings, many of which had been packed with raw rubber ready for stowage aboard outbound U-boats.[4] It was the final 100-aircraft strike made by XX Bomber Command, and although raids on Singapore continued into March the high-altitude American B-29s scattered their ordnance throughout the target area with little effect on the thinly spread German personnel below. More dangerous were the sporadically laid mines, B-29s dropping the lethal traps in the Johore Strait east of Singapore as well as in the immediate approaches to the harbour. Both the USAAF and RAF also mined Penang's approaches on a regular basis, beginning on 26 January and ending in April.

The first quarter of 1945 brought the rapid disintegration of the defensive fronts held by both Japan and Germany. Tokyo, Nagoya, Osaka and Kobe suffered severe fire-bombing, while in the Philippines American troops battered Japanese resistance to an end. The island of Iwo Jima fell to US Marines at the end of March and the first pre-invasion bombardment of Okinawa then began: the assault had finally reached Japanese soil. Concurrently in Burma, British, Indian and Commonwealth troops steadily pushed back a desperate Japanese defence until the Burma Road was reached on 31 March after eight months of bitter and costly fighting.

Meanwhile Hitler's gamble in the Ardennes, spearheaded by elite *Wehrmacht* and *Waffen-SS* units, had failed, and a similar attempt in Hungary was also sledge-hammered into retreat by overpowering Soviet forces. The final barrier in the west, the River Rhine, was crossed on 7 March when men of the US 9th Armored Division straddled the great natural defensive line at Remagen, their bridgehead soon expanded and troops racing deep into the German heartland.

At sea Dönitz's U-boats were a spent force. Putting to sea with the wisdom of their deployment unquestioned, the German submarine force was being steadily bludgeoned to death in a staggeringly ill-matched battle of attrition. To maintain the illusion of co-operation with the Imperial Japanese Navy, Dönitz issued a statement via the monthly *Kriegsmarine* magazine in January 1945 that he was willing to despatch German U-boats into the Pacific to aid the Japanese in their fight. Tokyo in turn expressed its gratitude and pushed for details of the proposed German commitment—which Dönitz in all probability had no intention of keeping. His priority remained the transfer of raw materials to Europe for Germany's war effort, and BdU ordered Wenneker to pass instructions to Dommes to step up the tempo of sailings from Java. Dommes had already enquired of BdU what the latest timetable would be for departures from his harbours during December 1944:

> Submarine bases Penang asked the latest date for non-*Schnorchel* boats from the East Asia area to start their homeward journey, to be able to still proceed through the Iceland Passage despite the advanced season (daylight).
>
> BdU replied: The end of August is the latest date for non-*Schnorchel* boats to pass the Iceland Passage with a daily run of 120–125 miles, i.e. they must leave Jakarta at the latest by the middle of January. Large boats with higher daily run can leave later.

BdU assumes that *U 181*, *U 510* and *U 532* will leave by 15 January. According to this, *U 537* and *U 183* will not be joining them. A decision on the use of *U 183* until she begins her return journey will be taken when she has completed a change of battery.[5]

Within the tempest of battle that scoured the Atlantic Ocean and North Sea, boats still planned to reach Java with supplies from Germany and those inbound carrying the raw materials so scarce within the belea-guered *Reich* gamely struggled to survive. From Norway the Type VIIF *U 1060* and Type IXD2 *U 864* put to sea for the voyage east. *U 1060*, laden with base supplies and 39 torpedoes, lasted only two days before being attacked by Fireflies of 1771 NAS west of Velfjord. His boat se-verely damaged, *Oberleutnant zur See* Herbert Brammer ran her aground on the island of Fliena, where British and Czechoslovakian bombers finished her off, the wreck sliding stern first into deeper water with sixteen dead aboard her, including Brammer.[6]

The fate awaiting *U 864* was no better. *Korvettenkapitän* Ralf-Reimar Wolfram took his U-boat from Bergen on 5 February 1945, laden with mercury, radar and torpedo parts among other items, as well as a dis-mantled Messerschmitt Me 262 jet fighter. The U-boat was two days from port and running submerged when Wolfram's periscope and *Schnorchel* mast were visually detected by the patrolling submarine HMS *Venturer*. The British boat was also submerged, and Lt J. S. Launders crept carefully along a parallel course for an hour before using hydro-phone bearings to fire four torpedoes. A single explosion followed by the sound of breaking bulkheads and wreckage plunging to the sea floor marked the end of the German. Launders surfaced and retrieved debris from a huge pool of diesel oil—evidence of the only successful attack between two submerged submarines to take place during the Second World War.

It was on 24 March that the last attempt to break through to Japan began from Kiel—a mission that still provokes controversy because of the unusual cargo involved. The Type XB *U 234* was the first U-boat command of *Kapitänleutnant* Johann-Heinrich Fehler, a former explo-sives officer aboard the raider *Atlantis*. The dynamic and aggressive Fehler, initially disappointed to have been given command of a mine-layer, had officially taken charge of his boat a year before at *U 234*'s commissioning ceremony. The construction process had begun in Oct-ober 1941 but had been delayed because of a bomb hit received during an air raid in May 1943, when an entire forward section was so severely damaged that it required replacement.

Trials within the Baltic were frequently postponed on account of Allied minelaying and it was not until 5 September 1944 that *U 234* returned to the Germaniawerft yards for the usual overhaul prior to active service. There was, however, more work scheduled since she was being redesigned for primary use as a transport rather than as a minelayer craft. In addition to maintenance work and the installation of a *Schnorchel*, the outboard mineshafts on each flank were reconfigured as cargo compartments. These were loaded with horizontal tubes, originally above-deck torpedo containers, shortened somewhat and installed for cargo stowage. *U 234* then carried six cargo containers in the mine chutes forward and amidships. Six vertical containers were placed in the chutes on either side, and in each of the four cargo spaces were eight horizontally placed cargo tubes. Four cargo containers, two on either side above decks, completed the loading bays. Fehler was aghast at the tasks that BdU decided he could complete on this his first combat voyage: as well as acting as a cargo and passenger transport and a torpedo attack vessel armed with eight torpedoes, his boat was also expected to carry out the 'Operational Order Cape Town and Colombo' that had been planned on 22 November 1944: 21 mines were to be deployed in each harbour at a depth no greater than 350m, although it was emphasised that this was a role secondary to Fehler's transport duties.

The cargo loading included 109 tons of mercury, steel, lead and optical glass within the keel and bilges. A disassembled Messerschmitt Me 262 fighter plane, 43 tons of aircraft blueprints, instruments, weapons and medical supplies, five tons of ammunition for 2cm and 3.7cm cannon, six tons of spares for the eastern U-boat stations and one ton of mail and films were stored in every available space as the boat prepared for sea. Much was stored within pressurised cargo containers, but several tubes were given over to the most unusual cargo items—ten small, cube-shaped metal cases, stamped with the number 'U-235'. At first the crew were perplexed, believing that they had another boat's cargo before realising that the containers carried uranium oxide ore, highly radioactive and a key ingredient in the manufacture of nuclear weaponry.

Amidst the chaos and ruin of a nightmarish Kiel, battered by bombing, Fehler and his men were under no illusion about the likely outcome of the war that was nearing its climax. Fehler even envisaged being able to put ashore somewhere should Germany collapse totally, using weaponry stowed aboard—both the official armaments and the unofficial 'extras' gleaned in Kiel—for self-defence while he and his men laid low and watched to see whether Germany would be devoured by the sinister Morgenthau Plan that was being touted as one option for the vanquished Reich—the transformation of Germany into a pastoral nation unable ever again to wage war in any shape or form:

> Among her many official assignments the *U 234* was supposed to carry ammunition to Japanese-controlled Penang . . . I was pleased by this assignment. I felt that the ammunition might prove of considerable use, but not in the way intended by its senders. For I had no confidence in the Japanese. I felt sure that, with the collapse of Germany, our Eastern Allies would consider we had outlived our uses and would treat us no better (perhaps worse) than the other Europeans who had been unfortunate enough to be caught in the Co-Prosperity Sphere. I did not relish the prospect.
>
> In the general pandemonium that was now spreading across the Reich, no one seemed to have the time, nor the inclination, to notice our peculiar preparations . . . we bartered with a army unit for tents; we traded with a stores department for mosquito netting; and we scrounged a small outboard motor, in order to turn one of our rubber boats into a scout, for exploring strange coasts and rivers.
>
> [Meanwhile] everywhere the military police and SS were active, seizing any personnel they could lay their hands upon and rushing them into the line . . . Short shrift was rendered to anyone suspect. The forests were full of corpses . . . of men who hung from trees.[7]

Correspondingly, with his desire to remain out of the clutches of the Japanese if Germany's war ended—as he knew it must—Fehler's heart sank when two of the passengers to be crammed aboard the already well-laden boat turned out to be Japanese engineering officers. Fehler had fought long and hard to reduce an original demand for him to carry 26 passengers to the East, the compromise solution of twelve still sitting uneasily on his mind. Eleven boarded at Kiel and one at Horten in Norway. The two Japanese officers were *Taisa* Genzo Soshi of the Japanese Air Force and *Taisa* Hideo Tomonaga of the IJN, who had originally reached Europe aboard *U 180*. The nine remaining 'guests' who came aboard in Germany proved a disparate assembly of men. Amongst them were the *Luftwaffe* officers *Oberst* Fritz von Sandrath, former head of Bremen's flak defenses and an anti-aircraft specialist; *Oberst* Erich Menzel, technical aide to the Air Attaché and communications specialist; and *Leutnant-Oberst* Kai Nieschling, a Nazi military judge appointed to investigate allegations of corruption amongst German military and diplomatic staff in Japan, and those implicated in the Richard Sorge spy scandal. The *Kriegsmarine* officers were *Kapitänleutnant* Heinrich Hellendorn, a specialist in naval flak gunnery; *Kapitän* (honorary) Heinz Schlicke, a radar, infra-red and direction-finding scientist; *Kapitän* Gerhard Falk, a shipbuilder; and *Kapitänleutnant* Richard Bulla, a specialist in air–sea co-operation and acting IWO of *U 234*, replacing the boat's appointed IWO, *Leutnant zur See* Klingenberg (to whom Fehler had an aversion, Bulla also having served aboard the *Atlantis*). Two civilians completed the ten Germans who boarded in Kiel—August Bringewald, senior Messerschmitt engineer and a specialist on the Me 262 and Me 263 designs and general rocketry; and Franz Ruf, a procurement specialist for Messerschmitt.

The final overhaul and fitting-out of *U 234* took until 24 March to complete and the U-boat, under escort by, and in company with, *U 516* and another Type VIIC U-boat, sailed that evening from Kiel for Horten, where Fehler intended to carry out some last-minute training with the newly installed *Schnorchel*. Fehler arrived at Horten two days later, having crept through seas heavily patrolled by Allied aircraft, and began eight days of *Schnorchel* trials. During the exercises, and while proceeding at *Schnorchel* depth, *U 234* was rammed by a Type VIIC boat carrying out similar tests. The Type XB's No 1 diving tank and adjacent fuel cell ruptured, but repairs had been completed at Kristiansand by 5 April and *U 234* topped up with provisions. Initially there had been no drydock available for the repair work, so Fehler improvised by flooding the forward diving tanks, submerging the boat's bow so that the damaged stern rose from the water, which enabled the crew to get to work with welding rods and sheet steel. At Horten Fehler had also embarked his final passenger, the flamboyant and outspoken *Luftwaffe General* Ulrich Kessler, destined for a new post as *Luftwaffe Attaché* in Tokyo and soon at odds with some of the more devout National Socialists among the other passengers—particularly offending Kai Nieschling with ribald jokes about Nazi officials. Fehler's boat was hardly a happy one when it sailed from Norway. *U 234* finally left Kristiansand on 15 April, Fehler informing his crew that, although their official destination was indeed Japan, he was firmly convinced in his own mind that it would never be reached.

Meanwhile attempts by U-boats to return from Malaysia and Penang with supplies for the Fatherland had continued apace. On 19 October 1944 the veteran *U 181* had slipped from Jakarta, tungsten and tin in her keel and hull, raw rubber distributed amongst the freeflooding superstructure and several buoyancy tanks, and crates and tins of opium, quinine, caffeine and molybdenum within the pressure hull. Sailing into the Indian Ocean, *Kapitän zur See* Kurt Freiwald went on to the offensive. He had only two torpedoes aboard his crowded boat but he managed to sink the American turbine tanker SS *Fort Lee* on 2 November 1944. *Fort Lee*, intercepted while travelling alone from Abadan, Iran, to Brisbane carrying 93,000 barrels of Navy Bunker C fuel, was the only Allied merchant ship lost to U-boat attack that month within the Indian Ocean. As Freiwald continued on his way to the Cape of Good Hope, the lack of maintenance facilities and spare parts in the East finally defeated him. On 26 November he reported serious mechanical problems to BdU: '*U 181* reports badly burned bearings. Three already running on bronze, no replacements left. Main bearings peeling. Reason believed to be dirty oil and tired bearing metal. Requesting rendezvous.'

With no spares available with which to make a rendezvous within the ocean, Freiwald was ordered to abort his sortie the following day. He arrived at Jakarta on 6 January 1945 after passing whatever spare fuel he had to the outbound *U 843*. *U 181* would spend one day in port before transferring to Singapore for major repair work, including the fitting of an ingenious, locally made, rigid *Schnorchel*. It was while stationed there that IIWO Johann Limbach received notification of the award of the Knight's Cross, bestowed on him for his long and exemplary service. His was the fifth awarded to men in the Indian Ocean, and it was also the last.

Kapitänleutnant Oskar Herwatz's *U 843* took fuel from both *U 195* and *U 181* as she sailed for the Atlantic, passing out of the Indian Ocean during mid-January and successfully dodging enemy patrols to arrive in Bergen on 3 April 1945. Herwatz and his men received a hero's welcome in the Norwegian bastion of German strength, departing again three days later, rested and preparing to head for a battered Kiel, where their cargo could be unloaded. In what can only be described as a cruel twist of fate for the 44 men aboard *U 843*, they were sighted in the Kattegat as the boat passed within miles of northbound *U 804* and *U 1065* and attacked by a Mosquito of the Banff Strike Wing. The two north-bound boats had come under fire earlier from 34 Mosquitos and both had been sunk during the fierce onslaught, after which a single Mos-quito from No 235 Squadron had flown off to escort a fellow-aircraft damaged during the battle and flying on one engine. Returning to the scene of the battle after his comrade had said they that he could make it alone, Fg Off. A. J. Randell sighted *U 843* and dived to let loose rock-ets, cannon and machine gun fire in the face of heavy flak. After the first attack the defending fire diminished and Randell made a second straf-ing pass, leaving *U 843* smoking and stationary before departing low on fuel. Behind Randell *U 843* lazily sank below the waves, taking with her 144 tons of valuable cargo and all the crewmen.

Korvettenkapitän Jürgen Oesten's *U 861* made a successful landfall in Norway 87 days after leaving Surabaya. After their initial arrival in Penang the previous November and ample rest and recreation on Penang Hill, Oesten and his men had taken *U 861* onward, initially to Singapore before being redirected to Surabaya to avoid the overcrowding within Singapore's drydocks. The *Propaganda Kompanie* reporter Kiefer, who had sailed on board *U 861*, stayed in Penang while Oesten had his boat placed into Surabaya's drydock so that the keel cargo could be removed and replaced with goods for Germany. Finally, on 15 January 1945 the 'Black Panther' boat put to sea from Surabaya bound for Norway, Oesten later describing the voyage in his usual unassuming manner:

> Although a submarine is a poor cargo boat, the best storage possibility was the ballast keel, that could load 100–120 metric tons. We took quicksilver [mer-cury], optical equipment and some other gadgets I don't recollect to Surabaya, where we changed the cargo in drydock. We loaded molybdenum ore (concen-trate) in cast tin boxes, rubber in some of the fuel tanks and within the boat opium for medical purposes as well as manganese in the torpedo tubes, ce-ramic jugs filled with iodine, quinine and even rock crystals!
>
> On the way home we had a meeting about 900 miles south of Madagascar with *U 510*, *U 532*, and *U 195*. I gave 60 tons of fuel to *U 510*, while *U 195* gave sufficient fuel to *U 532* and returned to Indonesia. *U 510* wanted more fuel and got some from *U 532* in addition. I could not afford to give more fuel to *U 510* as some of my fuel tanks were filled with rubber.
>
> The return journey to Norway was a routine job, [although] from the Cape Town longitude our gyrocompass was beyond repair and we had to fall back on a small magnetic compass, which is rather problematic on a submarine. In mid-Atlantic we chased a ship without result as she was too fast. We went to the ice border between Greenland and Iceland and along the ice border through the Denmark Strait and then to Trondheim, Norway.[8]

Once again Oesten had survived against the odds, his boat tying up at the pier where he and his crew were greeted by the Flotilla Commander and assembled U-boat officers on 19 April 1945. Though the end of the war was approaching fast, there was still one more transport boat to make a European landfall.

Kapitänleutnant Alfred Eick's *U 510* had sailed from Jakarta four days before Oesten had put to sea, heading for the Indian Ocean and into the South Atlantic. A single sinking was made on 23 February when Eick torpedoed the Canadian steamer SS *Point Pleasant Park* north-west of Cape Town—the sole success of the voyage—as *U 510* inched northward towards Norway. However, the Type IXC had been scheduled to refuel from whatever vessels became available, the diesel situation having become increasingly perilous after the meeting with *U 861* and *U 532* in the Indian Ocean. The sea miles clicked by, no U-boats within the Atlantic surviving long enough to make a rendezvous with Eick. Finally the situation reached desperation point and, also anxious that the boat obtain a *Schnorchel* before attempting to reach Norway, BdU redirected *U 510* to enter St-Nazaire, which she did on 23 April 1945 after slipping through numerous enemy naval groups—the last boat to reach Europe from the Far East. Eick's boat sailed into the bunkers of a port under siege by the American army. Periodic shellfire battered the remains of a smashed city, *Kriegsmarine* personnel having been impressed into the trenches in an infantry war of attrition that they could never win. The Germans within the surrounded port, hemmed in by closely patrolling naval forces to seaward, had been left to wither on the vine while the final dramatic moments of the war were played out hundreds of miles away. With worn batteries, no spare parts and ultimately little hope of fitting a *Schnorchel*, *U 510* and her precious cargo lay within the huge monolithic pens, stranded for the last few days of hostilities.

The day before Eick's landfall in France *Kapitänleutnant* Fritz Schneewind's *U 183*, one of the original *Monsun* boats, sailed from Jakarta flying a Japanese naval ensign for recognition and carrying extra fuel within her diving bunkers, preventing her from submerging. Unable to reach Europe unaided because of his Type IXC U-boat's range, Schneewind had instead been released by BdU to make a combat patrol into the Pacific as part of the support promised for Japan. With fresh batteries obtained at Kobe, Schneewind headed to the seas north of Dutch

New Guinea, where he planned to attack American supply lines within the region. However, he communicated his recognition signals and estimated travel plan (with times) to the Japanese and was promptly intercepted by FRUMEL, who despatched a boat of their own to lay in ambush.

Two days from port Cdr H. E. Miller sighted the zig-zagging *U 183* through the periscope of the USS *Besugo*. Within minutes six torpedoes raced towards Schneewind's boat, the ensuing blast rupturing the German's hull and sending her plunging to her doom. *Besugo* rescued a single German survivor from the crew of 55.

A final westbound U-boat was still at sea as the war dragged to its inevitable conclusion. *Fregattenkapitän* Ottoheinrich Junker's *U 532*, sporting a new propeller brought to Singapore by *U 843* in June 1944, had left Jakarta on 13 January and made course for the Indian Ocean. Junker had taken fuel from *U 195* on 9 February when the latter was forced to break off her own return to Europe, begun six days after Junker's. *U 195*, still commanded by Steinfeldt, had departed Jakarta for Norway, but her diesels had soon developed serious trouble. Directed to pass all spare fuel over to Junker, *U 195* limped back to Jakarta and from there on to Surabaya, where her load was removed and the boat put into dock for repairs.

Junker pressed onward, rounding the Cape of Good Hope and entering the Atlantic Ocean during late February. There *U 532* attacked and sank two ships, the British steamer SS *Baron Jedburgh* west-south-west of Ascension on 10 March and the American tanker SS *Oklahoma* west of the Cape Verde Islands on 28 March. With her final two victories secured, *U 532* sailed onward, and she was approaching the last leg of her journey north of the British Isles when an urgent broadcast was received on 2 May 1945: BdU relayed the news that Adolf Hitler had 'met a hero's death' and that Dönitz was now head of state and asking for allegiance in the last days of combat. Aboard *U 532* the men's emotions were strained to breaking point by the uncertainty over the future and their awareness of the perils they still faced at sea. Finally BdU broadcast a message at 0500hrs on 5 May that dispelled any final doubts: 'As from 5 May 0800hrs cease fire. Attacks forbidden. Break off pursuit of enemy. Return to Norwegian harbours.'

The war was over.

NOTES

1. Diary of H. Haake, Bremen, 23/8–12/12 1944. Copy held by Author.
2. Interview with Hans-Joachim Krug, 3 May 2003.
3. BdU KTB, 26 October 1944, Message from IJN Naval War Staff (4th Division), Va.
4. As a result of this bombardment, the Japanese withdrew their last two remaining battleships from South-East Asia to home waters.
5. BdU KTB
6. Four of those killed were from *U 957*, 28 of whose crew were transferred aboard *U 1060* for transport to Bergen before Brammer headed for the Far East after their boat had been written off in a collision.
7. A. V. Sellwood, *Dynamite for Hire*, p. 144–6.
8. Collected interviews by author with Jürgen Oesten, 2003.

Eleven

Capitulation

THE UNCONDITIONAL surrender of Germany was formally taken into effect from midnight on 8 May after *Admiral* von Friedeburg, promoted to Commander of the *Kriegsmarine* after Dönitz's accession to Head of State, and *General* Alfred Jodl signed the surrender document at SHAEF headquarters in Reims. Bound by the surrender of his Commander-in-Chief, Dommes, as *Chef im Süd-raum* ordered all U-boat personnel to relinquish their arms and conform to the demands placed upon troops of a defeated nation. News from Germany had been keenly followed in Singapore, where Dommes had authorised the close monitoring of Allied radio broadcasts. News of the death of the *Führer* had been followed by a memorial service on 3 May, where, in the presence of the Japanese General Tomoyuki Yamashita, Dommes delivered a eulogy to the fallen German leader, and a salute was fired by *Kriegsmarine* sailors at the beach of Pasir Panjang.

BdU pressed for Dommes to despatch at least Freiwald, promoted to Kapitän zur See on 1 April, to Europe and were even willing to allow the remaining boats to join *U 183*'s attempted support of Japanese operations in the Pacific. Dönitz, who continued to insist on the return of Freiwald to Germany, reluctantly accepted requests from Tokyo, hitherto refused, for *U 862* to drop Japanese agents in Madras. However, it was too late. Two days later, upon receipt of the radio instructions to end hostilities, Wenneker replied from Tokyo, 'Combat action of East Asia U-boats has ceased. Return of U-boats impossible, since they are not ready for travelling.'

In the meantime Tokyo had been preparing for over a week to take emergency measures against German units within its sphere of influence should they prove necessary. However, both Wenneker and Dommes had taken it upon themselves to make their own arrangements concerning the U-boats still within Japanese harbours. According to the terms of the German surrender they were technically obliged to put to sea and hand themselves over to Allied authorities, but between themselves, after consultation with both Freiwald and Timm, whose boats were present in Singapore, a compromise solution had been reached which would protect German troops under the terms of their surrender but still show loyalty to an erstwhile ally.

On 6 May Wenneker issued the codeword 'Lübeck' to *U 181*, *U 195*, *U 219*, *U 862*, *UIT 24* and *UIT 25*. Wenneker was activating the result of a covert agreement with Tokyo that allowed the Imperial Japanese Navy to seize control of the surrendered German U-boats. Armed soldiers arrived in trucks to take possession of the submarines and intern the *Kriegsmarine* crews, allowing the Germans to save face while abiding by the terms of their general surrender since the Japanese were requisitioning the vessels 'by force'.

At Singapore the Japanese seized both *U 181* and *U 862*. Through the recent weeks of uncertainty and growing unease as the Japanese attitude toward their German guests had appeared to cool, conditions had remained as normal as possible aboard the two boats. On 7 April Dommes and Freiwald had presented the German Cross in Gold to *Stabsobermaschinist* Franz Persch, *Obermaschinistenmaat* Karl Kaiser and *Maschinist* Wilhelm Linka for completing two arduous and dangerous patrols from Europe to Singapore. On 6 May the complement from each boat was assembled above decks in the presence of their officers and Dommes as the two boats lay moored at Seletar following the transmission of the codeword 'Lübeck'. Shortly afterwards *Chujo* Fukudome Shigeru, Commander of the Japanese 13th Area Fleet, accompanied by three other admirals and staff officers in dress uniform, arrived at the No 101 Navy Repair Unit alongside the two U-boats. Fukudome informed the three ranking Germans that, since Germany had signed the act of capitulation, they were to be interned as potential enemies. However, the officers were invited to a 'European style' festive dinner in order to thank them for their past contributions to the Axis war effort.

At 1600hrs that day trucks arrived and disembarked armed Japanese troops, who assembled aboard the two boats while the *Kriegsmarine* ensigns were lowered and flags of the Rising Sun hauled up the boats' staffs in their place: *U 181* was to become *I-501* and *U 862 I-502* of the Imperial Japanese Navy. As the U-boat crews were driven off to an former British rubber plantation at Batu Pahat in southern Malaysia decisions regarding the usefulness of the two boats were being taken in Japan. Although both were soon ready for sea and allocated the task of supply runs between the Japanese mainland and isolated outpost, their new owners in the event used neither in action. Despite this, German crewmen were returned to the boats to instruct Japanese sailors in the use of their systems until the war against Japan ended in September 1945.

At Surabaya *U 195* was taken over in a similar fashion by the Japanese. Her commander, *Oberleutnant zur See* Steinfeldt, ordered the lowering of the *Kriegsmarine* standard as a Japanese patrol boat anchored next to the U-boat as she swung lazily at anchor within the harbour. The Japanese captain and several armed ratings boarded *U 195* and hoisted the ensign of the Rising Sun and the boat was later commissioned into the IJN as *I-506*. She was subsequently overhauled at Surabaya's No 102 Repair Unit and assigned to the 2nd Southern Expeditionary Fleet but she did not receive a crew before September 1945.

The transfer of command was just as easily handled in Jakarta aboard *U 219*:

> We had been scheduled to go to Surabaya, but it was very difficult to get space there so the idea would have been to go when time permitted. But I have a feeling that our captain, after his experiences in World War One, probably knew that we were getting very close to the end of the war. We of course didn't realise it at the time.
>
> When Germany surrendered, the Japanese had an arrangement to take over our boats. So when the war ended for us they came over and seized them. That way they saved us any dishonour of handing over our boats. They arrived with weapons and so on, but nothing happened. We took down our flag, they raised theirs and that was it. Then they sent us to the huge *U-Boot Weide* in the mountains, and they left us there with thousands of Indonesian workers for the remainder of 1945. Some of the men even stayed after the war. One of our Engineering Mates even became an Indonesian Navy admiral.[1]

Loaded and ready to make a return run, the boat was transferred first to Surabaya under *Korvettenkapitän* Burghagen's command and with his crew and some Japanese sailors aboard. At Surabaya she also was overhauled by the No 102 Repair Unit and, commissioned into the IJN as *I-505*, assigned to the 2nd Southern Expeditionary Fleet. Once again, however, as Steinfeldt's and Burghagen's crews were interned within an open camp nearby, no Japanese crew was allocated to the Type XB and she stayed at Surabaya for the remainder of her operational life.

Elsewhere fragments of the various German crews had taken up small arms almost immediately upon being interned by the Japanese as Malaysian, Indonesian and Chinese partisans began an assiduous and brutal war against the occupation forces, whose grasp on the reins of control weakened with each newly reported development at the front lines facing the Allies. Fortunately there was little direct aggression towards the German internees, who endeavoured to keep as low a profile as possible.

In Japan itself the two ex-Italian boats began a short stretch under the third Axis flag of their unusual war. Both were at the Kawasaki Works at Kobe undergoing maintenance when the German surrender came into effect. While there *UIT 25* had suffered a casualty during one of the increasingly regular and severe bombing raids on the Mitsubishi and Kawasaki shipyards, but her war ended with a handover to Japanese troops. *UIT 24* was recommissioned as *I-503* and *UIT 25* as *I-504*. Their crews lived out the remainder of the war against Japan in relative comfort in a small hotel outside of the city, purchased by the *Kriegsmarine* with funds largely derived from money paid by the Japanese for two successful supply round trips completed by the UIT boats.

The interned Europeans who were recruited to train Japanese personnel in their boats' systems found themselves in a peculiar situation. They shared little common ground with their Japanese counterparts and the shipyards in which the U-boats lay were continually under Allied air attack, placing their lives in extreme jeopardy. The bitter irony of the possibility of being killed as a non-combatant after having survived so long at war was not lost on them. Correspondingly, at least twice U-boat crews opened fire on attacking enemy aircraft: Italian gunners aboard *UIT 24* aided in the destruction of a B-25 Mitchell bomber over Kobe and Germans aboard *U 862* shot down an attacking Lightning fighter-bomber over Singapore long after their nations' war had ended.

At sea when the German surrender came into effect, *U 532* was ordered to surface and fly the black flag of capitulation until shepherded into Liverpool harbour. There the docks were thronged with people eager to glimpse a real example of the reviled and feared 'Grey Wolves' that had caused so much pain in a city populated with merchant seamen. The cargo of tin, rubber, quinine, opium and tungsten was unloaded and added to the British stockpile, long free from any serious threat of depradations at the hands of U-boats. Likewise in Trondheim Oesten's cargo was eventually unloaded by the British, the sacrifice and hardship of his crossing ultimately having been in vain.

On 29 May 1945. Johann-Heinrich Fehler's *U 234* and her mixed cargo entered the harbour at Portsmouth, New Hampshire, the captain's grandiose plans of evading capture and making for neutral or unpopulated lands crushed by the harsh realities of a world at war. The rust-streaked boat sailed into American hands, two of her passengers having opted for their own destiny: the Japanese engineering officers had committed suicide after deliberately overdosing on Luminol tablets. Their suicide note apologising for the fact that their *Bushido* code would not allow them to fall into the hands of the enemy wrenched at Fehler's feelings as he respected their wishes and let them die with dignity and by a method of their choosing. The two bodies were buried at sea along with their *Samurai* swords, which had been entrusted to Fehler's safekeeping at the beginning of the voyage.

While the German sailors stranded in Japan, Java and Malaysia remained unmolested by the Japanese despite fears of persecution now that they were no longer of use to their former Oriental allies, the men aboard *U 234* surrendered on American soil. With Halifax, Nova Scotia, the nearest port at which to hand himself and his crew over to the Allied authorities, Fehler deliberately misled approaching Canadian warships as to his location, fearing a rough reception from a country that had fought so long against Germany. However, he was mistaken in his belief that the Americans would prove more amenable. Their belongings were stolen, and amidst some measure of brutality they were imprisoned first in Portsmouth and then Boston jail, alongside the crew of Friedrich Steinhoff's *U 873*. This Type IXD2 boat had been scheduled for a run to the Far East according to plans worked out during December 1944 but repeated delays caused by to bombing and the deteriorating military situation in Germany changed Steinhoff's destination to the Caribbean. Steinhoff, one time captain of *U 511*—'*Marco Polo I*'— soon committed suicide after surrender, following a severe beating at the hands of American interrogators eager to learn of *U 511*'s rocket trials.

In the East the final act came in September 1945, the month following the virtual destruction of Hiroshima and Nagasaki with atomic weapons—perhaps incorporating some quantity of the uranium oxide that had been hurriedly unloaded from *U 234* at Portsmouth and had quickly vanished into military hands, leaving no visible 'paper trail' behind it. On 2 September Japanese officials aboard the battleship USS *Missouri* in Tokyo Bay signed the official act of surrender, outlying garrisons following suit with more regional Allied commanders. On 4 September *Chujo* Itagaki and *Chujo* Fukudome signed the Japanese agreement to hand over Singapore aboard HMS *Sussex*, although the official surrender ceremony would not occur until eight days later. On 5 September on Penang's Swettenham Pier, a site that remains linked with the *Monsun* boats' presence in Malaysia, a formal surrender ceremony took place signalling that Penang was again under British control.[2]

Throughout the East, German and some Italian sailors passed into British and American captivity, their presence a surprise to many Allied troops. Following the chaos of victory little thought was given as to how best to deal with these prisoners, their status unknown since they were no longer surrendered enemy personnel. Eventually the majority still in Malaysia were trooped across country to the infamous Changi Prison, led on foot to their destination by *Fregattenkapitän* Kurt Freiwald. Once there, 255 Germans were interned within the former guard's barracks, not the festering huts that had seen so much misery for Allied prisoners-of-war held by the Japanese. Before long German work groups were employed by the local Allied commands for various tasks, their unbroken morale and continued loyalty to their captains and officers often remarked upon by their British captors.

I-506, ex-*U 195*, would, ironically, see some form of action once again after the surrender of the Japanese. With the end of occupation she had surrendered within Surabaya's shipyard but the city was soon overrun by Indonesian rebels, who feared the return of their pre-war Dutch colonial masters. After seizing the ex-German boats there the rebels demolished the city's electrical powerplant before Nepalese Gurkhas spearheaded a British attack from Singapore and routed them after three weeks of intense combat, restoring order once more amidst the bloodied bedlam of Surabaya. With the White Ensign now hoisted above *I-506*, men of her former German crew were recruited to run the diesel engines in order to drive her generators, making electricity for the city.

Eventually the German internees were evacuated to Britain aboard the steamer SS *Empress of Australia*, which departed Singapore on 28 June 1946. Despite promises of an immediate return to Germany, months dragged by before the erstwhile U-boat men set foot in the ruins of their devastated homeland. For many their repatriation to Germany and a chance to begin rebuilding shattered lives did not come until 1948.

With the Second World War now long past, the legacy of the *Monsun* operations remains tangled in their enigmatic identity and purpose. Fundamentally it appears as a sometimes bizarre attempt at German–Italian–Japanese co-operation that breached the boundaries of the racial concepts which formed the very foundations of both Hitler's Third Reich and Japan's planned East Asian Empire. However, none of the three Axis powers was able, or perhaps willing, to co-ordinate either their basic war aims or the means of achieving them. This is starkly demonstrated by the difference in the German and Japanese concepts of submarine warfare. The Imperial Japanese Navy saw its submarines as a means of attacking enemy naval power, with merchant targets only of secondary importance—the exact opposite of German strategy.

Dönitz's U-boat campaign in the Indian Ocean has often been written off as an historical aside, an operation of interest owing to its unusual nature but little else. However, although the results gleaned through the arduous toil of his men at sea within the Indian Ocean amounted to little in comparison to the time and effort involved in achieving them, surely the extraordinary tribulations suffered by the U-boat crews merit a deeper understanding of the purpose of their deployment. According to the eminent historian Jürgen Rohwer, in the Indian Ocean proper, German U-boats destroyed only 133 ships, totalling around 687,500grt. By comparison, Japanese submarines had sunk almost 331,000 tons of merchant and military shipping by 23 October 1942, when *U 504* made the first German victory past the 20-degree longitude. Indeed by the war's end Japanese submarines had managed to destroy no more than a confirmed 596,840 tons of shipping within the Indian Ocean, their last days of success being during November 1944. Japanese attention had soon been drawn to the Pacific, leaving the Indian Ocean principally a German hunting ground. The relatively meagre results obtained by the large and ponderous German U-boats employed within a theatre far removed from European soil are also often judged in terms of opportunities missed rather than successes achieved.

However, hindsight is a gift that historians and analysts can wield with abandon and one must not forget that things would have appeared very different at the time. Although the entire Eastern U-boat deployment seems very much a case of a lost opportunity—forces deployed too late to have the real impact that they could have during 1940 or early 1941—the question of whether it was ever feasible to envisage the *Kriegsmarine* dominating the Indian Ocean remains the central issue. As events transpired, Dönitz considered that U-boat strength was needed within the Atlantic, in the battle with British-American convoys—itself a war of attrition that he could not win, particularly after the entry of the United States into the conflict. Keeping with Dönitz's mandate that a ship sunk anywhere still needed to be replaced with new construction, the Indian Ocean would seem to have offered easy pickings at first; but this is a seriously flawed argument.

First of all the bulk of the U-boats in action were small Type VIICs, unable to travel the distances required. Secondly, if the larger U-boats had indeed been able to disrupt supplies to the British Eighth Army in North Africa by controlling and destroying Indian Ocean convoy traffic, for how long could they have held that dominance? Logistical support for U-boats at such distances was problematic and required equipment to travel from Europe in vulnerable surface ships or submarines with very limited capacity. Japanese *matériel* was incompatible with German and it was in any case in desperately short supply for Imperial Japan's own beleaguered forces. On the other hand Allied troops could be directly supplied and reinforced from India, South Africa, East Africa and Australia. Thus in hindsight it was a German plan that was probably doomed to failure from the outset. Even Dönitz's rationale that new assaults in distant regions would entail the transfer of valuable escort ships away from the Atlantic failed, not least because of American shipbuilding power and Allies' breaking of the Enigma code network.

The question has also been posed as to why Dönitz failed to sanction attacks by his boats within the Pacific. The planned Australian operation answers this question. Four boats were tasked with it and three were destroyed at the very outset. The surviving U-boat achieved little more than extremely localised Allied confusion and brief panic. During 1945 the Germans' belated agreement to send combat boats into another region of the Pacific to interfere with Allied supply lines resulted in nothing more than the destruction of *U 183*. Once again the importance of codebreaking and hence of being forewarned of enemy activity had proved invaluable to the Allies. In any event the likelihood of German successes by means of surprise attacks—with frequently malfunctioning weaponry, and at an even greater distance from supplies shipped from Europe—remains doubtful. The added factors of overwhelming Allied military strength and unparalleled codebreaking performance rendered even a deployment in the Pacific, where the U-boats could perhaps still have been useful as late as 1945, completely futile.

So it can be seen that the combat capabilities of the Eastern U-boats could never have made their deployment particularly meaningful. This leaves the issue of blockade-running and the shuttling of supplies between Germany and Japan, particularly the importation to the *Reich* of important raw materials. Here, of course, the final German blunder was the assumption that U-boats would be capable of carrying sufficient quantities of raw materials from Japan at all. The amount brought through by U-boats was but a fraction of a single load that could be taken by surface blockade-runner. By doubling the roles of the *Monsun* boats as both transport and combat submarines their capabilities as either were blunted. Hundreds of tons of *matériel* were destroyed with U-boats lost in action, while conditions became intolerable for men cramped by goods stowed during war patrols—and U-boats were made even more unwieldy and slow to manoeuvre by their heavy burdens. The statistics relating to the major categories of goods transported from East to West illustrate the meagre quantities that the *Monsun* boats were able to bring back to Europe—611.4 tons safely transported from East to West, 0.58 per cent of the 104,552 tons shipped by the surface blockade-breakers.

Ultimately it is perhaps fair to say that Dönitz had little interest in the Indian Ocean until the war situation had passed the windows of opportunity which had once been open. The Atlantic struggle had taken precedence until he was forced to admit defeat in 1943. By then it was already too late in the Indian Ocean as well, and, with no cards left to play, the *Monsun* boats faded into history's footnotes despite the best valiant efforts of dedicated men.

NOTES

1. Interview with Hans-Joachim Krug, 3 May 2003.
2. Units of the British East Indies Fleet mounted Operation 'Jurist'—the codename for the occupation of Penang and other minor ports—during late August and September.

Appendices

1. U-BOATS FOR THE INDIAN OCEAN

A. U-Boat Departures from Europe for Operations in the Indian Ocean

Boat	Group or designation	Depart	Port	Planned operational area	Return	Port
U 172	Eisbär	19/8/42	Lorient	Cape Town	27/12/42	Lorient
U 504	Eisbär	19/8/42	Lorient	Cape Town	11/12/42	Lorient
U 459	Eisbär	19/8/42	St-Nazaire	Supporting tanker (Quadrant GG)	5/11/42	St-Nazaire
U 159	Eisbär	19/8/42	Lorient	Cape Town	5/1/43	Lorient
U 156	Eisbär	20/8/42	Lorient	Cape Town (aborted)	16/11/42	Lorient
U 68	Eisbär	20/8/42	Lorient	Cape Town	6/12/42	Lorient
U 179	Eisbär 2	20/8/42	Lorient	Cape Town	8/10/42	Sunk
U 178	Eisbär 2	8/9/42	Kiel	Cape Town	9/1/43	Bordeaux
U 181	Eisbär 2	12/9/42	Kiel	Cape Town	18/1/43	Bordeaux
U 177	Eisbär 2	17/9/42	Kiel	Cape Town	22/1/43	Bordeaux
U 182	Seehund	9/12/42	Horten	Cape Town	15/5/43	SUNK
U 506	Seehund	14/12/42	Lorient	Cape Town	8/5/43	Lorient
U 509	Seehund	23/12/42	Lorient	Cape Town	11/5/43	Lorient
U 516	Seehund	23/12/42	Lorient	Cape Town	4/5/43	Lorient
U 160	Seehund	5/1/43	Lorient	Cape Town/ Durban	10/5/43	Bordeaux
U 180	Independent	9/2/43	Kiel	Personnel/Equipment exchange with IJN	2/7/43	Bordeaux
U 198	Independent	9/3/43	Kiel	Durban/Madagascar	24/9/43	Bordeaux

U 196	Independent	13/3/43	Kiel	Mozambique Channel/Aden	23/10/43	Bordeaux
U 195	Independent	20/3/43	Kiel	Cape Town	23/7/43	Bordeaux
U 181	Independent	23/3/43	Bordeaux	Madagascar/ Mauritius	14/10/43	Bordeaux
U 178	Independent	28/3/43	Bordeaux	Mozambique Channel	27/8/43	Penang
U 177	Independent	1/4/43	Bordeaux	SE Africa	1/10/43	Bordeaux
U 197	Independent	3/4/43	Kiel	SE Africa	20/8/43	Sunk
U 511	Marco Polo	10/5/43	Lorient	Transfer to IJN 15/8/43	15/7/43 Kure	Penang
U 200	Monsun	12/6/43	Kiel	Indian Ocean	24/6/43	Sunk
U 487	Monsun (support)	15/6/43	Bordeaux	Tanker	13/7/43	Sunk
U 462	Monsun (support)	17/6/43	Bordeaux	Tanker (aborted)	23/6/43	Bordeaux
U 462	Monsun (support)	28/6/43	Bordeaux	Tanker (aborted)	6/7/43	Bordeaux
U 188	Monsun	30/6/43	Lorient	Indian Ocean	30/10/43	Penang
U 168	Monsun	3/7/43	Lorient	Indian Ocean	11/11/43	Penang
U 509	Monsun	3/7/43	Lorient	Indian Ocean	15/7/43	Sunk
U 514	Monsun	3/7/43	Lorient	Indian Ocean	8/7/43	Sunk
U 532	Monsun	3/7/43	Lorient	Indian Ocean	30/10/43	Penang
U 183	Monsun	3/7/43	Lorient	Indian Ocean	30/10/43	Penang
U 506	Monsun	6/7/43	Lorient	Indian Ocean	12/7/43	Sunk
U 533	Monsun	6/7/43	Lorient	Indian Ocean	16/10/43	Sunk
U 516	Monsun	8/7/43	Lorient	Indian Ocean (aborted)	23/8/43	Lorient
U 847	Monsun	29/7/43	Lorient	Indian Ocean (tanker)	27/8/43	Sunk
U 848	Monsun II	18/9/43	Kiel	Indian Ocean	5/11/43	Sunk
U 849	Monsun II	2/10/43	Kiel	Indian Ocean	25/11/43	Sunk
U 510	Monsun II	3/11/43	St-Nazaire	Durban/Aden/ Indian Ocean	5/4/44	Penang
U 850	Monsun II	18/11/43	Kiel	Indian Ocean	20/12/43	Sunk
U 172	Monsun II	22/11/43	St-Nazaire	Indian Ocean	13/12/43	Sunk
U 1062	Independent	18/12/43	Kiel	Supplies for Penang; damaged	23/12/43	Bergen
U 177	Independent	2/1/44	La Pallice	Indian Ocean	6/2/44	Sunk
U 1062	Independent	3/1/44	Bergen	Supplies for Penang	19/4/44	Penang
U 852	Independent	18/1/44	Kiel	Indian Ocean	3/5/44	Sunk
UIT 22	Independent	19/1/44	Bordeaux	Transport to Far East (aborted)	21/1/44	Bordeaux
UIT 22	Independent	26/1/44	Bordeaux	Transport to Far East	11/3/44	Sunk

U 1059	Independent	4/2/44	Kiel	Supplies for Penang	19/3/44	Sunk
U 843	Independent	10/2/44	Lorient	Indian Ocean	11/6/44	Jakarta (Batavia)
U 851	Independent	26/2/44	Kiel	Indian Ocean	3/44	Sunk
U 196	Independent	11/3/44	La Pallice	Indian Ocean	10/8/44	Penang
U 181	Independent	16/3/44	La Pallice	Indian Ocean	8/8/44	Penang
U 537	Independent	25/3/44	Lorient	Indian Ocean	2/8/44	Jakarta
U 1224	Marco Polo II	29/3/44	Kiel	Transfer to IJN	13/5/44	Sunk
U 859	Independent	4/4/44	Kiel	Indian Ocean	23/9/44	Sunk
U 860	Independent	11/4/44	Kiel	Indian Ocean	15/6/44	Sunk
U 198	Independent	20/4/44	La Pallice	Indian Ocean	12/8/44	Sunk
U 861	Independent	20/4/44	Kiel	Indian Ocean	22/9/44	Penang
U 490	Independent	4/5/44	Kiel	Indian Ocean tanker	12/6/44	Sunk
U 862	Independent	21/5/44	Kiel	Indian Ocean	9/9/44	Penang
U 863	Independent	26/7/44	Bergen	Indian Ocean	29/9/44	Sunk
U 180	Independent	22/8/44	Bordeaux	Supplies for Penang	24/8/44	Sunk
U 195	Independent	22/8/44	Bordeaux	Supplies for Far East	28/12/44	Jakarta
U 219	Monsun II	30/4/44	Bordeaux	Supplies for Penang (aborted)	22/5/44	La Pallice
U 219	Independent	24/8/44	Bordeaux	Supplies for Far East	11/12/44	Jakarta
U 871	Independent	31/8/44	Trondheim	Indian Ocean	26/9/44	Sunk
U 1060	Independent	25/10/44	Trondheim	Supplies for Far East	30/10/44	Sunk
U 864	Independent	5/2/45	Bergen	Indian Ocean	9/2/45	Sunk
U 234	Independent	24/3/45	Kiel	Passengers and supplies for Far East	29/5/45	Portsmouth (USA)

B. U-Boat Departures from Far Eastern Ports

Boat	Group or designation	Depart	Port	Planned operational area	Return	Port
U 178	Independent	27/11/43	Penang	Indian Ocean/ return to France	24/5/44	Bordeaux
U 188	Independent	14/12/43	Penang	Singapore (keel loading)	15/12/43	Singapore
U 188	Independent	29/12/43	Singapore	Penang	30/12/43	Penang
U 532	Independent	4/1/44	Penang	Indian Ocean/ return to France (aborted)	19/4/44	Penang
U 188	Independent	8/1/44	Penang	Indian Ocean/ return to France	19/6/44	Bordeaux

U 168	Independent	28/1/44	Penang	Indian Ocean/ return to France (aborted)	3/2/44	Penang
UIT 24	Independent	2/2/44	Singapore	Transport	3/2/44	Penang
U 168	Independent	7/2/44	Penang	Indian Ocean/ return to France (aborted)	24/3/44	Jakarta
UIT 24	Independent	8/2/44	Penang	Transport to Europe (aborted)	3/4/44	Penang
UIT 25	Independent	8/2/44	Singapore	Transport	10/2/44	Penang
U 183	Independent	10/2/44	Penang	Indian Ocean/ return to France (aborted)	3/4/44	Penang
UIT 23	Independent	14/2/44	Singapore	Supplies for Penang	15/2/44	Sunk
UIT 25	Independent	7/3/44	Penang	Transport	11/3/44	Surabaya
UIT 24	Independent	5/4/44	Penang	Transport	6/4/44	Singapore
U 510	Independent	12/4/44	Penang	Refit	13/4/44	Singapore
U 532	Independent	5/44	Penang	Refit	6/5/44	Jakarta
U 183	Independent	3/5/44	Penang	Indian Ocean/ return to France (aborted)	5/5/44	Penang
U 183	Independent	17/5/44	Penang	Indian Ocean/ return to France (aborted)	7/7/44	Penang
UIT 24	Independent	25/5/44	Singapore	Refit	6/6/44	Kobe
UIT 25	Independent	10/6/44	Surabaya	Transport	25/6/44	Tama
U 843	Independent	13/6/44	Jakarta	Removal of keel cargo	15/6/44	Singapore
U 1062	Independent	19/6/44	Penang	Indian Ocean/ return to France (aborted)	2/7/44	Penang
U 510	Independent	26/6/44	Singapore	Battery replace- ment	7/7/44	Kobe
UIT 25	Independent	7/44	Tama	Refit	7/44	Kobe
U 1062	Independent	15/7/44	Penang	Indian Ocean/ return to France	4/10/44	Sunk
U 532	Independent	29/7/44	Jakarta	Battery replace- ment	29/9/44	Kobe
U 183	Independent	8/44	Penang	Maintenance	8/44	Singapore
UIT 24	Independent	5/9/44	Kobe	Transport	20/9/44	Singapore
U 862	Independent	12/9/44	Penang	Removal of keel cargo	13/9/44	Singapore
U 861	Independent	23/9/44	Penang	Transfer to Sura- baya	11/11/44	Surabaya
UIT 24	Independent	28/9/44	Singapore	Transport	28/9/44	Penang
U 168	Independent	5/10/44	Jakarta	Transfer to Sura- baya (prep. for Australia)	7/10/44	Sunk

U 510	Independent	7/10/44	Kobe	Return to active duty	19/10/44	Jakarta
U 196	Independent	9/10/44	Penang	Removal of keel cargo	11/10/44	Singapore
UIT 24	Independent	10/10/44	Penang	Transport	12/10/44	Singapore
U 183	Independent	16/10/44	Singapore	Battery replacement	29/10/44	Kobe
U 181	Independent	19/10/44	Jakarta	Indian Ocean/ return to France (aborted)	6/1/45	Jakarta
U 537	Independent	?/10/44	Jakarta	Relocation	?/10/44	Surabaya
U 862	Independent	6/11/44	Singapore	Return to active duty	8/11/44	Jakarta
U 537	Independent	9/11/44	Surabaya	Australia	9/11/44	Sunk
U 862	Independent	18/11/44	Jakarta	Australia	15/2/45	Jakarta
U 510	Independent	26/11/44	Jakarta	Indian Ocean/ return to France (aborted)	3/12/44	Jakarta
U 843	Independent	?/11/44	Singapore	Return to active service	?/11/44	Jakarta
U 196	Independent	30/11/44	Jakarta	Indian Ocean, Australia, on to Japan	30/11/44	Sunk
U 532	Independent	9/12/44	Kobe	Transfer	23/12/44	Jakarta
U 843	Independent	10/12/44	Jakarta	Indian Ocean/ return to Germany	9/4/45	Sunk
U 510	Independent	11/1/45	Jakarta	Indian Ocean/ return to France	24/4/45	St-Nazaire
U 532	Independent	13/1/45	Jakarta	Indian Ocean/ return to Germany	10/5/45	Liverpool
U 861	Independent	15/1/45	Surabaya	Indian Ocean/ return to Norway	19/4/45	Trondheim
UIT 24	Independent	15/1/45	Singapore	Refit	18/2/45	Kobe
U 195	Independent	19/1/45	Jakarta	Indian Ocean/ return to France (aborted)	4/3/45	Jakarta
U 862	Independent	18/2/45	Jakarta	Refit	20/2/45	Singapore
U 183	Independent	22/2/45	Kobe	Keel ballast installed	9/3/45	Jakarta
U 183	Independent	21/4/45	Jakarta	Indian Ocean/ return to France	23/4/45	Sunk

2. U-BOAT TRANSPORT OF MEN AND *MATÉRIEL* BETWEEN EUROPE AND THE FAR EAST, 1944–1945

Passenger Numbers and Tons of *Matériel* from Europe to the Far East

	Shipped	Arrived (% of total sent)		Lost	Turned back	En route at war's end
Passengers	96	64		22	–	10
Mercury (tons)	926.7	396.1	(43)	506.5	–	24.1
Lead (tons)	860.3	383.1	(45)	310.2	100.3	67.1
Aluminium (tons)	88.0	63.0	(72)	25.0	–	–
Optical glass (tons)	41.4	12.1	(29)	22.7	–	6.6
Steel (tons)	153.7	14.7	(9.6)	128.3	–	10.7
Totals (tons)	2,070.1	869.0	(42)	992.7	100.3	108.5

Passenger Numbers and Tons of *Matériel* from the Far East to Europe

	Shipped	Arrived (% of total sent)		Lost	Turned back	En route at war's end
Passengers	89	74		15	–	–
Tin (tons)	1,200.8	327.7	(27)	311.5	445.6	116.4
Rubber (tons)	731.6	172.4	(24)	219.8	303.1	36.3
Tungsten (tons)	595.5	99.8	(17)	213.0	164.5	118.2
Quinine (tons)	24.8	5.7	(23)	9.9	8.9	0.3
Opium (tons)	17.7	2.2	(12)	7.4	7.9	0.2
Totals (tons)	2,570.4	607.8	(24)	761.1	930.0	271.4

Figures from Hirama, Krug, Sander-Nagashima and Niestlé, *Reluctant Allies: German–Japanese Naval Relations in World War II*, Naval Institute Press (Annapolis, 2001).

Sources

UNPUBLISHED MATERIAL

BdU, *Kriegstagebuch*. NARA microfilm T1022, Rolls 3979–81, 4063–67.

Bordzeitung U861. Onboard newspaper. Provided by courtesy of Jürgen Oesten.

Catalina Association Newsletter (Cape Town Branch), No 279, June 2001.

German Espionage and Sabotage Against the United States, Office of Naval Intelligence Review 1, No 3 (Jan. 1946): pp. 3–38.

Haake, H., *Privat Tagebuch*, Bremen, 23 August 1944–12 December 1944.

Kriegsmarine Handbook: Penang, OKM Berlin, 1944.

Kriegsmarine Handbook: Shonan-to, OKM Berlin, 1944.

Monthly Anti-Submarine Reports. Held at Royal Navy Submarine Museum, Gosport.

Russell, Cdr Jerry C., *Ultra and the Campaign Against the U-Boats in World War II*.

US Army War College, Individual Study Project, 20 May 1980.

US Navy Report on interrogation of the crew of *U 860*, 6 July 1944.

US Navy Report on interrogation of the crew of *U 490*, 4 September 1944.

US Navy Report on interrogation of the crew of *U 234*, 27 June 1945.

ARTICLES

Gibson, Charles Dana, 'The Far East Odyssey of UIT 24', *Naval History*, Winter 1990.

Hui, Lee Ting, 'Singapore Under the Japanese', History Honours Thesis, University of Malaya, 1956. Reproduced by the South Seas Society.

Kratoska, Paul H., 'War and Occupation in Penang, 1941–1945', Department of History, National University of Singapore.

Mielke, Otto, 'Als U-Boot-Versorger im Indischen Ozean', *SOS*, Nr 68, Moewig Verlag, 1955.

Reberac, Fabien, 'Les Sous-Marins Allemands dans l'Océan Indien', *Histoire de Guerre*, March 2000.

Rosselli, Alberto, 'Italian Submarines and Surface Vessels in the Far East: 1940–45', http://64.224.13.60/others/fareast/

Saville, Allison W., 'German Submarines in the Far East', *USNI Proceedings*, August 1961.

Wise, James and Giese, Otto, *Hitler's Monsoon Boats*, Sea Classics, June 1991.

PUBLISHED BOOKS

Baba Ahmed bin Ahmed, Captain J. P., *Panaklukan Jepun: Suka Duka di Georgetown*, Media Indah Sdn. Bhd., 1992.

Bergmeier, Horst J. P., and Lotz, Rainer E., *Hitler's Airwaves*, Yale University Press, 1997.

Blair, Clay, *Hitler's U-Boat War*, Vols 1 & 2, Weidenfeld & Nicolson/Random House, 1998.

Brennecke, Jochen, *Haie im Paradies*, Preetz/Holstein, 1961.

———, *The Hunters and the Hunted*, Burke, 1958.

Brown, David (Editor), *The British Pacific and East Indies Fleets*, Brodie, 1995.

Dönitz, Karl, *Memoirs: Ten Years and Twenty Days*, Greenhill Books, 1990.

Farago, Ladislas, *The Tenth Fleet*, Obolensky, 1962.

Franks, Norman, *Search, Find and Kill*, Grub Street, 1995.

Giese, Otto, *Shooting the War*, Naval Institute Press, 1994.

Gunton, Dennis, *The Penang Submarines*, City Council of Georgetown, Penang, 1970.

Hashimoto, Mochitsura, *Sunk*, Holt & Company, 1954.

Herzog, Bodo, *Deutsche U-Boote, 1906–1966*, Karl Müller Verlag, 1996.

Hessler, Günter, *The U-Boat War in the Atlantic*, HMSO, 1989.

Hezlet, Arthur, *HMS Trenchant*, Pen & Sword, 2001.

Hirschfeld, Wolfgang, *The Secret Diary of a U-Boat*, Leo Cooper, 1996.

Howarth, Stephen, and Law, Derek (eds), *The Battle of the Atlantic: The 50th International Naval Conference*, GreenhillBooks/Naval Institute Press, 1994.

Kershaw, Ian, *Hitler: Nemesis, 1936–1945*, Allen Lane, 2000.

Köhl, Fritz and Niestlé, *Vom Original zum Modell: Uboottyp IX*, Bernard & Graefe, 1990.

Krug, Hans-Joachim; Hirama, Yôichi; Krug, Hans-Joachim; Sander-Nagashima, Berthold; and Niestlé, Axel, *Reluctant Allies: German–Japanese Naval Relations in World War II*, Naval Institute Press, 2001.

Lamont-Brown, Raymond, *Kempeitai: Japan's Dreaded Military Police*, Sutton Publishing, 1998.

Leasor, James, *The Sea Wolves (Boarding Party)*, Heinemann, 1978.

Lohmann, W., and Hildebrand, H., *Kriegsmarine 1939 – 1945*, Podzun-Verlag, 1956.

Merten, Karl-Friedrich, *Schicksalswaffe U-Boot*, Verlagsgruppe Weltbild, 1994.

Niestlé, Axel, *German U-Boat Losses during World War Two*, Greenhill Books/Naval Institute Press, 1998.

Paterson, Lawrence, *First U-Boat Flotilla*, Pen & Sword/Naval Institute Press, 2002.

———, *Second U-Boat Flotilla*, Pen & Sword/Naval Institute Press, 2003.

Rohwer, Jürgen, *Allied Submarine Attacks of World War Two*, Greenhill Books/Naval Institute Press, 1997.

———, *Axis Submarine Successes*, Greenhill Books/Naval Institute Press, 1983.

Rohwer, Jürgen, and Hümmelchen, Gerhard, *Chronik des Seekrieges, 1939–45*, Manfred Pawlak, 1968.

Rössler, Eberhard, *The U-Boat*, Arms & Armour Press, 1981.

Savas, Theodore (ed.), *Silent Hunters*, Savas Publishing, 1997.

Sellwood, A. V., *Dynamite for Hire*, T. Werner Laurie, 1956.

Showell, Jak Mallmann, *Wolfpacks at War*, Ian Allen, 2001.

Stevens, David, *U-Boat Far from Home*, Allen & Unwin, 1997.

Thomer, Egbert, *Unter Nippons Sonne*, Wilhelm Koehler Verlag, 1959.

Turner, L., Gordon-Cumming, H., and Betzler. J., *War in the Southern Oceans*, Oxford University Press, 1961.

Vause, Jordan, *Wolf*, Airlife/Naval Institute Press, 1997.

Wiggins, Melanie, *U-Boat Adventures*, Naval Institute Press, 1999.

Wynn, Kenneth, *U-Boat Operations of the Second World War*, Vols. 1 & 2, Chatham Publishing, 1997.

Y'Blood, William T., *Hunter-Killer*, Naval Institute Press, 1984.

Yasunaga, Hiroshi, *Shito no Suiteitai*, Asahi Sonorama, 1994.

SUGGESTED WEBSITES

Deutsche U-Boote 1935–1945 (http://www.u-boot-archiv.de)

Grey Wolf (http://www.u-boot-greywolf.de)

International Submarine Art Gallery (http://www.subart.net)

U-Boat Archive: Photographs and Records of the U-boat War (http://www.uboatarchive.net/)

U-Boat War, The (http://www.uboatwar.net)

U-Boat.net (http://www.uboat.net)

U-Bootwaffe & Kriegsmarine history (http://www.ubootwaffe.net)

Index